READING HARRY POTTER

Recent Titles in
Contributions to the Study of Popular Culture

The Detective in American Fiction, Film, and Television
Jerome H. Delamater and Ruth Prigozy, editors

Imagining the Worst: Stephen King and the Representation of Women
Kathleen Margaret Lant and Theresa Thompson, editors

Bleep! Censoring Rock and Rap Music
Betty Houchin Winfield and Sandra Davidson, editors

The Cowboy Way: The Western Leader in Film, 1945-1995
Ralph Lamar Turner and Robert J. Higgs

Parody as Film Genre: "Never Give a Saga an Even Break"
Wes D. Gehring

Shape-Shifting: Images of Native Americans in Popular Fiction
Andrew Macdonald, Gina Macdonald, and MaryAnn Sheridan

Noir, Now and Then: Film Noir Originals and Remakes (1944–1999)
Ronald Schwartz

Shaman or Sherlock? The Native American Detective
Gina Macdonald, Andrew Macdonald, and MaryAnn Sheridan

The Devil Himself: Villainy in Detective Fiction and Film
Stacy Gillis and Philippa Gates, editors

Scorned Literature: Essays on the History and Criticism of Popular Mass-Produced Fiction in America
Lydia Cushman Schurman and Deidre Johnson, editors

A Storied Singer: Frank Sinatra as Literary Conceit
Gilbert L. Gigliotti

Strange TV: Innovative Television Series from *The Twilight Zone* to *The X-Files*
M. Keith Booker

READING
HARRY POTTER
Critical Essays

Edited by Giselle Liza Anatol

Contributions to the Study of Popular Culture, Number 78

Westport, Connecticut
London

Library of Congress Cataloging-in-Publication Data

Reading Harry Potter : critical essays / edited by Giselle Liza Anatol.
p. cm. — (Contributions to the study of popular culture,
ISSN 0198-9871 ; no. 78)
Includes bibliographical references and index.
ISBN 0–313–32067–5 (alk. paper)
1. Rowling, J. K.—Criticism and interpretation. 2. Children's stories, English—
History and criticism. 3. Fantasy fiction, English—History and criticism.
4. Rowling, J. K.—Characters—Harry Potter. 5. Potter, Harry (Fictitious
character) 6. Wizards in literature. 7. Magic in literature. I. Anatol, Giselle Liza,
1970– II. Series.

PR6068.O93 Z83 2003
823'.914—dc21   2002032973

British Library Cataloguing in Publication Data is available.

Library of Congress Catalog Card Number: 2002032973
ISBN: 0–313–32067–5
ISSN: 0198-9871

First published in 2003

Praeger Publishers, 88 Post Road West, Westport, CT 06881
An imprint of Greenwood Publishing Group, Inc.
www.praeger.com

Printed in the United States of America

∞™

The paper used in this book complies with the
Permanent Paper Standard issued by the National
Information Standards Organization (Z39.48–1984).

10 9 8 7 6 5 4 3 2

Contents

III. Morality and Social Values: Issues of Power

Acknowledgments

I offer profuse thanks to the contributors for their time and efforts, and particularly for their enduring patience in seeing this project through to the end. I am grateful to my children's literature students at the University of Kansas, whose enthusiasm for the books kept me invigorated, and whose classroom discussions stimulated my own thinking about the books in new and exciting ways. I also deeply appreciate all of the people who snipped newspaper articles, sent websites, shared their own (or their children's) readings of *Harry Potter*, listened to ideas, challenged them, read drafts, and provided general support and encouragement: members of the Department of English at Spelman College, members of the Department of English at the University of Kansas, SAGE's Academics Anonymous, AHAA, Laura Hines, Katie Conrad, Anna Neill, Kirk Branch, Kim Dayton, Phil Wedge, Yo Jackson, Tami Albin, Sherrie Tucker, Carla Moore, James Abraham, Joo Ok Kim, and Marina Scheer and Jasmine Chandler, who deserve particular thanks for their hard work at the initial and final stages of the project. For their emotional and intellectual support on this project, and in my life, I would acknowledge D, Julie Crawford, Liza Yukins, Rhonda Frederick, Tonia Poteat, and my family. Finally, I offer deepest thanks to my mother, who taught me to read when I was three years old and showed me that "hitting the books" and loving them are not mutually exclusive.

Introduction

"I love your books—the real ones, I mean, I haven't read the ones for children, of course!"

—Ursula K. Le Guin, reporting on the comments of
some of her adult admirers[1]

By the end of the twentieth century, there were few people in the English-speaking world who had never heard of a boy named Harry Potter. British author Joanne Kathleen Rowling—better known by the androgynous initials "J. K."—achieved astounding commercial success with her series of novels focusing on the young wizard with the lightning-bolt forehead scar who finds out about his magical powers on the morning of his eleventh birthday. *Harry Potter and the Philosopher's/Sorcerer's Stone,*[2] the first book of a planned seven, each of which follows the protagonist through one year of his education at Hogwarts School of Witchcraft and Wizardry, won the 1997 British Book Awards Children's Book of the Year, the 1998 New York Public Library Best Book of the Year, and the 1998 *Parenting* magazine Book of the Year Award. It was named "one of the best books of 1998" by *Publishers Weekly, School Library Journal,* and *Booklist* in the United States. An illustration of Harry Potter on the cover of *Time* magazine made Rowling the first children's writer to be featured in a *Time* cover story.

The popularity of *Philosopher's/Sorcerer's Stone* and the ensuing two novels—*Harry Potter and the Chamber of Secrets* (U.K. 1998; U.S. 1999) and *Harry Potter and the Prisoner of Azkaban* (also 1998/1999)—led British children to vote Rowling the winner of the Gold Medal Smarties Prize for three years in a row. In the States, her books dominated the top three places on *The New York Times* bestseller list for over twenty months. At the time that book IV, *Harry Potter and the Goblet of Fire* (2000), was about to be released and promised to win a fourth spot on the list, the *Times* launched a surprising innovation—their Children's Bestseller List, comprised of fifteen titles. Unsurprisingly, the Potter books captured the top four places.

The *Times* decision angered many, who claimed that the new list unfairly ghettoizes literature for children and young adults—perhaps much in the same way that the speaker in my epigraph insisted upon separating Le Guin's work—on the other hand, supporters of the list expressed enthusiasm for a change that gives more children's writers publicity and children's book buyers more information about available texts. A similar controversy was instigated when committee members of the prestigious British Whitbread Book of the Year Award modified rules in 2000 to allow children's books into consideration for that prize. Regardless of which side critics fall in these ideological debates, it is clear that the Potter books have initiated momentous cultural change.

And this upheaval is not limited to Britain and the States. Also in the year 2000, the state-owned People's Literature Publishing House in China began an unprecedented printing campaign, translating Rowling's first three novels and packaging them as a boxed set. The 600,000-unit first printing was the largest ever for commercial release in that country. One of the translators confessed delight in shifting the focus from stringently didactic stories and bringing more imagination, creativity, and aspects of the fantastical ghost story of Chinese folk tradition to an audience of Chinese children. Internationally, *Goblet of Fire* had the largest first printing in publishing history—3.8 million copies in United States alone—and by July 1, 2000, Amazon.com had taken 282,650 advance orders, with the number reaching 350,000 by the following week. Over thirty million copies of *Goblet* were sold worldwide as of July 31, 2000, and Rowling was reported to be the world's highest-earning writer of that year.[3]

THE APPEAL OF THE HARRY POTTER SERIES

What is it about Rowling's texts that mesmerizes so many readers of so many ages around the globe? Does the "cosmic" battle between good and evil hold universal appeal? Or, in this age of Jerry Springer and reality television, are we all seedily enticed by the book-bannings in places such as Minnesota, Michigan, California, South Carolina, and New Zealand, and the accusations of the corruption of young, impressionable minds?[4] Or the plagiarism controversy surrounding Rowling and American Nancy K. Stouffer, author of *The Legend of Rah and the Muggles* (1984)? Is it that the stories are grounded in conventional morality, and yet not overtly didactic, moralizing, or formally educational?[5] Does the incredible range of genres woven together in the novels—fairy tale, bildungsroman, boarding school narrative, detective novel, adventure story, fantasy quest tale—allow each reader to satisfy her preferences?

Salon.com contributor Christine Schoefer identifies the lure as the "glittering mystery and nail-biting suspense, compelling language and colorful imagery, magical feats juxtaposed with real-life concerns."[6] These "real-life concerns" hold powerful resonance. In *Philosopher's/Sorcerer's Stone*, Harry worries upon entry into Hogwarts that he will be discovered as a fraud and told his admission was in error; in *Prisoner of Azkaban*, Professor Lupin's students must learn to handle the boggart—a creature that takes the shape of one's worst fear. The boggart transforms into Professor Snape (a menacing authority figure against whom students have no power because he is a teacher, and also because he is an adult); a bloody mummy, a bloody eyeball, and a severed hand (all directly out of Hollywood horror movies: one, a creature representing death and decay; the others, symbolic, perhaps, of the lack of privacy and control that children have); a banshee (a terrifying figure from folk stories); a rat, a rattlesnake, and a spider ("real" animals that can cause pain and possibly death).[7] Thus Rowling's books give forceful voice to childhood qualms, even on the most basic level.

The fascination with the stories is not limited to the preteen set, however. At the 2001 annual meeting of the American Psychiatric Association, one session was dedicated entirely to the Harry Potter books. As the conversation revolved around ways the stories could help therapists to establish a rapport with young patients and begin to tease out their responses to certain situations, it was revealed that almost everyone in the audience of approximately one hundred attendees had read at least one of the novels, and more than half had read all four. In Britain, publishers have distributed a separate set of the books with black and white photos on the covers to appeal to an adult audience (purportedly, the adults' and children's editions contained identical text but sold for different prices).

During the frenzy that preceded the official July 8, 2000, 12:01 A.M. sale time of *Goblet of Fire*, a group of adult readers dressed in magic-world attire showed up between platforms nine and ten at the King's Cross Station in London, perhaps hoping to witness an event more spectacular than the steam engine copy of the Hogwarts Express displayed prior to the release of the paperback *Chamber of Secrets*. In New York City, fans of all ages stood in line for more than two hours at Books of Wonder on West Eighteenth Street, and by a few minutes to midnight, over three hundred people—both adults and children—had lined up outside an Upper West Side Barnes & Noble Bookstore. Also present at the scene: a falconer with an Asiatic barn owl; staff members decked out in wizardly robes and hats; temporary lightning-bolt tattoos, plastic spiders, cauldrons, and star-shaped balloons.

One of the book reviewers waiting his turn in line remarked: "This is the most demented thing I've ever seen."[8] The U.S. children's literature scholar Jack Zipes would agree; he expresses much doubt regarding publishers' claim that as long as any book gets children to read, and read with such enthusiasm, this proves its inherent value. Because so much of the media hype surrounding Rowling's novels has dealt with the *event* of the releases and not the texts themselves, one might challenge how much children's literacy is truly at issue. According to

Zipes, serialized literature—from adult popular romances such as Harlequin Romances to the young adult Goosebumps, Sweet Valley High, and Babysitters Club series—is about literature transformed into product. These series are designed not to stimulate *readers'* imagination and intellectual processes but rather to stimulate *customers* to "buy and rebuy" not only books, but also CDs, audio- and videotapes, computer games, sugared cereals, and clothing.[9] Thus, purchasing and reading become an addiction, and our commodity culture makes the individual who does not participate—especially the child who is hyper-aware of "belonging" and of what is considered "normal"—aberrant.

The publication of black market Harry Potter novels in South Vietnam would appear to fit the trend. The books include pronunciation keys for the names, preserved in their English spellings, and sketchlike illustrations. Most strikingly, the books are being published serially, so that the first installment of *Stone* contains only the first three chapters of the novel, while Part 14 of book II, translated *Harry Potter & Phòng Chứ'a Bí Mật*, contains only Chapters 15 ("Aragog") and 16 ("The Chamber of Secrets") of Rowling's second novel. While buying each installment might allow a greater number of children to access the narratives and the delights of reading more easily, one cannot fail to notice that the serialized form encourages the type of addiction to which Zipes refers. Putting out a small amount of money every few days or weeks is more readily justified, and readers "must" buy the next book, and the next, and the next, in order to satisfy their cravings for the resolution of the story.

The seductiveness of the novels has also been linked to Rowling's personal history. The story of the author's incredible rise from welfare state to commercial success resembles the traditional fairy tale of the rags-to-riches princess who lives "happily ever after" and also echoes the Horatio Alger myth of the tattered urchin who diligently works his way up the ladder of achievement. The same drive for economic and social accomplishment that has long brought people to the United States as the Land of Opportunity, while no longer overtly influenced by stories of streets paved with gold, still holds sway for those who believe that hard work and wit will inevitably lead even the most downtrodden to triumph.

This ideology is evident in Rowling's fiction as well as in the myths surrounding her own story: Harry Potter, the champion of Good, with his unruly hair, broken glasses, and slight frame, is the nerdy underdog-turned-hero for whom we are conditioned to cheer. His adventures and continued successes allow adults to indulge in whimsy and recapture the "golden world" of childhood for which they are often nostalgic—a completely fair and just world, where the good and disciplined prosper. Childhood is typically further idealized by adults as a period without true responsibilities, and Rowling's formulaic "happy endings" offer older readers with complex and not-so-orderly lives comfort in the fact that everything will work out for the best.

At the same time, however, child readers can feel vindicated by observing how much heavy responsibility Harry Potter and his friends—and by extension, they themselves—must and can shoulder. Rowling's novels allow children to identify with a character who triumphs even though he, like them, appears powerless. In their daily lives, children lack control of things that adults can take for granted (what to eat, when to eat, what time to go to bed, what clothes are in their closets or which outfit to wear on what occasion, which chores are done at what time, and so forth). Children feel small in size and influence, especially if they are expected to be "seen and not heard." As a mere infant, the tiny and apparently helpless Harry Potter reveals that he possesses tremendous power when he deflects the fatal spell of the mighty wizard Voldemort. As each novel opens, Harry has no sense of control or influence in the Dursley household; he is then "rescued" from this existence by his magical abilities. As one who displays natural talents in this area, Harry is allowed to attend Hogwarts School of Witchcraft and Wizardry, where he is not only celebrated for the power exemplified in his early defeat of the "Dark Lord" Voldemort, but also has the chance to prove his academic abilities, athletic talents, and command over his own decisions and actions again and again.

To add to the appeal for children, throughout the series admirable adults are willing to admit error. At one point, rather than expel Harry and his best friend, Ron Weasley, for again breaking the rules, as he had promised, Headmaster Albus Dumbledore claims: "[T]he best of us must sometimes eat our words." He then bestows the boys with Special Awards for Services to the School.[10] And when Harry spends vacation time at Ron's home, he serves as the expert about what nonmagical people do: Mr. Weasley, an adult, and an important wizard with a position at the Ministry of Magic, likes to sit next to Harry at dinner and shower him with questions about "life with Muggles." He inquires with excitement about such banal things as electrical plugs and mail delivery.[11] The incredible number of characters and intricate details in the books similarly allow the child reader to feel intellectual power: by participating in quiz shows and trivia games, she can display a mastery of the written materials as well as feel that she is an insider, a compatriot with the characters who experience the fictional incidents.

WHY ENGAGE IN THIS PROJECT?

What is to be made of the Harry Potter phenomenon? Roger Sutton, editor of *The Horn Book*, claims he was "suckered ... by the cosmic forces that have ordained that this likable but critically insignificant series become widely popular and therefore news."[12] Along similar lines, Jack Zipes posits that the "phenomenal" aspect of the reception of the Harry Potter books has obscured the criteria "for anyone who wants to take literature for young people seriously." He continues: "The ordinary becomes extraordinary, and we are so taken by the phenomenon that we admire, worship, and idolize it without grasping fully why we regard it with so much reverence and awe."[13]

I would argue that it is exactly because the series has become so widely popular that it is both critically significant and should be taken quite seriously. As
the British children's literature scholar Peter Hunt argues, the authors read by
the greatest number of children are those who must be examined most carefully: it is these writers "whose attitudes and politics are most likely to be
stamped (through subconscious osmosis) into the national consciousness."[14]
Educator Bernice Cullinan concurs: in her textbook *Literature and the Child*,
she describes how stories can be soaked up "into the bloodstream" of young
readers. This vivid metaphor speaks to the ways children unconsciously absorb
not only the plot of the tales, but also the values imbedded within. Cullinan
goes on to argue that contemporary books reflect current social values "no less
than the 'teach and preach' books of [U.S.] Colonial days mirrored the Puritan
ethic."[15]

Children are not the bastions of wholesome innocence that is often purported, but they are impressionable and can be physically, emotionally, and in-
tellectually vulnerable to the ideological constructs underlying all texts, from
picture books to history textbooks to television commercials.[16] Adults involved
in children's literature must not necessarily look for ideas that young readers
will repeat immediately after reading a particular text—who knows whether or
not they will be able to articulate a particular concept?—but also for their emotional responses to the characters and situations that present the possibly submerged ethos as either attractive, detestable, or somewhere in between.
Interpreting the foundational messages and themes is vital for understanding
the ways that young people perceive the world and the ways that, as adults
raised with these narratives, we interact with each other in contemporary society.

The body of children's literature contains a massive number of texts, yet
very few have been the subject of sustained critical interpretation. When this
type of exploration does occur, it is often considered self-indulgent and ridicu-
lously overanalyzed by nonacademic readers, or a trivial, "dumbed-down" version of the conventional analysis associated with more canonical "adult"
literature, which is deemed deserving and worthy of deeper thought.

In terms of the former, critic M. Daphne Kutzer has noted that the belief that
children's literature (and fantasy in particular) is devoid of any contemplative
purpose made Frederick Crews's 1963 *The Pooh Perplex* incredibly popular: the
"humor rests on the assumption that serious commentary of the Pooh books is
comical by definition."[17] This, in turn, led to the tendency among some scholars to under-theorize children's fiction, remaining in the realm of simple categorization and description of the stories. Like feminist scholar Pamela Banting,
who argues for the translation of feminist discourse into nonacademic arenas, I
contest the idea that conversations produced within university settings cannot
be shared, understood, interpreted, or answered from outside the academy. "I
am not convinced that theory cannot and does not take place outside the walls
of the institution."[18]

For proof of the latter assumption of the trivial nature of works for children, one need only glance at the article published in the *New York Times* by William Safire, who claimed that "the Harry Potter phenomenon needs a little perspective. These are children's books."[19] Safire's condescending attitude towards children's literature suggests that these materials are insipid versions of adult fiction; the genre concerns itself merely with plot and action without considerations of character, philosophical ideas, and a variety of perspectives that allow the reader to enter the mind of another and expand her own. Critiquing the "infantilization of adult culture," Safire laments that "scholarly tomes" about the Potter novels will undoubtedly be written. The current collection of essays no doubt fits the bill.

We make no claims for justifying the adult readership of Rowling's fiction. The primary goal of this volume is to take a rigorous critical view of the books, precisely because they have received such widespread acclaim. The Potter series could become some of this generation's most formative narratives, and it needs exploration and study rather than rejection as simply pulp, pop culture, or the latest fad. Neglecting the potency of the novels and relegating them to the category of childhood trivia can result in the dangerously mistaken conclusions that the books do not reflect and/or comment upon the cultural assumptions and ideological tensions of contemporary society, and that they have no effect on the intellectual and social development of today's children and tomorrow's adults. As one letter-writer reacting to Safire's essay so articulately proclaimed: "Children's literature is important. It is today's young readers who will become tomorrow's adult readers and thinkers. There is nothing 'lesser' about children or the books they are inspired to read."[20] One may be reminded of C. S. Lewis, who stated that on becoming a man, he "put away childish things, including the fear of childishness and the desire to be very grown up."[21] Lewis also claimed that "no book is really worth reading at the age of ten which is not equally (and often far more) worth reading at the age of fifty."[22]

It cannot be stated enough times that works for children and young adults have incredible influence. This body of literature is a powerful tool for inculcating social roles and behaviors, moral guides, desires, and fears. Whether these books serve as "time-passers," literacy training, exercise for the imagination or the logical-thinking process, teachers of social norms, models for dealing with problems, and/or a means for improving a cantankerous or melancholy mood, they can affect and sway their readers. And in literature written specifically for children, the "appropriate" life paths and desires are usually more transparent and forcefully presented than in adult fiction.[23]

Some adult readers will reject this collection of essays, desiring simply to read J. K. Rowling's phenomenally successful Harry Potter books as a means of idyllic escape, and not as a site also subject to the ideological structures that motivate all actions and underpin the workings of our daily world. This resistance echoes the phrase many instructors have heard from students in their introductory-level literature classes: "You're reading too much into it."

Likewise, Schoefer comments on the parents who enjoy reading the stories as much as their children and resent any points that seem at all critical of the books. She wonders: "Is our longing for a magical world so deep, our hunger to be surprised and amazed so intense, our gratitude for a well-told story so great that we are willing to abdicate our critical judgement? Or are the stereotypes in the story so integral to our fascination—do we feel comforted by a world in which conventional roles are firmly in place?"[24] The purpose of this volume is not to destroy the world of fantasy, but merely to interrogate the many layers that surround the texts in an effort to help us see our own world more clearly. The contributors examine not only what the stories explicitly state, but also what they disguise and what they assume. It is to be hoped the chapters that follow will help to loosen up the restrictive boundaries between "pleasure" and "intellectual pursuit" and allow enjoyment at the same time as a critical engagement with the texts.

Of course, children process written materials very differently than more mature, experienced adults; according to Piaget's child development model, the typical thirteen-year-old will understand a text in vastly more complex ways than the typical eight-year-old. In the concrete-operations stage (at the age of about seven), children can deal with generalizations but rarely interpret language beyond the literal textual meaning; by the age of about eleven, they reach the formal-operations stage and can deal with abstractions and ambiguity; eventually, the mature reader can reflect upon and comprehend motivations and underlying actions. As such scholars as Karín Lesnik-Oberstein and Maria Nikolajeva point out, however, we must be careful of theories that posit a singular, nonindividualized "real" or "normal" child reader who is indistinguishable from any other child reader. In other words, while employing the Piagetian model, one should recognize that a child of eight might be able to read Professor Severus Snape as symbolically snakelike or make connections between his antagonism towards Harry's father—and, by extension, towards Harry—and Ron Weasley's submerged jealousy of all the attention Harry receives. Children's interpretative skills can be affected by numerous factors, including the child's age, the era in which he grows up, nationality, culture, racial or ethnic background, education, gender, position in the sibling lineup, and socioeconomic class. Because of this, what children will take from the Harry Potter books is impossible to pinpoint or to project. A more valuable approach, I believe, is considering what they *might* pick up on: topics *some* children might question—either as they read, a few weeks down the road, or years into the future—or areas in which they could be challenged.

THE CHAPTERS

One of the allegations against the Harry Potter books is that they promote hatred and rebellion. Children's literature has long been read as subversive, whether because texts allow children to collude with the authors and each other against the adult world, or because they allow children a form of escape. And yet, Peter Hunt wonders how subversive these narratives can really be: "It could be argued that they share with much popular culture the disruptive surface which disguises a profound conservatism."[25] Many of the chapters in *Reading Harry Potter* will examine the ways in which Rowling tries to undermine conventional ideology and how successful she is at this project, if at all. These interpretative moves might seem perplexing to nonacademic readers: "[O]ne does not expect [Beatrix] Potter or [A.A.] Milne, for example, to be cloaking social or political messages beneath the whimsy of talking animals."[26] It is our hope, however, that each chapter will be perused with an open mind and stimulate thought for readers of all backgrounds.

The first part, "Reading Harry Potter Through Theories of Child Development," explores the ways that we can see the psychological and social developmental experiences of children replicated in Rowling's texts. Alice Mills takes a Jungian approach to contrast the archetypal child motifs in *Harry Potter* to the lost child hero in Diana Wynne Jones's fiction. She reads Voldemort as the "dark double" of Harry's father, and the series as a young boy's wish-fulfillment fantasies to compensate for his physical and psychological abuse at the hands of his relatives. Lisa Damour, in turn, employs Freudian theory to contemplate the ways in which Harry's adventures parallel the psychological challenges of making the developmental transition from childhood to adolescence; she asserts that the books aid the vast readership of children and early adolescents in making this transition themselves.

In her chapter on the procurement of knowledge in the wizarding world, Lisa Hopkins details the surprisingly slow and sometimes painful procedure by which Harry and his friends gain information. She maintains that these deliberate steps appeal to young readers who can also find knowledge acquisition a challenging process. Analyzing the sorting ritual and the traits of the Hogwarts students in each of the four dormitory houses, Chantel Lavoie explains how this process challenges the conventional notions of ambition and courage and encourages children's growing understanding of the murky ground between "good" and "bad," "black" and "white." Finally, Rebecca Stephens argues that what causes critics to condemn the Potter series for its depiction of a dark supernatural world and simultaneously praise C.S. Lewis's Narnia books, which also portray a mythical world engaged in the struggle of good versus evil, is whether the authors subvert or support traditional hierarchical power structures and figures of authority. Her chapter urges readers to avoid the impulse of simply dismissing *Potter* detractors: "Dismissal, rather than attempts at understanding, is the most likely act to turn a skirmish into an all-out war, and walling ourselves off into factions only fragments our culture further."

The chapters in part II explore some of the literary and historical contexts in which Rowling is grounded. Karen Manners Smith situates the Potter narratives in the tradition of the "public school story," which typically features: the initiation of the protagonist into school rites; a bully (and the defeat of the bully); a hero who is nearly led astray but is saved by a good friend; a godlike headmaster; and codes of honor. Thomas Hughes, author of *Tom Brown's Schooldays* (1857), is commonly identified as the founder of the genre;[27] other popular titles include F. W. Farrar's moralizing *Eric, or Little by Little* (1858) and *St. Winifred's* (1859), described by Richard Jenkyns as books where people lust, but for food, not sex, and there exists "a half-erotic morbidity" that strikes one as "bizarre."[28] Jenkyns's characterization reveals aspects of the homoerotic element of many schoolboys' novels, which Manners Smith also investigates in her chapter.

In *Sticks and Stones: The Troublesome Success of Children's Literature from Slovenly Peter to Harry Potter*, Jack Zipes presents a convincing argument about the conventionality of the Potter narratives, lumping Rowling in with "the predictable happy-end school of fairy-tale writers" who, as part of the contemporary trend of globalization, only serve in "fostering sameness throughout the world."[29] However, as many child development theorists have explained, repetition is, in fact, pleasurable to the child reader, who can master the "rules" of the story and gain confidence as she searches for and finds particular patterns. This renders formulaic stories such as fairy tales appealing, perhaps, in part, because it implies a certain amount of "order and consistency in the world around [the child reader]."[30] In her contribution to this volume, Elaine Ostry details the fairy tale motifs in the Potter stories and the common theme of the battle between good and evil to show how Rowling attempts to combat the present-day evils of racism and materialism. As Joan Acocella has noted, the wizard world is caught up in "an overarching race war. ... [an] ethnic-cleansing campaign, led by Voldemort."[31] As Ostry reveals, however, by examining the representations of the symbolically racially "impure" Mudbloods—witches and wizards born to nonmagical parents or to one magical and one Muggle parent—and "mixed-race" characters like the half-giant Hagrid, Rowling's attempts are ambiguous at best.

Brycchan Carey also touches on issues of race as he lays forth the literary and historical abolitionist traditions out of which Rowling writes. Carey contends that the *Harry Potter and the Goblet of Fire* subplot of Hermione's campaign to emancipate the enslaved house-elves promotes political participation and encourages activism in young readers. And the last essay in this section compares technological development in Muggle and magical spheres to interrogate the ways that science works in the so-called real world; Margaret J. Oakes maintains that magic puts wizards on an equal footing, while technology leads to social distance and alienation among nonmagical peoples. Oakes, in concurrence with the theories of Jacques Ellul, which linked magic to the soul and the spiritual side of human development, demonstrates how the hi-tech world of the Muggles, especially the Dursleys, leads to lack of warmth and interpersonal bonds, while magic can satisfy these needs and teach readers about the importance of this "outdated" mode of interaction.

The final section of *Reading Harry Potter* deals explicitly with the inculcation of social values. Veronica L. Schanoes describes the complicated moral worlds of Harry Potter, interpreting this complexity through Rowling's ambivalent characterization of writing and reading in the series. In an exploration of Rowling's presentation of the rule of law, Susan Hall reveals weaknesses in the legal concepts of the wizarding world, contending that institutional corruption predestines the system to failure. I explore neocolonialism and xenophobia in the Potter stories, proposing that while the narratives' stance on the fall of the British empire appears to be positive, Rowling subtly reveals nostalgia for certain ways of old. Julia Park uses the works of Charles Dickens to investigate Rowling's attitudes toward socioeconomic class status. She asserts that Rowling reveals distinct middle-class prejudices in her descriptions of the characters, particularly the wealthy and snobbish Draco Malfoy, the financially impoverished but socially well-to-do Ron Weasley, and Hagrid, the half-giant.

And finally, Ximena Gallardo-C. and C. Jason Smith give us a reading of the gender dynamics in the novels. The topic of sexism has arisen on numerous occasions: Joan Acocella claimed that because many of the Quidditch champions are girls, and the school is coed, "[s]exism is not a major problem at Hogwarts."[32] On the other hand, Christine Schoefer points out the numerous instances of "Harry Potter's Girl Trouble," with Jenkyns, Zipes, and others following suit. For example, in *Harry Potter and the Philosopher's/Sorcerer's Stone,* Hermione often allows her emotions to overwhelm her intelligence: she comes across as the stereotypical hysterical female when confronted by the troll in the bathroom, and her panic paralyzes her reasoning process when she, Ron, and Harry land in the Devil's Snare plant near the conclusion of the book. Professor McGonagall serves as an excellent teacher of Transfiguration, but she is far from inspiring or charismatic for the students and she consistently defers to Dumbledore.[33] As Gallardo-C. and Smith point out, the profession of educator—like that of nurse or librarian—is one of the most conventional occupations for women. One cannot fail to notice while reading the series that Poppy Pomfrey serves as the stern but nurturing school nurse; Madam Pince, the librarian, is "a thin, irritable woman who looked like an underfed vulture," suggesting the typical miserable spinster;[34] and Professor Sprout, as the Herbology teacher, gets linked to gardening and fertility, traditional female domains as well.[35] Schoefer admits that she was spellbound by the Potter books and enjoyed them tremendously. She asks, however, very much in the spirit of this collection: "Is [enjoyment] a good reason to ignore what's been left out?"[36] Gallardo-C. and Smith acknowledge the ways the books can be interpreted as sexist but provide an alternative reading that allows us to think about the narrative in more expansive ways. They posit Harry as significantly passive at crucial moments in the texts, thus allowing cross-gender identification for girls and prohibiting easy gender stereotyping.

Of course, the volume's chapters could easily be reorganized and arranged into different section headings. Most of the contributors trace echoes of other works present in Rowling's texts, for example, so that at least three of the chapters discuss Rowling's employment of the fairy-tale tradition, and a separate three link Rowling to contemporary children's literature author Diana Wynne Jones. Like a creator of bricolage—art that is created from pieces taken from here and there—or palimpsest—a page that has been written on more than once, with the earlier writing incompletely erased—Rowling, whether consciously or not, makes allusions to myriad works. These references—both obvious and subtle—make her novels reminiscent of Judeo-Christian, ancient Greek and Roman, and Celtic myths; quest narratives, particularly Arthurian legend; European fairy tales; Victorian novels and orphan stories; adventure stories; contemporary popular culture narratives like Superman and Spiderman comic books, with the mild-mannered "nerd" saving the day, as well as *Star Wars*, in which Luke Skywalker battles the Dark Lord Darth Vader as he discovers the nature of his own powers and his true identity; and children's detective fiction series, including the Secret Seven, the Hardy Boys, Nancy Drew, Encyclopedia Brown, and numerous Sherlock Holmes adaptations. And of course, the Potter books build on the tradition of fantasy tales of alternative, magical worlds—especially those where children control destiny and effect change before returning to the "real" world.[37] The list of allusions, textual interweavings, and literary borrowings could fill an entire volume. Rather than simply dismiss Rowling as a talented mimic whose works lack originality, however, one should recall that many of the pieces listed here refer back to even earlier traditions. As Robert Louis Stevenson stated about his inspiration and influences for *Treasure Island:* "No doubt the parrot once belonged to Robinson Crusoe. No doubt the skeleton is conveyed from Poe. . . . The stockade, I am told, is from *Masterman Ready.*"[38] And as Salman Rushdie writes in *Haroun and the Sea of Stories:* "Nothing comes from nothing . . . ; no story comes from nowhere; new stories are born from old—it is the new combinations that make them new."[39]

This book does not lay claim to any "correct" answers that can fit the experiences of every member of every community. Some of the issues presented in the project have many defensible positions; we simply present them as topics to think about and explore. All literary works contain "gaps" that allow individual readers to make individual inferences, link ideas, build metaphors, and conceptualize characters in certain ways. By interpreting a text, filling in the gaps, and creating meaning from the words on the page, the reader "makes choices. . . . [and no] reader"—neither child nor adult—"can ever exhaust the full potential of any text."[40] Using writer Alan Garner's metaphor of his books as onions, we might read *Harry Potter* as a pungent fruit which we peel down, layer by layer, consuming as much as we desire, or as we are able.

The writers of chapters are quite varied—they currently reside in the United States, Canada, Britain, and Australia. While most are literary scholars, the professions of child psychology, journalism, and law are also represented. Similarly, readers of this collection could also be quite varied: students interested in investigating the field of children's literature, writers of children's texts, librarians, teachers, sociologists, stay-at-home parents, those who want to know more about the books that have captivated the attention of the children in their lives, nonspecialists in English who are interested in delving deeper into the meanings of *Harry Potter* or are simply curious about what a few academics have to say about the series. Even though all of these readers will have different backgrounds, purposes, and understandings of what Rowling's books do (or aim to do), we hope that *Reading Harry Potter* will stimulate thought and discussion and prove to be "an inspirational area for a productive interaction between adult, child and book."[41]

NOTES

1. Ursula K. Le Guin, *Earthsea Revisioned* (Cambridge: Children's Literature New England and Green Bay Publications, 1993), 49.

2. The novel was published in Britain under the title *Harry Potter and the Philosopher's Stone* (London: Bloomsbury, 1997) and in the United States under the title *Harry Potter and the Sorcerer's Stone* (New York: Scholastic Inc., 1997).

3. Sales figures have been compared to numerous other high-grossing children's books and authors: G. A. Henty, one of the most popular writers for boys during his time, sold approximately 25 million copies between 1871 and 1906—a thirty-five year period as compared to Rowling's one. Children's literature scholar Peter Hunt identifies Roald Dahl as the most popular writer of all time, followed closely by Enid Blyton, who wrote more than six hundred works between 1922 and 1968, and whose Famous Five books ranked first as the most popular series in a 1999 British study. He further describes Eleanor Porter's *Pollyanna* (1913) as a phenomenal bestseller, with forty-seven printings between 1913 and 1920; A. A. Milne's *Winnie-the-Pooh* (1926) and *The House at Pooh Corner* (1928) as likely "unrivalled in worldwide sales and marketing success of *any* books of the twentieth century"; E. B. White's *Charlotte's Web* (1952) as reputedly "the most-read children's book in the USA, by virtue of being a school textbook." Peter Hunt, *Children's Literature* (Malden, MA: Blackwell Publishers Ltd., 2001), 100 and 154. It would not be difficult to believe that all of these giants have fallen before Rowling's pen and the global market economy. The Potter books have reportedly been translated into more than twenty-eight languages in more than 130 nations.

4. The American Library Association (ALA) cosponsors Banned Books Week each September, which promotes and celebrates the freedom to read and respect all individuals' choices about what they and their families want to read. J. K. Rowling held the number one position on the ALA's list of most challenged books for the years 2000 and 2001. When *Sorcerer's Stone* debuted on the list in 2000, it rose to the top after only three months. Complaints included the promotion of occult/Satanic themes, antifamily messages, and excessive violence. Rowling ranked forty-eighth on the ALA's list of one hundred books that parents, library patrons, and/or other community members most often requested be removed from public library or school shelves between 1990 and 1999.

For many of those who condemn the Potter books for their setting in the "wiz-ardly world," magic is inherently tied to Satanism. Ironically, the word *magic* stems from "Magi"—the "Wise Men of the East" and "the Three Kings" in Matthew 2 who followed the star of Bethlehem to bestow gifts upon the newborn Jesus. Historically, the Magi were a priestly caste of ancient Persia, revered for their wisdom and reputed power over evil spirits. Regarding the actual plot of Rowling's novels, various readers have noted that Harry is an infant celebrated for his defeat of Voldemort, a lord of darkness parallel to Satan, and is therefore suggestive of the baby Jesus, who is also adored and glorified at birth. Where the wizards exclaim "Rejoice" (Rowling, *Sorcerer's Stone*, 5), the house-elf Dobby proclaims: "If [Harry Potter] knew what he means to us, to the lowly, the enslaved, we dregs of the magical world!" He describes how Harry's triumph over the Dark Lord created "a new dawn," with the boy shining "like a beacon of hope" for those who believed the "Dark days" might last forever. Rowling, *Harry Potter and the Chamber of Secrets* (New York: Scholastic Press, 1999), 178–79. Harry is a symbolic savior and protector of the meek, and therefore comparable to Christ and his advocacy for the poor, lepers, prostitutes, and children.

5. A comparison could be drawn here to Roald Dahl's 1964 *Charlie and the Choco-late Factory*. Amidst the "apparent anarchy" is "a straightforward moral tale with solid nineteenth-century origins. Those children who are lazy, stupid or spoiled come to suit-ably sticky ends: the poor and pure child is rewarded." Hunt, *Children's Literature*, 58.

6. Christine Schoefer, "Harry Potter's Girl Trouble." 13 January 2000; http://www.salon.com (accessed 18 July 2001), n.p.

7. Rowling, *Harry Potter and the Prisoner of Azkaban* (New York: Scholastic Press, 1999), 137–38. In response to the question of whether or not the books are too scary for young children, Roni Natov asserts: "Children need to see their feelings, particularly the darkest ones, reflected in their stories. Mitigating the darkness in the fairy tales takes away their power to reassure children that they are not alone in their fearful imagin-ings, that they are shared and can be addressed" (320). Roni Natov, "Harry Potter and the Extraordinariness of the Ordinary," *The Lion and the Unicorn* 25, 2 (2001): 310–27.

8. Laura Miller, "Pottermania at Midnight," 8 July 2000; http://www.salon.com/books/feature/2000/07/08/potter.html (accessed 20 July 2001).

9. Jack Zipes, *Sticks and Stones: The Troublesome Success of Children's Literature from Slovenly Peter to Harry Potter* (New York: Routledge, 2001), 6. Audiobook sales of the Potter series have been high; the film versions of *Harry Potter and the Sorcerer's Stone*, released in mid-November 2001, and *Harry Potter and the Chamber of Secrets*, released in mid-November of 2002, sold record numbers of tickets; Warner Brothers stores across the United States sell a plethora of Harry Potter paraphernalia, including trading cards, lunchboxes, board games, computer games, video games, broomsticks, paja-mas, Hogwarts caps and sweatshirts, sweatshirts, model figures, and stuffed animals; re-cently, while looking up David Kamish's picture book, *The Night Scary Beasties Popped out of My Head*, on Amazon.com, I noted that on the side of the screen was the promo-tional line: "Books Hagrid Would Tell You to Read." This is not to say that the readers of these books cannot resist market forces and/or engage with the texts in intellectual and creative ways: simply that capitalism seeks to create as much profit as possible.

10. Rowling, *Chamber of Secrets*, 331.

11. Ibid., 42.

12. Quoted in Zipes, *Sticks and Stones*, 188n.

13. Ibid., 171 and 173, respectively. In the past few years, a variety of readers have compared Rowling to fantasy favorites C. S. Lewis and J. R. R. Tolkien and found her lacking; however, Rowling's fans have been known to lambaste any critics. Hunt draws a comparison between Rowling and Lewis, commenting on the long period of time that passed by before readers recognized that it was possible to criticize Lewis's writing: "There [was and still] is a preoccupation with the range of his imaginative synthesizing and the potency of his symbols, *plus a tendency to discipleship rather than analysis.*" Hunt, *Children's Literature*, 201, emphasis added. Like that of Lewis, Rowling's work incites powerful loyalties, and "[t]he critic who has the temerity to question the pleasure given to children by this series is very likely to be met with incredulity"—if not hostility. Ibid.

14. Hunt, *Children's Literature*, 36.

15. Bernice E. Cullinan, in collaboration with Mary K. Karrer and Arlene M. Pillar, *Literature and the Child* (New York: Harcourt Brace Jovanovich, 1981), 226 and 509, respectively. This is not to say, however, that each writer is necessarily conscious of espousing a particular set of values. As Pulitzer Prize–winning author N. Scott Momaday proclaimed: "Writers are very frequently astounded by their work. ... They have perceptions and intuitions in the writing that they don't understand. ... [There are] insights which I think are valid, but those insights are not fully conscious ... . They exist beneath the level of everyday consciousness, but they are nonetheless real." Charles L. Woodard, *Ancestral Voice: Conversations with N. Scott Momaday* (Lincoln: University of Nebraska Press, 1989), 125.

16. Michael Benton cites a 1992 study of 115 eighth and eleventh grade students' responses to magazine advertisements and short fiction. The researchers found that their readers tended to blur fiction and reality when speaking about the magazine images and were unlikely to respond critically to any of the materials. And thus, while most Harry Potter child readers would probably be able to distinguish the magical acts of Rowling's novels as fiction, I wonder about their understanding of the social interactions that occur in the magical world. Michael Benton, "Readers, Texts, Contexts: Reader-Response Criticism," *Understanding Children's Literature: Key Essays from the International Companion Encyclopedia of Children's Literature*, Peter Hunt, ed. (New York: Routledge, 1999), 81–99.

17. M. Daphne Kutzer, *Empire's Children: Empire and Imperialism in Classic British Children's Books* (New York: Garland, 2000), 79.

18. Pamela Banting, "S(M)other Tongue?: Feminism, Academic Discourse, Translation," in *Collaboration in the Feminine: Writings on Women and Culture from Tessera*, Barbara Godard, ed. (Toronto: Second Story Press, 1994), 172.

19. William Safire, "Besotted with Potter," *New York Times*, 27 January 2000, A27.

20. See Nancy Smiler Levinson's Letter to the Editor in "The Magic of Harry Potter, for All: Readers React to Safire's Essay," http://www.cesnur.org/recens/potter_013.htm (accessed 20 July 2001).

21. Quoted in Hunt, *Children's Literature*, 200.

22. Quoted in Cullinan, *Literature and the Child*, 5.

23. Jack Zipes is biting in his assessment of the influence of children's books and other cultural tools of the socialization process, especially in the United States. He describes the ways in which adults "engage social and political forces on the battlefield of children's bodies and minds" (xii), claiming the ways we socialize children is "nothing short of barbaric" (x).

24. Schoefer, "Girl Trouble," n.p.

25. Peter Hunt, ed., Introduction, *Understanding Children's Literature*, 5.

26. Kutzer, *Empire's Children*, 79.

27. It has been suggested, however, that Hughes drew together elements from earlier sources, such as Sarah Fielding's *The Governess* (1749) and Harriet Martineau's *The Crofton Boys* (1802). These texts by early women writers, however, have virtually disappeared from the shelves in comparison with the continued popularity of *Tom Brown*.

28. Richard Jenkyns, "Potter in the Past," *Prospect* (October 2000): 38–43, 39.

29. Zipes, *Sticks and Stones*, 182 and 173.

30. Cullinan, *Literature and the Child*, 163.

31. Joan Acocella, "Under the Spell," *The New Yorker* (31 July 2000): 74–78, 77.

32. Ibid., 77. The logic of this statement does not quite follow through; it suggests that coed schools, workplaces, clubs, and entire societies should never have trouble with imbalances of power between men and women.

33. In *Goblet of Fire*, when the poltergeist, Peeves, ignores her orders to stop pelting students with water bombs, she threatens to summon the headmaster (172), enforcing her subordinate status. This novel also seems to carry a dangerous undercurrent in terms of the presentation of maternal influence. Barty Crouch, Jr.'s mother saves him from Azkaban by convincing her husband to rescue their son as her dying wish. Like Lily Potter's protection of the infant Harry, Mrs. Crouch's action saves her son, but her influence over Mr. Crouch means that one of Voldemort's most ardent supporters is released. Similarly, Winky cares for Barty, pities him, and persuades his father to give him occasional rewards for good behavior, like attending the World Quidditch Cup. This is where Barty steals Harry's wand and sends up the Dark Mark, again revealing the dangers of female compassion and the ability of women to convince and disrupt patriarchal authority.

34. Rowling, *Chamber of Secrets*, 163.

35. In her 1981 textbook, Cullinan laments that year after year, girls who are asked what they want to be when they grow up respond "mommy, nurse, teacher, actress" while boys respond with such answers as "astronaut, president, doctor, fireman." When I attended my five-year-old cousin's kindergarten graduation in the spring of 2001 and learned that the students would be replying to the same question, I wondered what changes I would witness, two decades after the publication of Cullinan's text. I was happy to hear that several young girls wanted to be veterinarians and zookeepers, countering the handful of "ballerinas" and somewhat breaking out of the traditional model. What disturbed me most, however, was the ways in which children could begin to push the envelope but then get curbed and contained by popular images. Three girls expressed

the desire to explore space; however, rather than say they wanted to be astronauts, each of them stated that she wanted to be "Barbie in Space." The feminist movement might have taken a few steps forward, but capitalist systems and the images presented in the media push hard in the opposite direction. While there may be some strong and arguably positive role models such as Buffy the Vampire Slayer and the PowerPuff Girls, these are primarily young girls and teens; adult women in powerful positions are rarely shown.

36. Schoefer, "Girl Trouble," n.p.

37. Such narratives include James M. Barrie's *Peter Pan;* P. L. Travers's *Mary Poppins;* L. Frank Baum's *The Wonderful Wizard of Oz;* Madeleine L'Engle's *A Wrinkle in Time* trilogy; Lewis Carroll's *Alice's Adventures in Wonderland;* C. S. Lewis's Narnia Chronicles, such as *The Lion, the Witch, and the Wardrobe;* and Maurice Sendak's picture book *Where the Wild Things Are,* which allowed children the fantasy space to validate and ride out emotions of fear, anger, hate, frustration, and rebellion. More like Roald Dahl's fantasy narratives in some ways, Rowling's hero finds more happiness in the magical world than in the relative safety (where Voldemort is concerned) of the Dursleys' home. Other innovative writers often mentioned in conjunction with Rowling are J. R. R. Tolkien, Ursula K. Le Guin, Joan Aiken, Lloyd Alexander, Natalie Babbitt, Jane Yolen, William Mayne, Francesca Lia Block, Henrietta Branford, and Philip Pullman.

38. Quoted in Hunt, *Children's Literature,* 234. Hunt identifies other cherished (and less scrutinized) books as part of older traditions to defend Rowling against claims of lack of originality: "Dahl's *Charlie and the Chocolate Factory* is little more than an extended *Struwwelpeter* with Belloc rhymes; and Blyton's fantasies are pot-pourris of late-nineteenth-century versions of fairy- and folk-tales; and Grahame's *Wind in the Willows* is merely a compilation of fashionable Thames river stories and echoes of music hall sketches." Hunt, *Children's Literature,* 123.

39. Salman Rushdie, *Haroun and the Sea of Stories: A Novel* (New York: Penguin Group, 1990), 86.

40. Cullinan, *Literature and the Child,* 7.

41. Hunt, *Children's Literature,* 263. One of the many fruitful areas not covered by this text is pedagogy. For more information on this subject, see Elizabeth D. Schafer, *Beacham's Sourcebooks for Teaching Young Adult Fiction: Exploring Harry Potter* (Osprey, FL: Beacham Publishing Corp., 2000). This sourcebook does not present critical arguments to the reader but is instead designed to furnish background material, websites, bibliographies, discussion questions, and ideas for classroom assignments.

I

Reading Harry Potter through Theories of Child Development

Archetypes and the Unconscious in *Harry Potter* and Diana Wynne Jones's *Fire and Hemlock* and *Dogsbody*

Alice Mills

J. K. Rowling's Harry Potter series offers a highly entertaining set of variations on three stock formulae for children's fiction: the initiation of a wizard, the boys' school story, and the story of an orphan recovering from loss to find a place in the world. Especially in the first and fourth volumes (to date, the most recent of the series to be published), these realist and fantasy elements deepen into the mythic. The Forbidden Forest holds creatures from both Greek and medieval Western myth, including centaur and unicorn, in the style of C. S. Lewis's Narnia books. The three-headed dog, Fluffy, of the first book, *Harry Potter and the Philosopher's Stone*[1] (published in the United States under the title *Harry Potter and the Sorcerer's Stone*) is a comical version of the three-headed dog Cerberus that guards the path to the underworld of Greek myth. The Hogwarts crisis of book I concerns the mythic theme of a search for eternal life. Rowling endows unicorn's blood with the power to give life to its drinker, much like the soul-saving blood of Christ, which unicorn's blood represents in medieval bestiary lore, and also like Harry's blood in *Harry Potter and the Goblet of Fire*.[2] This parallel among unicorn, Christ, and Harry is accentuated when the villain, Lord Voldemort, tortures the young wizard with the forbidden Cruciatus Curse in book IV. Furthering the Christian allusions, Hogwarts's headmaster, Albus Dumbledore, has a phoenix in his study, which has the power to heal any wound with its tears. As in ancient myth, this bird voluntarily dies in flames in order to revive in youthful vitality.[3] Like its miraculous healing virtues, its resurrection from the dead connects it with the figure of Christ.[4] All of these mythic figures, apart from the centaurs, are linked to the human longing to transcend time and death, whether by descending to the underworld and returning unscathed, or by magically gaining eternal life through the use of a talisman, or by being resurrected from death.

Among the human characters who triumph over death, Harry is the most innocent. His first victory occurs before the action of book I begins, when as a one-year-old child he not only survives Voldemort's attack but somehow strips the villain of most of his magical powers. The least innocent of the books' seekers after eternal life is Voldemort, a psychic and physical vampire in book I; in book IV he demands that others give their bone, blood, and flesh so that he can reconstitute his body, Medea-style, in a cauldron. Harry Potter and Voldemort are destined to function as each other's antagonists from the moment when the older wizard's powers mysteriously fail against the infant Harry.

First as a baby and then year by year at Hogwarts School, Harry confronts the much older figure of evil, a man as old as Harry's father would have been if he had not been murdered. The father's murderer, Voldemort, can be understood in terms of the Jungian personal unconscious as the dark double of Harry's father, in light of both their old rivalry and their current significance for Harry (indeed, for all the good wizards). Jung argues that the contents of the personal unconscious have a compensatory function to balance consciousness.[5] What Harry learns about his dead father constitutes James Potter as an ego-ideal for his son, someone to be looked up to as a model; Voldemort functions as a compensatory, monstrous father-figure, repeatedly erupting from the unconscious in terror and malignancy. The struggles between Harry and Voldemort can thus be interpreted as an Oedipal power struggle between the son, ignorant of the whole truth about his past, and the monstrous father-figure, out to destroy his son before his son kills him.[6]

Voldemort has an uncanny resemblance to Harry himself, as both are uncomfortably aware. As an aspect of Harry's shadow, his relationship to the boy becomes ever more complex. In book IV, Voldemort assimilates part of Harry's body when he uses Harry's blood to rebuild an adult human shape for himself. At this point he becomes magically blood-related to Harry, a son to Harry as father, by way of the all-male ritual of his rebirth. As usual, Rowling stresses Harry's innocence, his ignorance of what has been planned, and his complete lack of accountability for Voldemort's acts. Harry is compelled to give blood and bears no responsibility for the monstrous "child" that emerges from the cauldron's womb.

While Harry's innocence is sustained throughout, his conscious participation in confrontations with Voldemort increases from book to book. No one (except, perhaps, Dumbledore) knows exactly how Harry survived his first confrontation as a baby, but Harry's knowledge of what happened to his parents is gradually built up by both information from others and magical evocations of the past. At the climax of book I, Harry lapses into unconsciousness while struggling against Voldemort and remains ignorant of exactly how the villain is defeated. In book II,[7] he clings to consciousness while fighting the basilisk. He kills, but does not murder, for he has no awareness that stabbing Riddle's diary will annihilate the Riddle schoolboy manifestation of Voldemort. Here Harry has only slightly more responsibility for his triumph over Voldemort than previously. Book III[8] confronts Harry with the dementors, who, according to Dumbledore, are Voldemort's natural allies, though they are currently policing the wizards' prison. In the course of this third volume, Harry learns how to stay conscious in their presence, and he is fully conscious at the climax of this book when he demonstrates compassion for Voldemort's helper, Peter Pettigrew (like the compassion that Tolkien's hobbits, Bilbo in *The Hobbit* and Frodo in *The Lord of the Rings*, show towards Gollum). By Rowling's fourth volume, Harry is able to fight off unconsciousness in Voldemort's presence and cast off his curse, though not to overcome him. Such endings help the series to continue, as a decisive confrontation with Voldemort is postponed on each occasion; they also suggest, in a Jungian context, that Voldemort exists both as an external threat and as part of Harry's unconscious. The Oedipal struggle between father and son is also an internal struggle within Harry to bring to consciousness, and thus resolve, shadowy contents of his personal unconscious.

The whole series to date can be read, in part, as Harry's wish-fulfillment fantasies that compensate for his abuse at the hands of his family. Voldemort is a more powerful fantasy version of Mr. Dursley, and the glories of surviving Voldemort's attacks in the fantasy world of wizardry compensate for the humiliations and punishments that Harry must endure from those who function as his father and mother in ordinary Muggle consensus reality. Harry's friends at Hogwarts compensate for his solitary confinement at home, and his mastery of flight compensates for his life in a cupboard under the stairs. In such a reading, "uncle" and "aunt" are the shadow sides of Harry's fantasy ideal parents, both unavailable through death; equally, Harry's dead parents are the shadow side of his abusive living parents. Following Bruno Bettelheim's analysis of those fairy tales in which a dead ideal mother is replaced by a wholly negative stepmother,[9] Harry's dead ideal parents and horrible substitute parents can be read as split parts of whole human beings as experienced by the protagonist. Murderous rage against a parent is defended against psychologically in the Harry Potter series as in fairy tales by splitting, a typical maneuver practiced by abused children. For many such children, the terrible abuser is understood to be not the real parent—who must therefore be missing, probably dead—but a replacement: a stepparent or more distant relative. The Dursleys would thus be Harry's abusive parents against whom he defends himself psychologically by splitting, so that he fantasizes ideal dead parents, the most powerful, most beloved, and most lamented of all wizards. He further distances himself by doubling Mr. Dursley in the fantasy world with a villain, Voldemort (both of them opposed to his dead father), to legitimate his own murderous impulses. These are not "really" directed against a wicked father but are socially applauded efforts against a villain who threatens everyone in the fantasy world. Similarly, Harry's hatred for Dudley Dursley, the favored son, is duplicated in the fantasy world in his hatred for the spoilt Draco Malfoy.

Yet even the psychological defense of splitting is not potent enough to legit-imate Harry's murderous feelings towards the monstrous father. When he is in a position to act against Voldemort, Harry at first lapses into unconsciousness and is always exonerated from any murderous intent. In ordinary consensus reality as understood in the Muggle world (a different consensus reality is shared by Rowling's magical beings and a few select Muggles), his defenses against Mr. Dursley and his son become increasingly, though not altogether, ef-fective, as he resorts to flight (through the window at the start of *Harry Potter and the Chamber of Secrets*), bluff (as when he pretends to be casting a spell against Dudley at the start of *Harry Potter and the Prisoner of Azkaban*), and threat (at the end of *Prisoner of Azkaban* and the start of *Goblet of Fire*, he threatens to inform his "convicted murderer" godfather of any mistreatment by the Dursleys[10]). Harry's increasing ability to stay conscious when con-fronting the fantasy bad father gives hope that in the abusive family he may also become able eventually to confront consciously rather than avoid, flee, and take refuge in fantasy.

In such a reading, it is only the male figures in the abusive family that Harry is as yet capable of resisting, even in fantasy. His dead ideal mother is doubled, in the world of wizards, by the maternal Mrs. Weasley, as his dead ideal father is doubled by Dumbledore, but there is no female equivalent for Petunia Durs-ley. The only wicked adult female appears in book IV, in the nonhuman form of a huge snake writhing around in the vicinity of Voldemort. Harry can face the villain but has no dealings with this snake. The cauldron in which Voldemort is reborn is a symbolic womb, but again there is no way in which Harry confronts this feminine agent of evil. In comparison with Rowling's exploration of the fa-ther archetype, the mother is so far in the series completely idealized.[11]

A Jungian reading of the Harry Potter books in terms of the personal uncon-scious and the abused child accounts well psychologically for the death of Harry's good parents in his infancy, for the doubling of Mr. Dursley and Volde-mort, and for many of the contrasts between the ordinary everyday Muggle world and the world of wizardry. It does not, however, account so well for the episodes where Voldemort is depicted as a child, or for the novels' persistent theme of a search for eternal life, or for their frequent episodes of initiation, re-birth, and resurrection, or for their mythic elements. My Jungian reading of these aspects of the series moves from considering consciousness and the per-sonal unconscious to an archetypal interpretation in which I argue that Rowl-ing's characters are driven not only by the personal trauma of abuse but also by deeper and more universal forces of the collective unconscious.

Preeminent among *Harry Potter*'s archetypal images is the child. As Jung points out, the archetypal child is not to be identified with the chronological child nor equated with individual human beings.[12] The archetypal child is, like all archetypes, unknowable in itself, but recognizable indirectly by the images it stirs in the minds of dreamers, the mentally disturbed, and artists and writ-ers, and by its manifestations in beginnings, newness, upheaval, insurgency, the unknown, spontaneity, play, lostness. Some of Hogwarts's child and adolescent figures, like Hagrid and Harry, are strongly associated with the archetypal child; others, like Percy and Draco, align themselves with the past, parents, or institutions, traditions, and/or regulations that are the antithesis of child energy. James Hillman qualifies Jungian theory by arguing for a polarized archetype, *puer/senex*, rather than a single child archetype.[13] *Puer*, his version of the Jungian child archetype, is balanced as a force of beginning by *senex* as a force of ending; *puer* as a disturber of order is matched by *senex* as maintainer of order; *puer* as new entails *senex* as old. The Latin terms are gendered, but Hillman's *puer/senex*, like the Jungian child archetype, is gender-free and not necessarily manifest in human beings. Volcanic eruptions are as much *puer* as the act of being born in Hillman's schema. In my archetypal interpretation of *Harry Potter*, I adopt Hillman's pairing of *puer* and *senex* rather than an unpaired Jungian child archetype, while also placing Rowling's fiction in the context of Jung's *Archetypes and the Collective Unconscious*.

Archetypal energy depersonalizes human beings, insofar as it possesses them and drives their behavior. Percy as a *senex* figure and (to a lesser extent) the Hermione of book I are less than fully human in their allegiance to rules and authority. In contrast, the Weasley twins, George and Fred, are not individualized personalities but indistinguishable trickster figures.[14] When the archetypal energy of scapegoating possesses Harry's schoolfellows, their individual consciousness abates and they act collectively against him. As this energy fades, individual Hogwarts students regain the ability to think for themselves, feel shame, and apologize.

In the wretched Dursley household the scapegoat archetype remains in possession, manifest in different family members in turn, but principally in Harry as victim and in the sinister and comic Mr. Dursley as scapegoater. Irrational, driven, and obsessive, Mr. Dursley is a cartoon character rather than a consciously functioning human able to reflect or feel a wide range of emotions. The Dursleys' misadventures and punishments against them are as much a matter of sadistic scapegoating as is their treatment of Harry and are not so funny when understood in this way. Dudley's scapegoat punishments of being partially transformed into a pig in book I and having his tongue grossly extended in book IV—while hilariously funny to tricksters Fred and George—are not much funnier than Harry's incarceration in a cupboard. It might seem surprising that the Ministry of Magic does not step in to eradicate such evidence of wizardry as the sprouting of Dudley's pig tail, as it does for almost all other magical interventions in the Muggle world. However, in the context of the scapegoat archetype, it is appropriate for the Dursleys' fear and shame to be long drawn out.

Harry is a *puer* figure whenever he is lost, ignorant, or about to enter a new quest; he is a *puer* figure whenever he begins a new course of study or faces a new peril. As Jung comments, the archetypal child is paradoxically both helplessly vulnerable and superhumanly powerful: a savior figure yet at great risk of death.[15] Harry's championship tasks in book IV demonstrate these paradoxes as well as many of the archetypal child motifs listed by Jung, including the golden egg and the mandala. The manifestations of the child archetype, according to Jung, are sometimes influenced by Christianity but more often develop "from earlier, altogether non-Christian levels—that is to say, out of chthonic animals such as crocodiles, dragons, serpents or monkeys. Sometimes the child appears in the cup of a flower, or out of a golden egg, or as the centre of a mandala."[16] The *puer* archetype is not, however, simply associated with Harry and the *senex* with his older antagonist, Voldemort. Harry is also *senex* in that he has already, before the action of book I starts, ended Voldemort's reign and restored the rule of good among the wizards. His present is always shaped by the past, as he increasingly comes to understand.

As Harry learns more, as his place among the wizards becomes confirmed and he survives each struggle with Voldemort, he becomes more closely associated with *senex* characteristics of confidence, knowledge, familiarity, memory, and tradition. After book I, the role of naïve beginner falls less to Harry than to Ginny, the terrified novice of book II, and to the spontaneous and rule-defying Hagrid. Voldemort is also a *puer* character in that he keeps trying to overthrow Dumbledore's authority. He has the physical smallness and vulnerability of an infant. He asks Wormtail to milk the snake, for example, so that he can be fed during the night. "Milk" here refers to snake venom, but his mention of milk casts Voldemort in the role of an unweaned baby.

Rowling's novels are unusual among quest fantasies in their frequent and explicit shifts of archetypal imagery between characters: the *puer* between the weakened Voldemort and the innocent Harry; the *senex* between Voldemort as Dark Lord and Harry as hero; the trickster between the Weasley twins and the plotting Dark Lord and his followers; the scapegoat between Harry and the scapepig Dudley. This pattern in the Harry Potter books renders them trickster texts; they are far from simplistic in their treatment of (generally) formulaic material. Among contemporary fantasy writers, only Diana Wynne Jones is as expert a shifter of archetypal roles among her characters. She, too, writes trickster texts, with increasingly complicated plots in which few characters are as they appear to be. It is premature to evaluate Rowling's overall achievement as a fantasy writer against Jones's accomplishments: Rowling is aiming in the course of seven books to tangle and disentangle her plot threads and to represent the maturing of her adolescent main characters, as Jones has done in the course of single books. A fairer point of comparison is to be found in the two writers' treatment of the same themes: the longing for eternal life, the abused child, the archetypes of child, *senex*, and rebirth. I draw comparisons in the remainder of this chapter between the *Harry Potter* books and Jones's *Fire and Hemlock* (1985) and *Dogsbody* (1975), two of her most compelling books about the lost child.[17]

In *Fire and Hemlock*, Jones cites myths and fairy tales about the living dead, resurrection from the sleep of death, the restoration of human form to an enchanted prince, the ritual sacrifice of an old king, and a never-aging queen. The book's heroine, Polly, reads in *The Golden Bough* about the ritual killing of the king or his substitute at the end of a year or when he ages, to ensure the health of the kingdom by providing a youthful companion to the ageless fairy queen. The faerie world of Jones's novel is dominated by this ritual, in which the eternal queen's human consort evades death through the sacrifice of another man, every nine years, and where the queen herself pretends to die every eighty-one years, bequeathing her possessions to a female "descendant"—really her immortal self—so that she can continue to be accepted in human society as a normal human being.[18]

The men in this story are all victims or potential victims, in danger of ritual scapegoat death so that fairy queen Laurel's consort may live on with renewed vitality. Almost all the book's male characters are Laurel's lovers or potential lovers. Leroy, the aging king, has a son, Sebastian, who is terrified throughout of succeeding to his father's post as consort; it is not quite clear whether Laurel is Sebastian's mother or stepmother. At the end of the book, Leroy descends, probably to hell, and his son becomes his father's replacement as Laurel's husband. This produces an incestuous hell on earth, as the reluctant son replaces his father in the bed of his mother/stepmother. It also produces, in an archetypal reading, a series of shifts between *puer* and *senex*. As the aging king clinging to his power, desperate for the nourishment of someone else's death, Leroy is a psychic vampire like Rowling's Voldemort. As a consort millennia younger than his wife, he is a *puer* devoured by his mother, to be replaced by a son in an eternally repeated series of beginnings. Sebastian is the book's most hopelessly lost child as an unwilling king-consort. And Polly represents yet another *puer* figure, determined to overthrow the order of faerie, in conflict with the *senex* Laurel, a Voldemort-like psychic vampire unaffected by time and determined to keep repeating the ritual of human sacrifice. Like Rowling's Harry, Polly is also a *senex* figure in her desire for a different kind of order and permanence, one set of memories and one true lover.

Polly suffers child abuse in the form of neglect at the hands of her unloving parents and is as touching a lost child as Harry suffering at the hands of the Dursleys. As the plot unfolds in both works, however, it becomes unclear how much of what happens to the children is accidental and how much due to the malign influence of magic-wielders. The pet rat of Harry's best friend, Ron Weasley, turns out to be a disguised follower of Voldemort in book III, prepared to hide for twelve years until Harry arrives at Hogwarts and can become his victim. Polly's memories are twofold, and at first it seems as though one set is absolutely true and the other imposed by magic upon her, but it becomes more and more difficult to decide which are rigged and which accidental, until all come to seem equally controlled by the almost all-powerful world of faerie. Similarly, as Rowling's plots grow in complexity, no detail of Harry's life seems incidental, for each may be part of Dumbledore's master plan to defeat Voldemort or Voldemort's plan to defeat Dumbledore.

At the end of *Fire and Hemlock* it is Polly who is the least lost; she functions as the most powerful, wise, and healing character. She arrives at this power and understanding by surviving the onslaught of the child archetype in its help-lessness and lostness. She has been persecuted, scapegoated, neglected, emo-tionally undernourished, never adequately loved by either parent. She learns from her sufferings so that she can remain conscious and strong-willed at the novel's climax, when the powers of faerie try to confuse, embarrass, and outwit her. Harry Potter, in learning to resist the dementors and Voldemort, is on the same path.

Jones's earlier fantasy novel, *Dogsbody,* also has a lost child as heroine: Kath-leen, reluctantly fostered by her uncle and his hateful wife when her own fa-ther is imprisoned. Kathleen is a *puer* Cinderella figure, despised by the ugly stepmother figure of Aunt Duffie, bullied by her cousin, neglected by her uncle. She is little more than a suffering drudge until she rescues a drowning puppy who turns out to be a celestial prince, lord of the sphere of Sirius. Her version of the Cinderella story does not have a totally happy ending; she remains a *puer* figure to the end of the book, longing for a new beginning with her precious dog. Her inadequate foster parents similarly keep their *senex* qualities, living out a loveless marriage of convenience and habit. It is in the character of Sirius that the archetypal energies of *puer* and *senex* shift. As a star-lord he is a *senex* figure millennia old, who should be responsible for the perturbations of his sphere. Sirius begins the novel as the besotted lover of his wicked consort, and he clings on, *senex*-style, to an unchanging image of her even when it is likely to cost him his life. However, his gusts of rage are *puer,* and when reborn as a puppy, Sirius has the *puer* characteristics of living for the moment, the inabil-ity to remember, playfulness, and lostness. Much of *Dogsbody* concerns Sirius's gradual regaining of star consciousness, the return of his memories, and the putting right of starry wrongs. He learns the *senex* virtues of justice and re-sponsibility and how to balance them with *puer* love and play, rather than al-ternating between *puer* rage and *senex* stubbornness to his own mortal peril.

Jones's Sirius, the lord of a celestial sphere transformed into a dog, is a hu-morous variation on the Greek myth of Sirius, the canine translated after death to the heavens as the dog-star. Rowling's Sirius Black also changes his shape between human and dog, having acquired the skill through long train-ing. Rowling's choice of the name "Sirius" for this character suggests, how-ever, that his weredog transformations may be innate as much as acquired. Similarly, the name of her werewolf character, Professor Lupin, hints at an in-nate wolf nature via the Latin for wolf, *lupus.* In contrast, the author's two other shape-changers, Peter Pettigrew and James Potter, have nothing of the rat or the stag about their human names. For all four, shape-shifting does not entail immortality, a place in the starry heavens, or a permanent place in the mythically charged Forbidden Forest of Hogwarts. Rather, it is a trickster at-tribute that leads to mischievous pranks. Sometimes the consequences of shape-shifting are more serious. For Lupin, his shape-shifting must be hidden lest he be persecuted and killed; for Sirius Black, it is only his dog-consciousness that enables him to trick his way out of madness and death.

The most perplexing character in *Dogsbody* is another shape-shifter who appears only briefly at the end of the novel, when Sirius and Kathleen each earn a wish by travelling with the Wild Hunt. The Master of the Hunt is an enigmatic being. Kathleen and her cousin Robin, being exceptionally well read in myth, note his connection with Arawn, lord of the underworld in Welsh myth, and wonder whether he may be Orion or Actaeon, torn to pieces by his own hounds in Greek myth. The Master is a dying and resurrected god, both leader of the pack and its antlered prey. At every running of the Wild Hunt, he replays the archetypal pattern played out on Earth and in the heavens by Sirius, who first dies as a star and is resurrected as a beast, and then dies as a beast and is resurrected as a celestial being.

Sirius has been given the body of a dog so that he can hunt down the truth about himself as star. His consort pursues him, but this hunt is to some extent choreographed and overseen by Sirius's starry judges as a way to bring him back to life as a star. For Kathleen, the Master of the Hunt plays a different role. He grants her a wish, and as a potent, mysterious, cautioning giver of supernatural gifts, he enacts the role of fairy godmother to Kathleen's Cinderella. His gift brings profound loss, for Kathleen asks to understand Sirius rather than to continue being his loving companion. She then plunges back into lost child helplessness and suffering when Sirius dies as a dog.

Surprisingly, the Master also asks Kathleen for a gift, when she is temporarily armed with a fearsome interstellar weapon: "I'm sick of being a child of night. My ancestors came out by day and didn't frighten or puzzle people. I want to be the same.... I want to walk Earth as you do."[19] This is a remarkable request by a chthonic archetypal figure, capable of nightly dying and coming back to life. The Master is said to be Earth's most unhappy child, though Jones does not expand on this remark. When he asks to be like a human, it is not clear whether his appeal entails the loss of his godlike powers of resurrection from the dead, but it resonates with Sirius's wish to be a mortal dog again in Kathleen's loving company. Like Sirius's yearning, and like Kathleen's greatest desire, this wish to surrender the dread of his presence and become part of the ordinary everyday human world is not granted.

Rowling's half-giant Rubeus Hagrid is not a mythic figure like the Master of the Hunt, but he, too, longs not to be an outsider. Of all the wizards, Hagrid is the most closely in touch with the mythic Forbidden Forest, where he alone can walk in safety. This character, like Jones's Master of the Hunt, is master of the Forbidden Forest's hunt—usually with a miniscule one-dog pack. He embodies the child archetype in both his mysterious parentage and his labors as a thrall.[20] As a menial servant, Hagrid is associated with the "little people" of the books— the house-elves, who are ruthlessly or benevolently enslaved by human magic-wielders. Like Hagrid, they embody the archetypal lost child. In addition, the Hogwarts groundskeeper has the *puer* qualities of naïveté, spontaneity, and playfulness. He longs to parent, but his desires, rather than fit the orderly, responsible *senex* role, are for a contraband nonhuman child, whether it be a flesh-eating spider or a wild dragon. Hagrid often takes the maternal role of nurturer and egg-protector; as such, he attempts to compensate for his own motherless childhood and compulsively re-enacts his own concealed parentage. Rowling hints that in Harry Potter books to come, giants may lose their stigma and be completely accepted into the world of wizards along with the house-elves. In order to do so, half-giant and house-elf may have to change roles, from lost and exploited child to child as hero, just like Harry in each book to date. Indications are that Hagrid's longing for acceptance will be more easily assuaged than the yearning of Jones's sad Master of the Hunt.

Jones's good female characters in *Fire and Hemlock* and *Dogsbody* are in love with eternity, while her good males long for the world of ordinary time, change, and death.[21] In *Fire and Hemlock*, Sebastian and Polly's beloved Thomas dreads the thought of becoming the ageless Laurel's next consort, and both see Polly as their possible savior. *Dogsbody's* Sirius tries to get back into the body of a dead dog so that he can be closer to Kathleen. Jones skillfully voices the yearning towards ordinary consensus reality—a yearning so strong that Sirius would rather live as a dog on earth than as a deity in the heavens. In Rowling's Harry Potter series, it is the evil male characters who seek the unchanging world of eternal life, which turns out to be identical to the world of eternal death. Harry repeatedly renounces the lure of eternal life in favor of ordinary existence, subject to time and death and surprises. He functions in his encounters with Voldemort's evil like a Quidditch Seeker, whose role is to bring the game to an end. Perhaps, as the series continues, Harry will succeed in connecting myth and consensus reality without attachment, so that the archetypes can be honored guests rather than calamitous visitors, so that the shadow side can be embraced rather than suppressed, so that child abuse can finally be healed.

NOTES

1. J. K. Rowling, *Harry Potter and the Philosopher's Stone* (London: Bloomsbury, 1997).

2. J. K. Rowling, *Harry Potter and the Goblet of Fire* (London: Bloomsbury, 2000).

3. While the phoenix in Western mythology is first recorded in ancient Greece and attributed to Egypt, its ability to resurrect itself from death led to its mediaeval interpretation as a type of Christ.

4. There are plenty of hints, however, that all is not as it seems in this episode, and that Dumbledore has set it up for long-term consequences, towards an ultimate complete victory over Voldemort.

5. C. G. Jung, *The Archetypes and the Collective Unconscious*, 2d ed., trans. R. Hull (Princeton, NJ: Princeton University Press, 1968).

6. For an extended Freudian and Kleinian investigation of Oedipal issues in the Harry Potter series, see Kelly Noel-Smith's "Harry Potter's Oedipal Issues" in *Psychoanalytic Studies* 3, 2 (2001): 199–207.

7. J.K. Rowling, *Harry Potter and the Chamber of Secrets* (London: Bloomsbury, 1998).

8. J.K. Rowling, *Harry Potter and the Prisoner of Azkaban* (London: Bloomsbury, 1999).

9. See, for example, Bettelheim's analysis of Cinderella in *The Uses of Enchantment: The Meaning and Importance of Fairy Tales* (New York: Alfred A. Knopf, 1977), 236–77.

10. Rowling, *Prisoner of Azkaban*, 317.

11. The power of a mother over a child is explained in archetypal terms by Hillman: "For the mothering attitude, it is always a matter of life and death ... because the mother's relation to the child is personal, not personal as related and particular, but *archetypally personal* in that the child's fate is delivered through the personal matrix of her fate." James Hillman, *Loose Ends: Primary Papers in Archetypal Psychology* (Dallas: Spring Publications, 1975), 36.

12. Jung, *Archetypes*, 161, fn. 21.

13. James Hillman, "Senex and Puer," *Puer Papers*, J. Hillman, ed. (Dallas: Spring Publications, 1979).

14. Jung writes at length about the psychology of the trickster in *The Archetypes and the Collective Unconscious*. Of particular relevance to the Weasley twins are the trickster traits of "fondness for ... jokes and malicious pranks" and the connection between the trickster archetype and carnival "reversal of the hierarchic order." Jung, *Archetypes*, 255.

15. *Ibid.*, 170.

16. *Ibid.*, 159.

17. Diana Wynne Jones, *Dogsbody* (London: Macmillan, 1975) and *Fire and Hemlock* (London: Methuen, 1985).

18. Like *The Golden Bough*, *Fire and Hemlock* extends its mythic references worldwide. The fairy queen, Laurel, has lived for at least as long as myths have been told and is represented as the source of all such stories rather than as an example of them.

19. Jones, *Dogsbody*, 179.

20. See Jung, *Archetypes*, 171. Hagrid conceals his giantess parentage until book IV for fear of being scapegoated.

21. While this pattern might seem to reinforce the sexist stereotype of the powerless, loving woman, Jones's most lethal, hateful, and powerful women in both books are older women: Laurel, Sirius's consort, and Duffie. A case could be made for Jones as biased against older women rather than a sexist writer, as almost all the older women in her fiction are evil.

2

Harry Potter and the Magical Looking Glass: Reading the Secret Life of the Preadolescent

Lisa Damour

In *The Uses of Enchantment: The Meaning and Importance of Fairy Tales,*[1] Bruno Bettelheim, a prominent psychoanalyst, asserts that the "classic" fantasy tales enjoy an enduring mass appeal because they speak to some of the critical psychological dilemmas of childhood. Bettelheim convincingly argues that tales such as "Little Red Riding Hood" and "Hansel and Gretel" symbolize and find resolutions for unconscious psychological conflicts typical among children: fears of abandonment, the tension between gratification and frustration, curiosity and confusion about adult sexuality, and so on. Using mass appeal as a gauge, it appears that the books of J. K. Rowling's Harry Potter series[2] may also address some of the significant developmental challenges facing their vast readership of children and preadolescents. Indeed, the opening acts of the Harry Potter series employ several popular fairy tale conventions. Harry lives with relatives, the Dursleys, who are inadequate, incompetent, and cruel stand-ins for his far superior *actual* parents who happen to be dead. The belief in having superior but absent parents is so commonplace among children that Sigmund Freud gives the construct a name of its own: the fantasy of the family romance.[3] In a similar vein, Harry's adventures allow children to indulge vicariously their wishes to defeat a dominating and indulged sibling and substitute all-good (Dumbledore) or all-bad (Voldemort) adult figures for their own perplexingly complex parents. However, Harry's childhood experiences are described only to set the stage for the real heart of the series—the challenges he faces as a preadolescent, a developmental period that runs roughly from ages eleven to fourteen years. The astounding popularity of the Harry Potter series may derive, in part, from the fidelity with which the stories speak to the dynamic and unconscious conflicts, fears, and wishes that arise when children set their sights on becoming adults.

Obviously, enjoyment of the Harry Potter series is not an entirely unconscious experience. Symbolic meanings aside, Rowling's stories are enormously appealing: the humor and suspense of the twisting plots and the highly detailed descriptions of the magical world are almost impossible to resist. Many parents await the next installment of the Harry Potter series with more excitement than their children do. If adults are so enthralled by Harry Potter, is it reasonable to suppose that the series' popularity stems from its depiction of the *preadolescent* experience? Certainly adults haven't cottoned to "Cinderella" and "Snow White," which reflect the experiences of early childhood, as they have to the tales of Harry Potter.

In fact, adults may delight in the Harry Potter series precisely *because* the stories speak of the preadolescent experience—a time of life that many grownups remember vividly. In contrast, the memories of earliest childhood are almost always unconsciously but deliberately forgotten—in psychoanalytic terms, repressed—in the course of development. This being the case, fairy tales meant for younger children appeal primarily to an audience of readers/listeners who are currently living through the unconscious conflicts mirrored in the tales, but are less interesting to adults who, as a fact of development, do not recall what it was like to be five. Grown-ups can enjoy Harry Potter because they *do* remember what it was like to be eleven, twelve, thirteen, and fourteen and take pleasure in recognizing and reliving a time when they were preparing to leave childhood behind.

It is nothing new to analyze a piece of literature through a psychoanalytic lens. However, many applications of psychoanalysis in the humanities leave aside an important dimension: psychoanalysis is a developmental theory. In other words, psychoanalytic theory views human development as a progression through a series of stages, each with its own qualities, tasks, and conflicts. Every stage is built on the foundation of those that went before and salient elements of each stage are recapitulated or reworked multiple times in the course of development. While psychoanalysis has provided an illuminating framework for understanding the symbolic meanings of many products of the liberal arts, it can be *especially* useful in addressing the question of why certain texts appeal to people of certain ages. Put another way, why do particular stories appeal to an audience sharing a particular developmental moment? Or, for the purposes of this chapter—what can psychoanalysis tell us about why Harry, his friends, and their adventures have such a devoted following among preadolescent readers?

Since psychoanalysis is a developmental theory with each phase building upon what went before, an analytic inquiry into the experience of the preadolescent reader necessitates a summary of the earlier developmental stages. Needless to say, volumes upon volumes of psychoanalytic literature have been devoted to the description of development from birth through adolescence. What follows is simply a brief description of the major phases and tasks of early life.

Freud[4] and his followers frame early development in terms of the successive concentration of libidinal and aggressive pleasures at different erogenous zones. For roughly the first eighteen months of life, the primary organizing experiences occur through the mouth (the oral stage). Pleasure arrives in the form of mouthing objects, sucking, and taking in nourishment. Aggression is also expressed through oral routes such as biting, spitting out, and crying. The oral stage is a time of massive vulnerability, with the infant's survival depending entirely on the provisions of the outside world. As such it lays down the foundation for an individual's sense of the world as a safe and reliable or inconstant and precarious place.

The anus succeeds the mouth as a primary site of erogenous activity. During the anal stage (roughly ages two and three), toddlers delight in the products of their own bowels and the developing ability to regulate their retention and expulsion. At a time when increased physical motility means that many actions are met with a strong parental "No!" most toddlers relish their sovereignty over their own anal activity, hence the frequent power struggles of potty-training. Anal aggression is sadistic and it usually involves gaining pleasure from teasing. The major developmental tasks of this stage involve adopting socialized values of what it means to be clean and replacing pleasure in sadism with the development of empathy and autonomy.

The genitals overtake the anus as the primary site of physical pleasure in children between the ages of four and six (known as the phallic stage). In addition to discovering that the genitals can be manipulated to produce pleasurable sensations, children in this stage begin to appreciate the difference that the genitals denote: what it means to be male or female. Some psychoanalysts and analytically minded cultural theorists attribute enormous emotional, personal, and political significance to the ownership of a penis or envy thereof. Modern psychoanalytic theory has staked out a position that is not only more agreeable, but almost certainly more in tune with what is actually on the mind of the four-year-old who realizes that his or her genitalia is not the same as everyone else's. Prior to the appreciation of genital difference, children believe that they can become everything and anything; little girls look forward to being daddies, little boys imagine their future pregnancies. The realization of genital difference has sweeping implications for children of both sexes, but not of the "phallus-as-source-of-all-social-power" sort. For the first time in their short lives, children are faced with the painful reality that their capacities, even their *potential* capacities, are limited. They cannot be men *and* women, mommies *and* daddies.

Enlightenment about genital difference can be a profound shock and disappointment causing some four-year-olds to construe their genital limitations as a form of punishment. But why so much concern with punishment, and especially punishment at the site of the genitals? The phallic stage of psychosexual development also happens to coincide with the occurrence of the Oedipus complex in which children long for an exclusive relationship with the parent of the opposite sex. The desire for such a relationship necessarily involves the wish to displace the same-sex parent. Even toddlers can appreciate that the same-sex parent might not take kindly to such feelings (hence the fear of being or having been punished) and that the special nature of the parental relationship has something to do with sexuality (hence the preoccupation with genital punishment). The Oedipus complex is resolved when children of both sexes realize that their attempt to displace the same-sex parent is futile, decide that "if you can't beat 'em, join 'em," and trade in their competitive feelings for wishes to imitate and be like the same-sex parent. As noted above, the memories of the Oedipus complex and all that led up to it (oral, anal, and phallic preoccupations) are repressed, thus paving the way for the next developmental stage: latency.

During latency (roughly ages seven to eleven) sexual and aggressive energies ease and are channeled—in psychoanalytic terms, sublimated—into socially appropriate behaviors such as sports, schoolwork, and developing friendships with other children. Though sexual and aggressive feelings are never truly latent, parents and children experience this phase as a time of relative calm between the stresses of early childhood and the upheavals of adolescence. The latency phase comes to a close when children experience a resurgence of sexual and aggressive drive energies, an occurrence that often coincides with the biological event of puberty.

When the Harry Potter tales begin, Harry's latency has just about come to an end. Indeed, the series kicks off with Harry's eleventh birthday and the accompanying news that he is, in fact, a magical boy. Each volume in the series covers a year of Harry's life and his birthdays (disappointing or joyous) are featured at the beginning of each book lest the reader forget his age. At the time of this writing the series has covered Harry's eleventh through fourteenth years, the period of preadolescence. Like each developmental phase, preadolescence brings its own challenges and anxieties and unlike most of the preceding phases, crucial elements of preadolescence are starkly different for boys and girls. While the surge in sexual and aggressive energies that occurs at the end of latency feels reminiscent of the phallic period for all children, boys and girls react to this upsurge in drive activity with diametrically opposed tendencies. As Peter Blos notes,[5] girls tend to counteract the reminder of their early childhood dependence on their mothers by throwing themselves toward heterosexual relationships. In contrast, boys, who often lag behind girls developmentally, avoid what feels like a renewal of the phallic-phase relationship with their mothers by doing it one better: regressing to an even earlier stage. Rather than reliving the phallic phase and its attendant peril (namely, castration anxiety), boys take refuge in the two-pronged pleasures of the anal phase: all-things-gross and sadism. Indeed, many mothers are shocked and disappointed when their previously charming schoolboys emerge in their tenth or eleventh year as connoisseurs of fart noises and torturers of ants.

For preadolescent readers looking to indulge their anal interests through sanctioned mediums like reading, the Harry Potter tales provide a lot to like.

Throughout the series, ample space is set aside for the gratuitous description of disgusting objects and for displays of sadistic behavior. On their first train ride to Hogwarts, Harry and Ron thoroughly enjoy eating Bertie Bott's Every Flavor Beans. They seem to like the grass and sardine flavored beans at least as much as the coconut and strawberry flavors. Ron even goes so far as to brag that his brother once got a jellybean that was "booger-flavored."[6] Confections are a source of delightful disgust throughout the series: Jelly Slugs, Cockroach Clusters, and blood-flavored lollipops are among the sundries available at the Honeydukes candy shop when Harry, Ron, and Hermione pay a visit as third-year students.[7]

The first day of classes in the fourth year includes a lesson from Professor Sprout about how to extract pus from the bobotuber plant. While the plants are described as ugly, sluglike, and disgusting, squeezing their pus is also characterized as "oddly satisfying," and the process, a clear analog of pimple-squeezing, is outlined in exquisite detail.[8] No account of anality in the Harry Potter series would be complete without noting that much of the plot action in book II takes place in a Hogwarts bathroom and involves a ghost, Moaning Myrtle, who lives in a toilet. Indeed each book in the series is peppered with the grotesque (e.g., Nearly-Headless Nick, the hairy-infant Voldemort of book IV, and so on). The point here is that occasionally repulsion is critical to the story line—but much of the time it's just for fun.

Sadism, the enjoyment of another's pain, is the most prominent form of anal-phase aggression and, like the anal-phase delight in anything repulsive, it is also heavily featured in the Harry Potter series. Naturally, every story with a villain has sadism in it—a villain isn't worth his salt if he does not enjoy the suffering of his victims, as Voldemort certainly does. But young readers whose superegos can already generate guilty feelings need not go to the dark side to have a little sadistic fun. Rowling has cleverly taken all of the shame out of sadistic pleasures by providing a wide range of deserving victims such as the Dursleys, Percy Weasley, and Draco Malfoy. Two of the earliest acts of magic in the entire series come at Dudley Dursley's expense when Harry unwittingly sets a boa constrictor on him and then, in a fit of anger, Hagrid tries to turn him into a pig but only succeeds in affixing a corkscrew tail to his bottom. The theme of torturing Dudley or his relatives (all of whom equally enjoy torturing Harry) repeats itself at the beginning of each new volume: in book II, flying owls and flying puddings ruin the Dursleys' dinner party for rich potential clients, Aunt Marge is turned into a blimp in book III, and in book IV, the Weasley twins trick Dudley into eating Ton-Tongue Toffee. While the Weasley twins are "good guys" within in the broader fight between good and evil chronicled in the series, they serve an important purpose as "bad boys" whose antics are enjoyed by all, and whose prank shop is ultimately funded by Harry. When minor characters like Fred and George Weasley carry out sadistic acts, the reader can fully enjoy the cruel behavior since doing so does not come at the expense of pleasurable identifications with the essentially moral young heroes:

Harry, Ron, and Hermione. Similarly, when Harry and Draco Malfoy argue in book IV, it is Mad-Eye Moody, not Harry, who turns Malfoy into a squealing, bouncing ferret.[9]

While regression to anal-phase pleasures characterizes preadolescent behavior in boys, the average preadolescent girl assuages her fear of revisiting a regressive relationship with her mother by actively pursuing heterosexual relationships. Unfortunately for the girl, her early romantic leanings are usually unrequited. As the foregoing description of psychological development in boys suggests, preadolescent boys are far more interested in being disgusting or sadistic than they are in being suitors. Indeed, when preadolescent boys do engage their female peers, it is often in the form of anal-phase behavior such as teasing them or trying to "gross them out." The lopsided relationship between girls and boys, with girls carrying all of the romantic interest, is also faithfully represented throughout the Harry Potter series. In book II, young Ginny Weasley has a mad crush on Harry and Hermione is equally enthralled with Gilderoy Lockhart. When Viktor Krum arrives at Hogwarts in book IV, he quickly develops a gaggle of female followers, one of whom hopes that he will sign her hat in lipstick.[10] The fictional description of the girls' crushes reflects a fact of preadolescent life: preadolescent girls' romantic pursuits often seem to be more aggressive than affectionate. Preadolescent boys are usually overwhelmed by the intensity of girls' heterosexual feelings, especially when such interests are paired with the reality that eleven and twelve-year-old girls are often taller and stronger than boys of the same age.

As noted above, the preadolescent boy regresses to anal-phase pleasures to avoid revisiting the unconscious castration anxieties of the Oedipal complex. This being the case, how does the young man react when his female age-mates mature into sexual aggressors? Usually, preadolescent boys protect themselves from the pervasive female threat by banding together in all-male groups where, conveniently, they are free to indulge their anal-phase interests. Certainly Harry and Ron resort to this tactic in the close friendship they share with each other, and Hermione makes a worthy third boy since her femininity is decidedly absent for much of the series. When Hermione does act like a girl, she is ridiculed by Harry and Ron, as is the case with her crush on Gilderoy Lockhart, or is unrecognizable, as when she arrives for the Yule Ball on Viktor Krum's arm.

The scene from book IV in which Harry takes a bath with his golden egg depicts, in exquisite detail, the particular dynamic of the dominating preadolescent girl in sexual pursuit of a preadolescent boy who is looking to indulge infantile, not adult heterosexual, interests. On Cedric Diggory's advice, Harry takes his golden egg to the prefects' bathroom in order to discern its clue. Harry is awed by the bathroom, its glorious tub, and the many-colored bath bubbles that flow from the tub's golden taps. After he gets into his bubble bath and is playing with the egg—a scene strikingly reminiscent of a toddler in the tub— Harry is outraged to discover that Moaning Myrtle is also in the bathroom and has likely seen him naked. She complains that he has been avoiding her, confesses that she often spies on boys as they bathe, makes nasty, competitive comments about an attractive mermaid who inhabits a portrait in the bathroom, and all the while delights in "bossing him around."[11] Harry benefits from Myrtle's advice about the egg but he is frightened and annoyed by her sexual curiosity. As he gets in and out of the tub, Harry angrily insists that Myrtle cover her eyes so as not to see him nude. Her peeping is an unwelcome act of aggression and lest the implied castration threat be lost on the reader (or, more likely, the reader's unconscious), the bathroom scene is revisited in a dream of Harry's shortly thereafter. In the dream, the seductive mermaid from the portrait has taken Harry's Firebolt and is holding it above his head while she taunts him and insists that he jump out of his bubble bath to retrieve it.[12] Even the recreational psychoanalyst can easily appreciate the symbolic potential of the Firebolt.

Harry expresses sexual interest in books III and IV, but the instances in which he possesses desire seem to be exceptions that prove the rule. Bulgaria's veela mascots enchant Harry as they dance for the crowds at the Quidditch World Cup in book IV.[13] Hypnotized, he prepares to jump out of his viewing box in the hopes of making a good impression. Harry may be in love but he is not the agent of a feeling, just the victim of a dangerous spell. Again, the preadolescent boy is an unwilling and vulnerable target of feminine sexuality. Interestingly, when Harry does develop a crush of his own, it is on Cho Chang, a girl who is sweet and kind and has little in common with her pushy female peers.

The foregoing description of preadolescent boys and girls suggests that they could not be less alike. But despite the poor match in the arena of psychosexual development, preadolescent boys and girls do share a great deal of common ground in their psychological experiences of puberty and of the adult world. Few experiences are more prominent in the lives of preadolescents than the onset of puberty. Though essentially a biological event, puberty abounds with psychological meaning; certainly most adults have salient, emotional memories of the onset of menses or nocturnal emissions.

At first glance, literal accounts of pubertal development seem to be notably absent from the Harry Potter series considering that, to date, the books have covered Harry, Ron, and Hermione's eleventh through fourteenth years. Passing references are made to pimples and their treatments: Moaning Myrtle usually picks at her chin while she talks and is taunted by Peeves for being "pimply."[14] Professor Sprout bemoans the fate of Eloise Midgen, whose failed attempt to curse her pimples away resulted in the temporary loss of her own nose.[15] Otherwise, the radical physical changes endured by Harry's age-mates appear to go unmentioned.

However, an understanding of how puberty is usually experienced by those caught in its clutches illuminates why young readers might enjoy the absence of any explicit descriptions of Harry's physical maturation. As noted above, preadolescence occurs in the wake of the developmental period known as latency, during which sexual and aggressive drives lose some of their early power and are channeled into socially appropriate endeavors. Latency is also a time when children usually enjoy an extended period of feeling comfortable with their own bodies. Having navigated the straits of the Oedipal period, the latency-age child is usually happily resigned to being a boy or a girl (not an adult, or a person of the opposite sex). Further, between ages seven and eleven the body changes much more slowly than it did in early life, thus providing an unprecedented continuity in the sense of self. And when the body does change, it is almost always for the better: latency-aged children become stronger and more coordinated, and often revel in burgeoning athletic skill.

Come puberty, the body no longer feels like a friend. The physical changes associated with preadolescence are usually experienced as unwelcome, embarrassing, and unhelpful. Formerly cute latency-aged children become homely adolescents; graceful athletes and dancers turn gangly and clumsy. Girls who did not give much thought to their bodies during latency must now manage the all-too-public affair of growing breasts and the beginning of menstruation—an event experienced by some girls as nothing short of traumatic.[16] Boys contend with awkwardly changing voices, unpredictable erections, and radical differences in the size and strength of their various male peers. Given how emotionally overwrought puberty can be, we can certainly appreciate that preadolescents might seek out recreational reading that provides a fantasy escape from, not an explicit description of, their own physical upheavals.

But even though the Harry Potter tales barely address the biological facts of puberty, they speak volumes to the psychological experience. Throughout the series, Harry, Ron, and Hermione endure several terrifying and bizarre physical changes. When Harry is injured by a rogue Bludger in book II, Lockhart's "cure" removes all of the bones in Harry's arm.[17] Shortly thereafter, Harry and Ron use Polyjuice Potion to turn themselves into Crabbe and Goyle (who are very far along in pubertal development), while Hermione accidentally morphs into a cat. Later in the series, Hermione must contend with the sudden eruption of yellow boils all over her hands,[18] while Harry grows gills and webbed feet to complete the second task of the Triwizard Tournament.[19] Harry, Ron, and Hermione mimic the experience of puberty by enduring one shocking physical change after another. Their feelings about these magical changes could equally describe the typical reaction to pubertal development: it is strange and unpleasant, yet sometimes marvelous.

Significantly, the stories not only mirror the physical disruptions of puberty, but also offer a magical solution. No matter how miserable the transformations, our heroes' bodies always return to their original states thanks to the passage of time or Madam Pomfrey's unfailing ministrations. Thus the preadolescent reader can enjoy in fantasy what is impossible in reality: a physical self (and closely associated psychological sense of self) that is continuous and invariable.

There is one notable exception to the rule that the protagonists' bodies always return to their original states. Hermione allows Madam Pomfrey to unknowingly overcorrect the size of her two front teeth after they are elongated by one of Malfoy's hexes.[20] In doing so, she procures a cosmetic change that her parents (both dentists) had not previously allowed. Here Hermione enacts a hopeful fantasy often associated with preadolescent development: that the indignities of puberty may be rewarded by the emergence of a physical form more elegant and glorious than ever before.

For both boys and girls, preadolescence consists (thankfully) of more than just the anxiety and suspense of pubertal development. Above all, the world of the preadolescent is a world of peers. Though still very much embedded in their families, eleven- and twelve-year-olds often prefer to be with their friends, not their parents. Preadolescence is the time when children conclude that their parents are far more embarrassing, restrictive, or just plain dorky than they had ever noticed before. Ideally, parents are able to tolerate their children's increasing demands for physical and psychological independence, especially as these early demands pave the way for a more complete separation, which usually occurs during late adolescence.

Again, the Harry Potter series happily indulges the preadolescent's fantasy life. Harry and his peers do not live with their families, but with their friends. They are each other's guardians and parents; Hermione in particular often serves as Harry's and Ron's mom-away-from-home. The Hogwarts house system provides the children with a sort of extended family with whom they eat and sleep. One might argue that many adults populate the Harry Potter tales. This is true, but in all cases, the children are characters while the adults are caricatures. Harry, Ron, and Hermione have grown increasingly psychologically complex with each new installment in the series. Harry feels anger and fear, grieves for his parents, and yearns for Cho Chang. Ron can be jealous and loyal, Hermione dutiful and caustic. But the adults are two-dimensional, even though they appear in one installation of the story after another. Dumbledore is good and wise; Snape is vindictive and cruel. The Dursley parents are stupid and cold-hearted; the Weasley parents are warm and loving. Even Sirius Black turns out to be a simple faithful protector once we learn that he is not just an evil murderer. Though the adults are critical to the story line, Rowling treats them as set pieces, while Harry, Ron, Hermione, and their peers get to be actors in an unfolding drama.

Much more could be said about how the Harry Potter tales faithfully represent the inner lives of children and preadolescents. Space does not allow for a consideration of the preadolescent's moral development and the myriad ways in which the Potter tales address what it means to be good, and what entices people to be bad. Similarly, the series deals admirably with Harry, Ron, and Hermione's maturing cognitive and emotional capacities and their increasingly complex understandings of themselves, each other, and the world around them. In these and other ways, Rowling has artfully created a textual looking-glass where young readers can observe their own unconscious conflicts in a displaced and imaginary form, indulge their fantasy lives, and find magical solutions to otherwise hopeless troubles.

NOTES

1. Bruno Bettelheim, *The Uses of Enchantment: The Meaning and Importance of Fairy Tales* (New York: Vintage Books, 1976).

2. J.K. Rowling, *Harry Potter and the Sorcerer's Stone* (New York: Scholastic Press, 1997); *Harry Potter and the Chamber of Secrets* (New York: Scholastic Press, 1999); *Harry Potter and the Prisoner of Azkaban* (New York: Scholastic Press, 1999); *Harry Potter and the Goblet of Fire* (New York: Scholastic Press, 2000).

3. Sigmund Freud, "Family Romances," in *Collected Papers, V* (London, Hogarth Press, 1950).

4. Sigmund Freud, *New Introductory Lectures on Psychoanalysis* (New York: W.W. Norton, 1933).

5. Peter Blos, *On Adolescence: A Psychoanalytic Interpretation* (New York: The Free Press, 1962), 67.

6. Rowling, *Sorcerer's Stone,* 104.

7. Rowling, *Prisoner of Azkaban,* 196–97.

8. Rowling, *Goblet of Fire,* 194–95.

9. Ibid., 204–6.

10. Ibid., 248.

11. Ibid., 462.

12. Ibid., 489.

13. Ibid., 103.

14. Rowling, *Chamber of Secrets,* 135.

15. Rowling, *Goblet of Fire,* 195.

16. J.S. Kestenberg, "Menarche," in *Adolescents: Psychoanalytic Approach to Problems and Therapy,* ed. S. Lorand and H.I. Schneer (New York: P.B. Hoeber, 1961).

17. Rowling, *Chamber of Secrets,* 173.

18. Rowling, *Goblet of Fire,* 541.

19. Ibid., 494.

20. Ibid., 405.

3

Harry Potter and the Acquisition of Knowledge

Lisa Hopkins

Lack of access to technological, commodified versions of knowledge such as tape-recorders and computers means that for Harry Potter, knowledge, which is crucial to his survival, must always be acquired slowly, painfully, and over a period of time. Indeed, from the outset, Hogwarts headmaster Albus Dumbledore insists on the importance of time and process when he explains to Professor McGonagall why Harry must live with the Dursleys, as part of the Muggle world, unaware of his own fame until he is "ready to take it"—until, presumably, he has the requisite emotional mechanisms to assist him in the assimilation of that knowledge.[1] Thus, ignorance becomes Harry's defining condition. As Hagrid says upon meeting him, "[the boy] knows nothin' abou'—about ANYTHING."[2] He knows nothing about the magic world, not even what he himself is—a celebrated wizard.

Indeed, Harry's first encounters with the magic world are full of reminders of his ignorance, as when he is subjected to an inquisition in Madam Malkin's robe shop by Draco Malfoy and is unable to answer any of his questions. Sometimes the young protagonist does not even know what he does not know: for example, not until Uncle Vernon asks him about it does he realize that he has no idea where Hogwarts is, just as in *Harry Potter and the Goblet of Fire*, he is shocked to realize that he has never thought to ask about Neville's parents, or, for that matter, about Hagrid's.[3] Instances such as these also serve to keep the reader constantly alarmed about what else Harry might not know, particularly, I shall argue below, in connection with his own family history.

Draco Malfoy, who already knows what house he will be in, disapproves of the very concept of acquired knowledge. He thinks that Muggle-borns should not be admitted to Hogwarts because they differ from the children of wizarding families in that they haven't "been brought up to know our ways."[4] He judges people by their surnames, evidence of their bloodlines. The wizarding world is, it seems, so small that one can identify a member of it by name alone, and he and Ron prove on the train that they have heard about each other's families, just as Hagrid will later be able to identify Ron as a Weasley by sight, on the basis of his red hair. However, Malfoy's very formulation undoes the basis of his own argument. When he pinpoints the nature of his objection to Muggle-borns as the fact that they have not "been brought up to know our ways," he effectively concedes that nurture has a role to play, and that wizarding is not innate but must be learned.[5]

Malfoy signals his commitment to ideas of heredity and nature by his proclaimed preference for Slytherin House, of which all his family have been members. The house for which he expresses particular dislike is, interestingly, not Gryffindor, which we will later come to identify as the natural opposite of Slytherin, but Hufflepuff.[6] Hagrid, whom readers have already learned to like, assures us that even though the students of Hufflepuff may not be the brightest, they are infinitely preferable to those of Slytherin, a house whose very name encodes the effortless entry of birthright, and which is, we subsequently learn, populated by students belonging precisely to the same hereditary caste valorized by Malfoy. The meritocratically selected Muggle-borns, such as Justin Finch-Fletchley in Hufflepuff and Hermione Granger in Gryffindor, gravitate to the other three houses.

It is highly suggestive that Malfoy should dislike Hufflepuff in particular. Despite the fact that there are plenty of the Muggle-born in the other houses—in addition to Hermione, Dean Thomas is selected for Gryffindor in Harry's first year, and Colin Creevey joins them in the next—and also purebloods represented in Hufflepuff—Quidditch Captain and Seeker Cedric Diggory, who comes to such prominence in *Goblet of Fire,* has a father who works in the Ministry of Magic—Hufflepuffs do appear generally slow on the uptake. Fred Weasley insists that Cedric's silence is the result of his having nothing to say, and Justin Finch-Fletchley is completely taken in by Professor Lockhart in *Harry Potter and the Chamber of Secrets,* while Ernie Macmillan and Hannah Abbott are easily seduced into believing that Harry must be the heir of Slytherin.[7] Moreover, Malfoy's prejudice seems reinforced by the Sorting Hat's reaction to Harry during the welcome feast ritual in book I: the hat debates between Gryffindor and Slytherin as possible houses for Harry, and comments on the quality of Harry's mind, as though toying with the prospect of Ravenclaw, but Hufflepuff is never explicitly considered. Hufflepuffs have many compensating qualities—they are loyal and hard-working, with their determined nature implied by their emblem of the badger and its associated connotations of "badgering someone"—but their comic aspect is simultaneously encapsulated in the very name Hufflepuff.

I argue here that Malfoy's scornful dismissal of the Hufflepuffs raises the issue of the relative merits of acquired versus innate knowledge, since Hufflepuffs rarely know how to do anything instinctively, but are prepared to work at it. Once Harry is at Hogwarts, there seems to be, both literally and metaphorically, a level playing field. Despite a wizarding background, Ron Weasley has no advantage over Harry, and certainly none over Hermione, because, as Hagrid has reassured Harry, each student "starts at the beginning at Hogwarts," mimicking, of course, the experience of the reader.[8] Even Ron Weasley, from a long-established wizarding family and with a father working at the Ministry of Magic, cannot use the combination of a magic wand and a spell he learned from one of his brothers to turn Scabbers yellow. Indeed, the sheer difficulty of finding one's way around Hogwarts means that everyone's attention must initially be focused on knowledge acquisition, with Muggle-born and wizard-born equally disadvantaged.

Most interestingly, we are early presented with a strongly marked contrast between Draco Malfoy, proud of his broomstick flying, who is immediately told that although he might have been doing it for years, he has been doing it improperly all that time, and Harry, who finds that he can fly effortlessly.[9] This is presumably a hereditary aptitude, since we later learn that the protagonist's father was a talented Quidditch player. However, this element of nature does not outweigh Rowling's general stress on nurture for two reasons. In the first place, Harry would never have known that he had a natural talent for flying until he had made the experiment. Second, he needs to practice, though he lacks what a Hufflepuff would have, which is the determination to keep trying even when the going is difficult. Harry is not invariably industrious; he would rather sleep than be shaken awake by Oliver Wood and is slow to try reading *Quidditch through the Ages*, though when he actually does, it turns out to be a book that he enjoys immensely and that teaches him things that will enable him to prepare himself for the match.[10] Indeed, throughout the four books published so far, Harry never stops learning things about Quidditch, picking up the idea of the Wronsky Feint from Viktor Krum at the World Quidditch Championships and regularly practicing new maneuvers at Oliver Wood's behest. And if they have taught him nothing else, Harry's years with the Dursleys have certainly honed his skills in speed, self-protection, and avoiding trouble, talents as useful on the Quidditch pitch as when facing Voldemort.[11]

Malfoy's contempt for Hufflepuffs therefore enables us to see that the ostensibly direct contrast between him and Harry is, in fact, interestingly triangulated. Malfoy puts his faith only in what he has always known: the fact that he has been "doing it wrong *for years*" (emphasis added) clearly indicates that he has been happy not to change, alter, or develop his technique in any way. Harry has natural aptitudes, but the inclusion of the Hufflepuff ethos of working diligently at improvement reminds us that natural ability in itself is not enough; thus, even when one has a predisposition to excel in certain areas, they must still be worked at. Harry himself may be both too clever and too averse to mechanical effort to have ever been considered for Hufflepuff by the Sorting Hat, but the very fact that Malfoy despises the Hufflepuff ethos should in itself be enough to indicate to the reader—especially the young child reader—that it must have merit. It is fitting that Cedric Diggory should attain almost heroic status in his death in *Goblet of Fire*, and that Dumbledore, in his closing address to the school, should pay tribute to Cedric as exemplifying the characteristics typical of Hufflepuff House.

Indeed, it is clear from the first book onwards that at Hogwarts, despite all its eccentricities, the philosophy of the school is unmistakably centered on discovery, teaching, and the slow, steady, cumulative acquisition of knowledge. The school's whole agenda might be summed up in Mad-Eye Moody's justification, twice reiterated, for showing students the Unforgivable Curses, *"you've got to know,"*[12] or in the second line of the school song, *"Teach us something please."*[13] The importance of knowledge is also strongly foregrounded by the centrality of the library. There might seem to be a faint echo here of another text with Gothic overtones set in a building which is inordinately difficult to find one's way around—Umberto Eco's *The Name of the Rose* (1980). In Eco, however, the contents of the book that lies at the heart of the narrative are never divulged, and the library becomes ultimately secondary to the labyrinth that leads off it. At Hogwarts, the library is crucial for its own sake.

Most notably, it is to the library that Harry, Ron, and Hermione turn to discover the identity of Nicolas Flamel, and we are immediately reminded of the importance of knowledge retrieval techniques in an age of information overload. Moreover, while Muggles might use apparently more direct techniques such as web searches, one of the most strongly marked advantages of books as represented in the Harry Potter series is that they often prove to reveal information that the reader did not even know he or she was looking for: thus *Magical Mediterranean Water-Plants and Their Properties*, ostensibly intended by the supposed Professor Moody to boost Neville's confidence in book IV, would in fact have told Harry about the potential of gillyweed, and would thus have saved him many hours of worry. Even Hagrid turns to the library when he acquires a dragon's egg and finds books useful, since the only other mode of proceeding available to him, trial and error, is too risky when there is a real, live dragon in question. Ron feels that even getting past Fluffy, the guardian of the Philosopher's Stone, could probably be learned from a book.[14] When Hermione exasperatedly exclaims "[D]on't you two read?"[15] the importance and usefulness of books reaches its apogee. It is even to the library that Harry goes first when he tries out his new Invisibility Cloak.

The importance of all the knowledge that Harry, Ron, and Hermione have been acquiring during their first year at Hogwarts is abundantly confirmed when it becomes apparent that the whole of their final adventure is structured as a symbolic test on what they have learned so far: as Harry aptly remarks, the trio is "lucky" that Hermione pays attention in Herbology.[16] The many evenings spent playing chess have not only taught Ron that he himself is the best player of the three, and must therefore direct the game, but have also honed his own skills. Harry himself uses his Quidditch skills to catch the key, and, as they eventually realize, Dumbledore has taught them "just enough to help,"[17] especially by giving Harry a prior sight of the Mirror of Erised, just as in *Goblet of Fire* Harry's acquisition of knowledge about summoning charms proves crucial to his survival, initially in the first task and then when, during his encounter with Voldemort, he is able to use one to summon the Triwizard Cup and be transported back to Hogwarts.

In the Harry Potter series, things are never mysteriously revealed. In many children's fictions involving magic, words are mysteriously "torn from the lips" of the young heroes or heroines, as in the following example from Alan Garner's *The Moon of Gomrath* (1963):

Colin turned. "*Esenaroth! Esenaroth!*" he cried. The words came to him and were torn from his lips independently of his will, and he heard them from a distance, as though they were from another's mouth.[18]

In Rowling's novels, however, knowledge must always be worked for and can often prove difficult to retain, as it is for ordinary children. At a crucial point of *Harry Potter and the Philosopher's Stone* (published in the United States as *Harry Potter and the Sorcerer's Stone*), Harry, Ron, and Hermione are anxious to consult Professor Dumbledore, but suddenly realize that they do not know where his study is. They have to ask Professor McGonagall, but she will not tell them and indeed heads them off, largely on the grounds that their knowledge base is insufficient and that they cannot, therefore, have anything important enough to say to warrant an audience with the headmaster. For Professor McGonagall, her pupils' belief that they can intervene productively in the question of the Philosopher's Stone is just another example of ludicrous presumption, such as that which she thinks was earlier demonstrated in Hermione's supposed single-handed tackling of the troll. Ironically, of course, she is mistaken: it is in fact her *own* knowledge base that is insufficient here, and her overconfidence in her own assumptions leads her to a potentially fatal error.

In the second volume, *Chamber of Secrets*, the continuing importance of books, already established in the first story, is further developed. It is signaled at an early stage by the queue outside Flourish & Blotts. The long line is caused not just by those who *must* buy school books but also, and indeed primarily, by those who *want* to buy Gilderoy Lockhart's books, presumably because the purchase of a book by Lockhart gives them access to something of the reflected glory of his glamorous image. Books are thus shown as not only an important but also an intensely pleasurable part of people's lives, as they are again in the vignette of Percy, lost in *Prefects Who Gained Power*. Unappetizing as this text appears to Harry, power is what Percy wants—Ron comments explicitly on his ambition—and, given what we have seen so far of the usefulness of books, there seems no reason to doubt that he is correct in identifying this book as something that can teach him how to gain it. How dynamic and transformative books can be is also shown by Riddle's diary, which ensnares (and nearly kills) Ginny Weasley, and by *Moste Potent Potions*, which allows Harry and Ron to transform themselves into the likenesses of Crabbe and Goyle.

Other kinds of knowledge are also important in *Chamber of Secrets*. In particular, Harry's lack of knowledge of his own family history forces him to fear that he could be descended from Salazar Slytherin, one of Hogwarts's four founders. Harry views several members of his family in the Mirror of Erised, but he has no means of identifying them. The identities of his parents may be obvious, but beyond that all he has to go on is guesswork.[19] The surprise revelation of his own ability to speak Parseltongue—a skill which is clearly not acquired through study, and so logically ought to have been inherited—is that which forces Harry to speculate on whether he is related to Slytherin, famous for that particular skill. Not until the end of the narrative does Dumbledore provide a rational explanation for Harry's proficiency as a Parselmouth—this, like others of Voldemort's powers, might have been inadvertently transmitted to the infant Harry when the Avada Kedavra Curse failed.

Dumbledore's suggestion that Harry acquired rather than inherited his ability to speak Parseltongue—though not necessarily establishing that Harry is *not* related to Slytherin or Voldemort—returns readers firmly to the books' general preference for nurture rather than nature, and this continues to be strongly stated. When it is revealed that Hagrid was born to a giantess, numerous members of the magical community allege that the brutal nature of giants will automatically be inherited and dominate his personality. In fact, Hagrid's upbringing by his gentle, diminutive father has given him an apparently inexhaustible supply of tolerance and patience. It is also notable that the villains, by contrast with the heroes, do not learn and tend to be dismissive of the modes and ideology of knowledge acquisition. Salazar Slytherin sought to deny education to Muggleborns. Harry reports that the first requirement for a peaceful life with the Dursleys is *"Don't ask questions."*[20] When the young wizard is allowed to move into Dudley's second bedroom, he finds that the books are the only unbroken things because Dudley has never touched them. Similarly, we are told that Mr. Dursley always sits in his office with his back facing the windows.[21] Cutting himself off from sources of fresh information means that Mr. Dursley will shortly be taken by the unpleasant surprise of magical intrusion into his ordered Muggle world. There is a sharp contrast here with Harry, who *does* notice an owl at King's Cross station and is accordingly able to deduce that the Weasleys are wizarding people and thus find his way onto the Hogwarts Express platform.

Vital though the acquisition of knowledge is, that does not always mean that it will be easy. In *Chamber of Secrets*, Harry learns to deal with the gnomes the hard way, through being bitten, and it is indeed remarkable how often his learning experiences are painful. In *Goblet of Fire*, for example, he must choose agony rather than oblivion when he fights the Cruciatus Curse. Much attention is also paid to how difficult Harry finds it to choose subjects for further study, not to mention which career he should pursue. The difficulties attendant on knowing things are also stressed when, in *Goblet of Fire*, Hermione insists that although Sirius will find out anyway that his godson has been entered for the Triwizard Tournament, he ought to hear it directly from Harry. In almost the same breath, Hermione explores the affective dimension of epistemology by explaining that Ron really does know that Harry did not enter himself, just as Harry ignores the fact that he knows that Ron did not mean to interrupt his conversation with Sirius in the Gryffindor common room. In both these instances, knowing things is severely complicated by the fact that apprehension is clearly revealed as not only an intellectual but also an emotional process.

Particularly striking is the way in which Harry's growing understanding of the facts of his past is shadowed by a parallel development of realizations about his future: at the same time that he learns about his original family, he also begins to perceive the principles on which any future family in which he may participate will be founded, for he goes through puberty. This process begins to become apparent in *Harry Potter and the Prisoner of Azkaban*—the idea of a milky-white patronus leaping from the end of one's wand is, after all, nothing if not phallic—and is well advanced in *Goblet of Fire*, where sexualization and gendering suddenly seem to be everywhere, from Hagrid's attempt to establish the gender of the Blast-Ended Skrewts to the unicorns' preference for girls, which is explicitly linked with the girls' own processes and degree of maturation.[22] The whole motif culminates in Ron's astonished observation of Hermione: "you *are* a girl,"[23] which precisely encapsulates the ways in which even what is obvious may still need to be emotionally internalized in order to be fully apprehended. Exceptionally noticeable is the fact that while people have been invariably referred to as witch or wizard rather than man or woman in the early books, in *Goblet of Fire*, several characters, particularly Rita Skeeter, are referred to as woman or man, thus emphasizing gender rather than magic.[24] Knowledge is also explicitly linked with a burgeoning sexuality when Krum uses visits to the library to get to know Hermione.

The centrality of puberty in the context of knowledge acquisition is by no means without literary precedent. Particularly pertinent forerunners are Diana Wynne Jones's Worlds of Chrestomanci books, which were first published from the 1970s onwards but have now been re-released and repackaged on the back of the Harry Potter phenomenon, accompanied, in the United Kingdom at least, by special bookshop displays and free bookmarks explicitly linking the two authors. In Jones's *Charmed Life* (1977), an orphaned young boy who has not previously known that he has magic powers is taken to a castle and taught magic there.[25] In *Witch Week* (1982), the pattern of young people discovering their magic is repeated. Here, unlike *Charmed Life* where Cat has unwittingly been an enchanter all along, the explicit statement that magic is not acquired until early adolescence clearly links it with the processes of puberty. Finally, just as Dobby appears in book II of Rowling's series to try to give Harry special information, the goddess appears on Christopher's bed in *The Lives of Christopher Chant* (1988) in a scene that can be interpreted as suggestive of the connection between budding sexuality and budding knowledge. Thus, although there may be no direct influence of Jones on Rowling, there is clearly at least a precedent for the parallel between the two kinds of knowledge.

There is also an interesting contrast here with the other author whose books are being extensively marketed in conjunction with Rowling's—Philip Pullman. In the *His Dark Materials* trilogy, puberty brings with it the end of magic: at the close of *The Amber Spyglass* (2000), Lyra Silvertongue loses her untaught ability to read the alethiometer. Further, at the very moment when she and Will discover their love for each other, they are forced to accept that they must part forever because they will never again be able to travel between worlds. Throughout the trilogy, Pullman vociferously opposes organized religion's traditional condemnation of sexual awakening as evil. The witch Ruta Skadi vigorously denounces the Church's use of fear and repression, and the war of astronomical proportions towards which the trilogy heads focuses on the presence of "Dust" in the universe. The Dust represents sin and the temptation of Eden's Tree of Knowledge to some, and an ethereal awakening of knowledge and creativity to others. The narrative insistently parallels the spiritual death produced by severance of humans from their daemons in an attempt to keep them pure and free of the Dust with castration.

Another interesting literary parallel lies between J. K. Rowling and Dorothy Dunnett, both highly popular authors who write long, elaborate series of interlinked books, both setting large parts of those books in Scotland.[26] Dunnett's series culminates with the revelation of an astonishing secret about the hero's birth. It certainly seems likely that the Potter series, too, will climax with a similar divulgence, which will presumably address the unanswered questions of why exactly Voldemort was so determined to kill Harry; why, as Tom Riddle remarks in *Chamber of Secrets*, the two have so many points in common and even look alike; and why the first time Harry hears the name Tom Riddle, "it . . . seemed to mean something to him, almost as though Riddle was a friend he'd had when he was very small, and half-forgotten."[27] Will this be Rowling's definitive demonstration of the importance of nurture rather than heredity?

It is also worth noting the strongly liberal sensibility of Dunnett's novels. Written during the 1960s, her Lymond chronicles contain drug use (albeit unwitting), homosexuality, and spiritualism. Dunnett's appropriation of the past to covertly argue for tolerance in the present alerts readers to a rather similar process that seems to be taking place in Rowling, who has spoken publicly in support of often-demonized single parents and against racial bigotry and the National Health Service's discriminatory treatment of multiple sclerosis victims. Tolerance for the difference of characters like the slow-witted Neville, the half-giant Hagrid, the werewolf Professor Lupin, and the falsely accused Sirius Black is clearly and warmly advocated by her books. One of the things Harry and his peers must evidently learn is tolerance of difference, though this in itself complicates the already multifaceted nature of the things he has to know. Indeed, one wonders whether he will, in the end, even have to accept the heroism of Professor Snape. After all, Dumbledore trusts him: at the end of *Goblet of Fire*, he has asked Snape to do something difficult and dangerous in the fight against Voldemort, and Snape has undertaken this task. Some of the Harry Potter websites at one point claimed that even Draco Malfoy is to be redeemed and will fight alongside Harry in book VII.[28] If Rowling does do this, or pull off some similar coup, she will not only have told a story but will have forced her readers to reflect on how they responded to that story and how accurately they were able to weigh and interpret the various clues along the way. She will, in short, have provided an object lesson in knowledge acquisition as well as a reflection on it.

I suspect that one reason for the books' phenomenal appeal to children is this emphasis on knowledge acquisition, and the opportunity to identify with a hero who, like all children, has to learn things. He does not always do so rapidly, and, as they are, he is always conscious of moving through time to an unpredictable future. There is certainly a notable contrast here with more traditional boys' books where narrative strategies often rely on readers' presumed previous knowledge—codes of honor, rules of games, and so on. There is almost as great a contrast with many fantasy texts—Roald Dahl would be an obvious example—where knowing things actually will not help one, since narrative developments are often so wildly unpredictable. Rowling herself has said that the Harry Potter books are not fantasy, a genre which, she explains, she does not like, and she will not break her own rules. For instance, she is insistent that, despite pleas from readers, Harry's parents will not be restored to life, because death, as in the real world, must be accepted as final. It is this grounding in the real and in readers' own experiences which, I think, accounts at least in part for the appeal of the books. It should be noted here that a surprising number of the spin-off products currently being marketed are knowledge-based, including customized versions of both Cluedo, in the shape of the board game Mystery at Hogwarts, and of Trivial Pursuit. Both games significantly depend on knowledge, intuition, and deduction. Mystery at Hogwarts in particular is also quite likely to lead to overt discussions among its players of epistemological processes, since it can be won either by logical deduction, inspired guesswork, or a combination of the two.

Most importantly, Harry Potter himself legitimizes the good behavior associated with learning in school. The Voldemort T-shirt that was initially marketed (in the United Kingdom at least) as part of the preparation for the release of the first film seems to me to miss the point of the books completely: evil is *not*, as so often, more glamorous than good. It is acceptable to say, like Ron, that you're not sure whether it's safe to enter the Triwizard Tournament because you don't know if you've learned enough.[29] It is also admirable and necessary—indeed, essential—to work hard, read books, and spend long hours in the library, because the things you learn there may just save the world.

NOTES

1. J. K. Rowling, *Harry Potter and the Philosopher's Stone* (London: Bloomsbury, 1997), 16. Rowling's repeated stress on the affective dimension of knowing is something to which I will return.

2. Rowling, *Philosopher's Stone*, 41.

3. J. K. Rowling, *Harry Potter and the Goblet of Fire* (London: Bloomsbury, 2000).

4. Rowling, *Philosopher's Stone*, 61.

5. The books themselves, of course, will later resoundingly underscore the superiority of nurture over nature by the neat device of having twin sisters Padma and Parvati Patil placed in different houses—Padma in Ravenclaw and Parvati in Gryffindor—something which looks for all the world like a direct rejoinder to the numerous studies that have used twins to show the importance of nature.

6. See Rowling, *Philosopher's Stone*, 60.

7. See Rowling, *Prisoner of Azkaban*, 127 and *Chamber of Secrets*, 73 and 149, respectively. J. K. Rowling, *Harry Potter and the Prisoner of Azkaban* (London: Bloomsbury, 1999) and *Harry Potter and the Chamber of Secrets* (London: Bloomsbury, 1998).

8. Rowling, *Philosopher's Stone*, 66.

9. Ibid., 109.

10. Ibid., 133.

11. The other thing that his upbringing has instilled in him, understanding of suffering, will also prove useful.

12. Rowling, *Goblet of Fire*, 192–93.

13. Rowling, *Philosopher's Stone*, 95.

14. Ibid., 180.

15. Ibid., 161.

16. Ibid., 202.

17. Ibid., 219.

18. Alan Garner, *The Moon of Gomrath* (London: William Collins, 1963), 44.

19. Significant at this point is the fact that all members of the Dursley family look strikingly unlike each other, with Dudley's tendency towards corpulence as an apparently acquired rather than an inherited characteristic: the presence or absence of a family likeness may not be a reliable guide.

20. Rowling, *Philosopher's Stone*, 20.

21. Ibid., 8.

22. Rowling, *Goblet of Fire*, 420.

23. Ibid., 348.

24. See ibid., 292, 383, 391, 392, 394, and 445 for explicit references to women, and 381, 385, 391, and 395 for explicit references to men.

25. Other parallels include: music is repeatedly compared to magic in *Charmed Life* just as it is by Dumbledore in *Philosopher's Stone*, 95; the Chrestomanci himself, whose combination of great power and aloof eccentricity foreshadows Dumbledore, is referred to as "You Know Who" by the Nostrums.

26. That this is the location of Hogwarts is made clear in *Chamber of Secrets* when the Weasleys' flying car is spotted over Peebles as it follows the Hogwarts Express. Both authors also end one of their books with a game of living chess.

27. Rowling, *Chamber of Secrets*, 174.

28. For example, http://www.harrypotterfans.net/rumors.html#bk5 (accessed 15 July 2001).

29. Rowling, *Goblet of Fire*, 168.

4

Safe as Houses:
Sorting and School Houses at Hogwarts

Chantel Lavoie

"It's a toast which should bind us all together and to those who've gone before, and who'll come after us here. It is the dear old School-house—the best house of the best school in England!"
— Thomas Hughes, *Tom Brown's Schooldays*[1]

In J. K. Rowling's Harry Potter series, as in other boarding school fiction in which the year is a cycle—both structured and endlessly varied—occasion is married to ritual. The capacious Great Hall at Hogwarts School of Witchcraft and Wizardry is home to many feasts, celebrating triumphs and community while containing keen rivalries in the form of the four houses that make up the academic institution. Each September first when students arrive aboard the Hogwarts Express, a special banquet awaits them and the aged Sorting Hat describes in song both archetypes and character traits associated with the four ancient wizard school founders and their choice pupils. Those who are bravest at heart belong in Gryffindor House and are set apart for having exceptional *"daring, nerve and chivalry."* The other houses are Hufflepuff, for the *"just and loyal"*; Ravenclaw, suited to those possessing *"wit and learning"*; and last, but not least, Slytherin, where *"cunning folk use any means / To achieve their ends."*[2]

The song, varied yearly (although Harry has thus far heard it only twice) links the past, present, and future. As each nervous new first year scampers to his or her house table, the process reminds returning students of where they themselves belong and why. This feast of initiation and homecoming reinforces two types of loyalties—that which each individual owes to the school, and that which is owing to one's house. The Sorting Hat thus brings the students together and simultaneously sets them apart.

The school, like each of the houses it contains, is both exclusive and inclusive in interesting ways. It is magical ability alone that determines acceptance to Hogwarts—not ethnicity, race,[3] or, for three of the four houses, family (the fourth, Slytherin, restricts itself to pureblood wizard families). Money and the lack of it do matter at Hogwarts, as Draco Malfoy's constant taunting of Ron Weasley proves, but it does not seem that anyone is prevented from attending Hogwarts for financial reasons. Most importantly, as the school predates any of the other boarding schools in Britain, its foundation over one thousand years ago demonstrates that differences such as gender were not—and should never be—an impediment to achievement.[4] Hogwarts was founded by two wizards and two witches, and there have been headmistresses as well as headmasters. The ratio of female to male professors seems equally matched or uneven on the side of women, including Madam Hooch, the Quidditch coach. Quidditch, the most popular sport in the wizarding world, has less to do with physical strength than with flying skill and, in the case of the Chasers, who score all the goals, eye-hand coordination; this determines the equitability of the sport for both sexes. That Hogwarts is coeducational seems especially important to Harry Potter's school house: Katie Bell, Alicia Spinnet, and Angelina Johnson are Chasers on the Gryffindor Quidditch team; Professor McGonagall, head of Gryffindor House and an excellent teacher, is deputy headmistress; Hermione Granger is at the top of her class.[5]

The four houses of Hogwarts may be equal in theory; however, two are "more equal" than the others. The most important school founders were obviously the males, who dominate in memory and tradition—Godric Gryffindor and Salazar Slytherin. The real fight between good magic and dark magic is between these two enduring entities and their houses. Slytherin broke off from all three of his cofounders, but the strong dual animosity can be seen in the Hogwarts crest, which consists of a large "H," the four corners of which are flanked by a lion, an eagle, a badger, and a snake. The Gryffindor lion and the Slytherin snake face one another at the top, as though prepared to wage war with the school as battleground, while the other two emblems appear in less combative stances.

Slytherin students, like their founder, seem a bad sort, and to have the kind of character that lands one in their house—a house "unpolluted" by Muggle-born wizards, a coed Quidditch team, generosity, or compassion—is evidently something to be feared. They are menacing. In *Harry Potter and the Prisoner of Azkaban*, both Lee Jordan and Harry notice that the Slytherin Quidditch team seems to be "going for size rather than skill,"[6] a tendency that conveys the impression of thuggery in Gryffindor's chief rivals. Marcus Flint, the Slytherin team captain, strikes Harry as having part troll ancestry.[7] Crabbe and Goyle, who behave as Draco Malfoy's bodyguards, guffaw loudly, flex their muscles, and remain speechless. The girls in Slytherin seem physically out of proportion, unbalanced. Millicent Bulstrode (the bull who strides into china shops?) is horse-faced, a lot bigger than Harry, and frighteningly rough in the dueling club with Hermione, whereas Pansy Parkinson's name says it all—she is frilly, simpering, nasty. Her first name is synonymous with a wimp, and her surname suggests a Nosy Parker. With puglike features, Pansy's unkind nature manifests itself in facial expressions, and, like Harry's Aunt Petunia—another unpleasant persnickety female named after a flower—her apparently concentrated femininity is not nourishing.[8] Indications of Pansy's blind devotion toward Malfoy are reminiscent of Petunia Dursley's slavish affection for her son, Dudley—both are examples of personal attachments that exclude *agape*. Most dominant among the students of Slytherin House is Harry's greatest child enemy, the clever Draco Malfoy—himself pale, small, similar in build to Harry and also a Seeker on his house Quidditch team.[9] Among other feckless actions, Malfoy's connivance with the hack journalist, Rita Skeeter, in *Harry Potter and the Goblet of Fire* testifies to his moral bankruptcy. In Slytherin, then, the combination of brute strength and cunning find a home.

Michael D. O'Brien complains that "[i]n a consistent display of authorial overkill Rowling depicts such 'bad' characters as ugly in appearance [and] ridicules the oafish bodies of the students who oppress Harry. In these details and a plethora of others throughout the series, the child reader is encouraged in his baser instincts while lip service is paid to morality."[10] But revolting descriptions of Slytherins are in keeping with the third-person narrator's empathy with Harry's perspective, as well as being consistent with the house system. Such a passionate, biased reaction is a cathartic part of house loyalty. To know that one's house is the best is to believe that the others are inferior, the chief rival in particular, and to take seriously one's obligations to house and team. Even non-Slytherins are not exempt from competitive resentment. On the way to the Quidditch World Cup in *Goblet of Fire*, Harry and the Weasleys meet up with the handsome Cedric Diggory, the captain and Seeker of Hufflepuff's Quidditch team. At Cedric's greeting, everyone returns his hello except for George and Fred, who only nod coolly; they have not forgiven Hufflepuff for defeating Gryffindor in the first Quidditch match of the previous school year.[11] Harry is initially more forgiving than the Weasley twins, but when Cedric takes Cho Chang to the Yule Ball, a different sort of rivalry rears its head as Harry now condemns Cedric as "a useless pretty-boy."[12]

Blind loyalty and the desire to imagine one's rivals as uniformly detestable is, of course, a problematic virtue. C. E. Montague pointed out as much in *Disenchantment*, a discussion of the prejudice that took the place of logic and objectivity in the Great War. Indeed, Montague links the demonization of the enemy in wartime propaganda to the passion aroused by seemingly innocuous school house rivalries:

If you cannot hit or kick during a fight, at any rate you can spit. But, to be happy in this arm of the service, you have to feel sure that the adversary is signally fit to be spat upon. Hence, on each side in every war, the civilian will-to-believe that the other side are a set of ogres, every man of them. ... A few choice spirits will even carry this fond observance into the milder climate of sport. A boy of this kidney, while looking on at a vital house match, will give his mind ease by telling his friend what "a lot of stinkers" the other house are.[13]

In the case of Slytherin versus Gryffindor, the reader, too, may give his or her mind ease, for there is no need to pause over one's responses, to decide where one's loyalties lie. Slytherin is separate from the other three houses in ways that exclude fair play entirely. They are signally fit to be spat upon.

Clearly there are different levels of loyalty at Hogwarts. Cedric Diggory's loyalty—a trait for which Hufflepuff is renowned—is not confined to his house, but to his school. Both he and Harry are school champions in *Goblet of Fire*, and Cedric's death follows a noble willingness to forego the Triwizard Cup and rare glory for his house in favor of fair play.[14] Later on the Hogwarts Express, Draco Malfoy taunts Harry about Cedric's death being the first of many at the hands of Lord Voldemort. With the simultaneous wand-work at which our favorite Gryffindors tend to excel, Harry, Ron, Hermione, Fred, and George hex Malfoy, Crabbe, and Goyle in retaliation for the taunt.[15] Whereas there are rivalries and temporary tensions between the Gryffindors and students of other school houses, there are also friendships: Percy Weasley has a Ravenclaw girlfriend, Harry may one day have as well. More often than not Gryffindors are united with Hufflepuffs and Ravenclaws in their abhorrence of Slytherin. At the final match between Gryffindor and Slytherin for the Quidditch school cup in *Prisoner of Azkaban*, Harry sees over three-quarters of the fans in the stands waving red Gryffindor flags or flourishing pro-Gryffindor banners.[16] Such loyalties confirm Slytherin's nearly universal lack of appeal.

All other house rivalries are healthy, fair, and challenging competition in comparison to the dark agenda of Salazar Slytherin and his infamous descendant: cheating, lies, prejudice, death. Even the locations of the entrances to the four house common rooms and dormitories speak to Slytherin's position as dark underbelly of the school. Whereas the students of Gryffindor and Ravenclaw are both housed in towers (the entrance to Hufflepuff has not been revealed), Slytherin is located in a dungeon. Why, then, are those students suited to Slytherin House allowed in the school? Why allow such a house at all?

Perhaps the most important reason is that courage must be tested and it is Slytherin's role to test Gryffindor, the house that values courage above all else. The importance of the house founded by Godric Gryffindor is made clear even before Harry arrives at Hogwarts. Harry first hears the house praised by Rubeus Hagrid, Hogwarts gamekeeper and himself a former Gryffindor, and then on the train by his new friend, Ron, whose entire family has been in that house. When Hagrid initially explains to Harry that there are four houses, with Hufflepuff students often identified as "duffers," Harry's initial certainty that he'll end up in Hufflepuff speaks to the young wizard's performance anxiety, whereas Hagrid's assertion—"Better Hufflepuff than Slytherin"—insists on a different type of criteria: better to be incompetent than to be skilled and use that skill badly.[17]

The Sorting Hat, in lingering over Harry Potter at that first feast, echoes the boy's own fears about where he belongs when it vacillates among his many attributes: courage, a sharp mind, talent, and "a nice thirst" to prove himself. When the hat intuits Harry's unvoiced plea for being placed anywhere but in Slytherin, its audible musings are not entirely comforting: "Are you sure? You could be great, you know. . . . "[18] Harry, relieved by the final declaration of "GRYFFINDOR!," continues to be troubled by the Sorting Hat's hesitation.

At the same time, readers have been given a hint that "a nice thirst" to prove oneself is not necessarily a bad characteristic. Indeed, the wording in the song—that each of the founders "did value different virtues"—suggests that ambition is a virtue.[19] But Slytherin House contains the daring of Gryffindor taken to extremes and to the exclusion of all other virtues; there is an emphasis on the sinister purity of ambition untempered by other important qualities. Rowling's novels thus imply that ambition should go hand in hand with daring but not overwhelm fair play. Both Slytherin and Gryffindor were (as wizards) and are (as houses) focused upon excellence but, as the Sorting Hat explains, the "cunning folk" of Slytherin "use any means / To achieve their ends."

Gryffindor and Slytherin need one another as worthy rivals. The contrast between the windowed tower in which Gryffindors spend their time and the dungeon where Slytherins meet and sleep on some level suggests the ego and the id. Both times that readers "hear" the Sorting Hat sing—first in *Harry Potter and the Philosopher's Stone* (published in the United States as *Harry Potter and the Sorcerer's Stone*) and then in *Goblet of Fire*—the order in which the founding wizards are mentioned is Gryffindor first and Slytherin last. In this way, visually within the poem, they are actually higher and lower on a column of lines. Although Slytherin House and its students are undesirable—certainly to most other students in the school—they also seem inevitable. Slytherin seems to be tolerated by Dumbledore, and acceptance of their behavior is marked by his silences. When he calls for a toast to honor Harry's courage in the fourth book, for example, Malfoy and many of the other Slytherins remain "defiantly" seated and refuse to raise their goblets. Harry concludes that Dumbledore does not see them, but one wonders if this is true.[20] Elsewhere, Dumbledore sees a great deal.

Rowling raises many questions in these books about what Joan Acocella identifies as "the kinship of evil. . . . Maybe it's the Miltonic idea of evil as merely good perverted. Or maybe not."[21] As Dumbledore explains to Harry near the end of *Prisoner of Azkaban*, by saving Peter Pettigrew's life, Harry has created "a certain bond" between himself and one of Voldemort's most ardent followers. As with his nebulous connection to the Dark Lord, Harry wants no such bond, yet, as Dumbledore explains, this inexplicable tie is the most profound type of magic.[22] In any case, this kinship between Slytherin and Gryffindor is not as simple as the former playing the bad guys to the latter.

Nevertheless, instinct and conditioning encourage the reader to interpret the relationship between the houses in this way. As readers young and old visit the many websites devoted to Harry Potter in order to fall more in thrall to Rowling's magical world, they encounter sites that provide the option to "get sorted" by the Sorting Hat. One internet location simplifies the process by instructing the reader to "think hard" about what house he or she would like to be in, and then click on a button which randomly calls up the description of one of the four houses.[23] In some ways, the unexpectedness and lack of control duplicate the moment of sorting in the novels. The effect of being placed in Slytherin would be unnerving for most. Did "thinking hard" have anything to do with this placement, or nothing? And, by extension, is wishing to possess particular qualities of no consequence when it comes to the manifestation of personality and who one truly is?

Another unofficial website allows the reader to be sorted into a house according to his or her choice among four attributes: Brave, Smart, Loyal, and Selfish.[24] The reduction of Slytherin to a house characterized by the flaw of selfishness—which is certainly implied but never explicitly stated by Rowling's Sorting Hat—illustrates the transformation of ambition into a purely negative trait. One witnesses an apparent unwillingness on the part of the web mistress to make Slytherin a serious choice for visitors to the site.

A third site poses two initial questions in order to sort the reader into a house: "What position would you play on your Quidditch House Team?" and "If you were faced with a troll, what would you do?"[25] Regardless of how one answers the first question (indeed, one need not answer it at all), as long as the response to the second is "Fight it" as opposed to "Get help," the player is put into Gryffindor. If the answer is "get help" other questions come up. Regarding a homework assignment that calls for two written parchments, for example, if one chooses to "Write three parchments because you wanted to," the player is put in Ravenclaw. Each of these methods of sorting reveal that courage is to be considered as a truer indicator of house spirit than any other quality. Were Hermione to answer the secondary question about schoolwork, she would certainly be in Ravenclaw, but because the troll scenario comes first in the sorting test, she would not be required to make this decision. The same is the case for Ron, who might well choose to "Copy a classmate's report"—a decision that lands the player in Slytherin. A similar quandary occurs with the final question, which asks how the player sees him or herself when looking into the Mirror of Erised. This magical mirror reflects one's deepest desires. If the answer is "surrounded by good friends," one is placed in Hufflepuff; if it is "as the most powerful wizard in the world," the suitable house is Slytherin. "Teaching at Hogwarts" places one in Ravenclaw, whereas "facing the Heir of Slytherin and defeating him" naturally sends the player to Gryffindor. Each of these choices makes sense, but none of them is the sight that greets either Harry or Ron when he first gazes into the mirror in book I: Harry sees himself enveloped by family; Ron envisions himself as Head Boy and Captain of the Quidditch team. Rowling's characters, and the houses in which the hat places them, are more complicated than the websites allow.

Slytherin proves no exception to such ambiguity. What, for instance, are we to make of the oily and unpleasant Severus Snape, head of Slytherin House? Snape blatantly favors the students of his own house and would gladly see Harry expelled. Yet he saves Harry's life in the first book, and we learn in *Goblet of Fire* that in the past he has acted as a spy for Dumbledore among the Death Eaters, risking his life in the process.[26] As his name suggests, the potions master is severe, sniping, even snakelike—evocative of Slytherin himself. He is not, however, and despite his position in Slytherin House, simply evil.[27]

The annual sorting ritual, then, is not deterministic but merely reflective. People are not one-dimensional, nor are the decisions with which they are faced. Such complication is demonstrated by instances of bravery, as Gryffindors are clearly not the only ones capable of exhibiting this trait. Samuel Johnson observed that "Courage is a quality so necessary for maintaining virtue, that it is always respected, even when it is associated with vice."[28] Although Rowling shows that bullies are often cowardly—neither Crabbe, Goyle, nor the more clever Draco Malfoy is actually brave when it comes to situations involving real danger—she also allows unlikable characters, including Professor Snape, to be impressively courageous. If this were not the case, Voldemort and his followers would present no threat. Certainly Barty Crouch, disguised as Mad-Eye Moody, is "ready to risk everything" and dare anything for his evil master.[29] Furthermore, just as every Slytherin student did not follow Voldemort, every Gryffindor throughout time did not stay the noble and more courageous path. Although in the first book Harry learns from Hagrid that Lord Voldemort's rise to power was supported by his fellow Slytherins—not one witch or wizard who "went bad" wasn't formerly in Slytherin[30]—the gamekeeper is not quite right on this point. It was a Gryffindor, Peter Pettigrew, who supported Voldemort and betrayed Harry's parents. We learn in *Prisoner of Azkaban* that Pettigrew has spent years in hiding as Scabbers, Ron Weasley's pet rat; forced to escape detection by scurrying into the sewers, Pettigrew reenacted physically the moral descent he had taken to the psychological dungeon of Slytherin. It is clear that the sniveling Pettigrew is a Slytherin at heart, even though, in effect, he turned Slytherin *after* leaving Hogwarts; ambition and self-love overwhelmed his other traits and he forsook his Gryffindor roots in favor of the Death Eaters. His explanation, a fear of being killed, is met by the true Gryffindor response when Black roars: "THEN YOU SHOULD HAVE . . . . DIED RATHER THAN BETRAY YOUR FRIENDS, AS WE WOULD HAVE DONE FOR YOU!"[31]

The powerful duality present in each character is first suggested in *Philosopher's Stone*. In chapter 1, before the reader has come to understand this enchanted world or even to meet Harry, Dumbledore states that Lord Voldemort has powers not possessed by himself, to which Professor McGonagall retorts that this is only because the headmaster is too honorable to use these forces.[32] Later, Harry purchases a wand that is a "brother" to that which killed his parents, causing the shopkeeper, Mr. Ollivander, to believe that tremendous things can be expected of the young wizard; after all, Voldemort accomplished "great things—terrible, yes, but great."[33] In the same book, Professor McGonagall's assertion that each house possesses a "noble history" and "outstanding" magical alumni reinforces the ambiguity and complex representation of the houses.[34] The words "great," "noble," and "outstanding" suggest that good and dark magic are two sides of one coin.[35]

Such duality is further emphasized in the curious similarities between Harry and Voldemort. Dark magic is obviously hidden magic, and Lord Voldemort is very much the father of lies. Yet Harry tells many lies as well, chiefly to his professors in order to execute a plan or protect a friend.[36] Tom Riddle, the young Voldemort, points to other striking resemblances: "Both half-bloods, orphans, raised by Muggles." They are also both Parselmouths, and "even look something alike."[37] These similarities, together with their the profound differences, point to ways in which Slytherin House and Gryffindor House are also "brothers," much like the two wands in the duel at the conclusion of *Goblet of Fire*. Voldemort's wand is put to destructive use, such as with the Cruciatus and Avada Kedavra (torture and killing) Curses; Harry's wand is used for preservation and recuperation when he employs Expelliarmus.[38]

Near the conclusion of book II, Harry admits another anxiety to Dumbledore: that the hat only placed him in Gryffindor because he so desperately asked not to be put in Slytherin. The headmaster's response is at once a relief and another puzzle. He claims that Harry's request is what distinguishes him so clearly from Tom Riddle. Dumbledore assures Harry that "[i]t is our choices … that show what we truly are, far more than our abilities."[39] In contrast to Harry's prolonged sorting, when it came time for Draco Malfoy to be sorted, the hat's decision was immediate: Slytherin.[40] Children, too, have important decisions to make, and Rowling's texts emphasize that they need to consider individual preference, conscience, and right and wrong rather than what the majority think and do. These choices should be informed, reflecting both self-reliance and cooperation—involving group or family loyalty and "grown-up" negotiations between those shifting boundaries. This idea is not something from which Rowling shies.[41]

In each book, Harry proves that he belongs in Gryffindor, for who is in more need of courage than the boy whom Lord Voldemort wants dead? But what are we to make of the other sorts who are sorted, especially Harry's housemates, whose position in Gryffindor seems less obvious at the outset than that of the Slytherins we encounter? The fearless Weasley twins seem to be in the right house—they are certainly not born Hufflepuffs, though they are diligent in mischief-making. Ron Weasley, neither especially clever nor hard-working, demonstrates his bravery in the first book by allowing himself to be knocked out—hard—in the game of chess that helps them reach the Philosopher's Stone, in the second book by seeking out the Chamber of Secrets with Harry, and in *Prisoner of Azkaban* by declaring that he will die alongside Harry if Sirius Black chooses to kill his best friend.

But why is Hermione Granger, who regularly achieves better than perfect marks on assignments, not in Ravenclaw among those who value wit and learning? Or even in hard-working Hufflepuff, where surely Percy Weasley belongs? What of Neville Longbottom, over whom the Sorting Hat also lingers in the first book? Is he merely Gryffindor by default, because he is neither clever, notably hard-working, nor ambitious? The reasons for Neville's position in this house are not apparent even to him. He chokes out that there is no need to tell him that he is not courageous enough to be a member of Gryffindor, since Malfoy has already taunted him with this accusation.[42] In the fourth book, we learn of Neville's parents, cursed so badly by Lord Voldemort that they have been driven insane, unable to recognize their son when he visits them in hospital. Surely Neville, though cringing and trembling around bullies like Professor Snape and Malfoy (both Slytherins), must draw on resources of courage simply to go on. His efforts to act in spite of his fears speak to a bravery that Dumbledore acknowledges by granting Neville the final points that win the school cup in *Philosopher's Stone*. He intones that confronting one's enemies requires great courage; however, it is important to realize that it can take "just as much to stand up to our friends."[43] It is fitting that Gryffindor win this first cup not for skill in Quidditch (which is what put Slytherin in first place before the daring retrieval of the Philosopher's Stone), but for bravery. Until this year, Harry's first at Hogwarts, Slytherin had won the house cup for seven years in a row—a reminder that, although the many dark wizards who followed Voldemort from his house were defeated, there is still power within it. Nor is Voldemort dead. Courage is needed because, as the grotesque form of Voldemort that inhabits Professor Quirrell in *Philosopher's Stone* asserts, there are always people willing to let him infiltrate "their hearts and minds."[44] Both of these locations—the heart and the mind—are essential to the emphasis on courage in Gryffindor House. One former student who speaks to the requisite "daring, nerve and chivalry" of Gryffindor is Professor Remus Lupin. Dumbledore once took a great risk in letting him, a boy who had been bitten by a werewolf, enter Hogwarts, and Lupin's affliction is seen very much as a handicap, difficult to overcome. It requires a special sort of courage—one in which he must hurt himself to protect others.[45] It is little wonder that the Sorting Hat placed Lupin in Gryffindor where, as it reminds us in book IV, "the bravest [are] / Prized far beyond the rest."[46]

C. S. Lewis argued that "Courage is not simply one of the virtues but the form of every virtue at its testing point."[47] Godric Gryffindor himself seems to have possessed the qualities that each of the other founders prized: he must have been not only courageous, but also hardworking, clever, and ambitious. His intelligence is demonstrated in that it was he who came up with the solution to the problem of perpetual sorting by taking from his own head the hat into which the four founders then placed brains.[48] True leaders, Rowling suggests, must have many strengths. The Aristotelian pronouncement that "Courage is the first of human qualities because it is the quality which guarantees the others" also holds true in these novels and is perhaps best exemplified by Hermione. *Philosopher's Stone* introduces Hermione as a girl with whom Harry and Ron share only tension and personality conflicts until an encounter with a troll unites them in a daring act of mutual preservation. It is their first conquest together, and from that moment onward, she becomes a true friend. In spite of a genuine respect for rules, Hermione risks expulsion from school to save Hagrid's baby dragon, Norbert, and to retrieve the Philosopher's Stone. She dares to make and use the risky Polyjuice Potion in *Harry Potter and the Chamber of Secrets* and aids in the escape of two condemned prisoners—Buckbeak the hippogriff and Sirius Black—in *Prisoner of Azkaban*. Here, too, she walks out of Professor Trelawney's Divination class, refusing to read (and read fear into) the future. She is an example to Harry in her scorn of the malicious *Daily Prophet* articles in *Goblet of Fire*, and her ability to disregard the taunts of Slytherins demonstrates a fearless sense of self-worth. Rooted in courage, such actions speak to Hermione's loyalty, compassion, confidence, and cleverness in the execution of various schemes. As the top student in her year, she is one of the most ambitious characters in the novels, but she is no Slytherin. Rather, as Hagrid tells Harry and Ron in the third volume, Hermione has "her heart in the right place."[49] Dumbledore's assertion, in his praise of Neville, that all kinds of courage exist is an important key to belonging in Gryffindor because, as the headmaster suggests, peer pressure can be more difficult to counter than external conflict. Hermione is also steadfast in her defense of the rights of house-elves in *Goblet of Fire*, despite an obvious lack of support from her house or her school. Indeed, her bravest moments are in *Prisoner of Azkaban* when she risks losing her two best friends, and for a time does so, because she cares more about Harry's safety than about their friendship. First, she tells Professor McGonagall about the broom Harry has received from an unknown source, and then she threatens to inform McGonagall if Harry risks his life by going into Hogsmeade.[50]

With a sense of belonging in a school house comes evident peer pressure. The worst punishment by far is the chilly silence of housemates whom one has let down by losing house points. Harry experiences this sick feeling more than once, and it is little wonder that when Professor McGonagall contemplates how to punish him and Ron for crashing the car into the Whomping Willow, Harry anxiously argues that since the term had not officially begun when they took the car, points should not be deducted from Gryffindor.[51] When Harry and Ron enter the Gryffindor common room afterward, they are applauded because, aside from detention, they more or less have gotten away with their "crime"; had each lost fifty house points on the first day of term, their reception would have been very different. Failure as well as success is shared by the house. The importance of winning Quidditch matches and the communal pride in Gryffindor when Harry is given a Firebolt in *Prisoner of Azkaban* emphasize the degree to which a superior broomstick is about success on three levels: individual, team, and house. House points are won and lost not only on the basis of individual behavior and athletic performance, but also according to academic achievement, which means that Hermione, considered a know-it-all by her housemates, wins considerable points for Gryffindor.

In the instances when transgressions of the rules actually hurt a gentle person to whom one owes loyalty (like Neville), or disappoint a teacher whom Harry respects (such as former Gryffindors Dumbledore and Lupin), guilt—a self-inflicted punishment—is far more onerous than any threats the malevolent Snape could levy. The potential for internal conflicts (and perhaps the problems facing Gryffindors in particular, given that courage is their principle aim) is anticipated in book I with Professor McGonagall's explanation that each house is like one's family at Hogwarts.[52] The familial metaphor is significant, as each of the central characters has a complicated family life of one sort or another: dead parents, Muggle parents, lost parents, and in Ron's case, the fragmented attention of busy parents.[53] When George Weasley tells his brother Percy not to sit with the other prefects at the Christmas banquet because Christmas is "for family," he seems to be referring not merely to himself, Fred, and Ron, but to the Gryffindor table, their house away from home.[54] Gryffindor fills a need in each of its students, and belonging to any family—as the personality conflicts and monetary troubles of the Weasley family testify—demands courage as well.

Harry, of course, has known only the Dursleys' version of family before his life at Hogwarts. The affection in this Muggle family—comprised of Uncle Vernon, Aunt Petunia, and Harry's cousin Dudley—is mixed, real and shallow, based in large part on material considerations and criticism of those outside their home. The Dursleys also seem to shape their family life around the very exclusion of Harry from their triumvirate of parents and only son, an effect which doubles the loss of his own family. By contrast, life at Hogwarts offers Harry glimpses into the parents he lost—tales about them as students, photographs, painful memories brought to the surface by the dementors. It also offers him, finally, somewhere to belong. Over the summer in *Chamber of Secrets*, Harry's longing for Hogwarts "was like having a constant stomachache"—a familiar symptom of homesickness.[55] Returning to the Gryffindor dormitory in *Prisoner of Azkaban*, although aware that a murderer intends to seek him out at Hogwarts, Harry "felt he was home at last."[56]

The Mirror of Erised, an imaginative portal to the gazer's deepest desire, reveals to the orphaned Harry Potter generations of his family in *Philosopher's Stone*, while it shows Ron Weasley a solitary glory, his arms full of awards. Like the school house system, the mirror demonstrates the importance both of inclusion and of exclusion. Hogwarts plays with these two desirable attributes in a school, reflective of our own tendencies in childhood for secret clubs, passwords, for a world apart from adults.[57] Harry's decision to heed Dumbledore's advice not to seek out the visions in the mirror, which distract him from concrete action, is yet another type of courage that validates his position within Gryffindor: he is able to walk away from fantasy toward reality, however unpleasant. Each book's conclusion thus far has contained a moment in which

Harry's attendants, Ron and/or Hermione, or Cedric, fall back, whereupon he is left alone, a child who is more than a child because he is a true Gryffindor, facing the most evil Slytherin of all time in unfair competition.

In their confrontation in book IV, Harry's archenemy challenges him to die "like a man," both "straight-backed and proud, the way your father died."[58] In times of trouble, the Gryffindor who comes most readily to Harry's mind is his father, James Potter, in whom Harry's two families—the Potters and the Gryffindors—meet and strengthen each other. Thanks to these two families, Harry's courage is both inherent and reinforced. Like his resistance to the Imperius Curse—which causes the mind to embrace ignorant bliss as an alternative to everything from grief to torture—Harry's courage brings first pain, then freedom. This is the opposite order in which these gifts come to Slytherin students who choose the powerful attraction of dark magic, follow Voldemort, and "eat death." Harry realizes independence as well as a sense of belonging at Hogwarts because within Gryffindor he is both first among equals and an equal among firsts in the best house at the best school in Britain.

NOTES

1. Thomas Hughes, *Tom Brown's Schooldays* (Oxford: Oxford UP, 1989), 125.

2. J.K. Rowling, *Harry Potter and the Philosopher's Stone* (1997; Vancouver: Raincoast Books, 2000), 88.

3. The school contains pupils of many races: Lee Jordan, in Gryffindor, has dreadlocks; the "very pretty" and distracting (to Harry) Cho Chang is in Ravenclaw, and identical twins Parvati and Padma Patil are in Gryffindor and Ravenclaw, respectively.

4. It is worth noting that, magic aside, Hogwarts has much higher expectations for genuine scholarship than Muggle schools: the eleven-year-olds who begin there have obviously mastered the basic skills not only of reading and math in order to carry on with their complicated history lessons, spells, summarizing of chapters, mixing of potions, and later Arithmancy; they also arrive capable of writing research essays, some of which are assigned over the summer.

5. That said, certain specialties at the school do seem to be obviously feminine: the school nurse is Madam Pomfrey, whereas Divination is the repertoire of the wispiest of witches—Professor Sibyll Trelawney. However, Charms, often associated with witches, not wizards, is significantly taught by a man. Transfiguration, among the most difficult types of magic, once taught by Headmaster Dumbledore, is now the domain of Professor McGonagall. Arithmancy, the magical equivalent of math—is also taught by a woman, Professor Vector.

6. J.K. Rowling, *Harry Potter and the Prisoner of Azkaban* (Vancouver: Raincoast Books, 1999), 225. The conflict between those who do and do not accept Muggle-born wizards dates back to Salazar Slytherin's defection from the school he helped establish and rages still outside the school, as well as within, chiefly between Slytherin and Gryffindor. Joan Acocella identifies Voldemort's role in this "overarching race war" as

initiating an "ethnic-cleansing campaign." Joan Acocella, "Under the Spell," *The New Yorker*, 31 July 2000, 74–78, 77. Nevertheless, Voldemort (himself half-Muggle) and his Death Eaters are willing to kill wizards, witches, and Muggles both for trying to stand in his way and for amusement.

7. Rowling, *Philosopher's Stone*, 136.

8. It is worth noting that Lily Potter, Harry's mother and Aunt Petunia's sister, also had a floral name, which in her case seems to connote a positive blossoming of femininity.

9. Rowling is particularly good with names. "Malfoy" is positively Spenserian.

10. Michael O'Brien, "Harry Potter and the Paganization of Children's Culture," *Catholic World Report* (April 2001), 52–61, 56.

11. J. K. Rowling, *Harry Potter and the Goblet of Fire* (London: Bloomsbury, 2000), 67.

12. Rowling, *Goblet of Fire*, 347.

13. C. E. Montague, *Disenchantment* (London: Chatto and Windus, 1922), 89.

14. Rowling, *Goblet of Fire*, 550.

15. Ibid., 633.

16. Rowling, *Prisoner of Azkaban*, 225.

17. Rowling, *Philosopher's Stone*, 61.

18. Ibid., 90–91.

19. Rowling, *Goblet of Fire*, 157.

20. Ibid., 627.

21. Acocella, "Under the Spell," 78.

22. Rowling, *Prisoner of Azkaban*, 311.

23. See http://www.mikids.com/harrypotter/sorting_hat.htm (accessed 12 August 2002).

24. See http://www.homestead.com/harrypotterbymegz/sort.html (accessed 12 August 2002). If one claims to be "brave" and therefore suitable for Gryffindor (as most visitors would?), he or she learns: "In Gryffindor we're all brave at heart ... even those that you least expect to be."

25. See http://www.harrypotterfansonline.com/SortingCap.htm (accessed 14 August 2002).

26. Rowling, *Goblet of Fire*, 513.

27. See Veronica L. Schanoes's chapter for further discussion of Rowling's complex portrayal of "good" and "evil."

28. Quoted in Boswell's *Life of Johnson*, 11 June, 1784 (1791).

29. Rowling, *Goblet of Fire*, 597.

30. Rowling, *Philosopher's Stone*, 61–62.

31. Rowling, *Prisoner of Azkaban*, 274–75.

32. Rowling, *Philosopher's Stone*, 14.

33. Ibid., 65.

34. Ibid., 85.

35. As Professor Binns explains to his History of Magic class: "Just because a wizard *doesn't* use Dark magic, doesn't mean he *can't*." The emphasis is on free will, and the

strength to resist exercising power merely because one has it. J. K. Rowling, *Harry Potter and the Chamber of Secrets* (1998; Vancouver: Raincoast Books, 1999), 115.

36. The profound falsehood by the most infamous graduate of Slytherin House, however, is very different from Harry's pranks and house loyalty in that it is unspeakable: Voldemort is referred to by most wizards as "You-Know-Who" or "The Dark Lord" or "He Who Must Not Be Named"; Salazar Slytherin's ancient basilisk is a monster whom even other monsters will not name in *Chamber of Secrets*. The difference between the house ghosts of the two dominant houses speak to the distinction between openness and secrecy, between being the resistant victim of wrongdoing and doing wrong. Gryffindor has Sir Nicholas de Mimsy-Porpington. Better known as Nearly Headless Nick, he endured forty-five blows to the neck with a blunt axe before succumbing to death. In contrast, the Slytherin ghost is the mysterious Bloody Baron, gaunt and covered in silver blood. When queried about how the Baron came to be in this state, Nearly Headless Nick murmurs tactfully, "I've never asked." Rowling, *Philosopher's Stone*, 179. The Baron elicits fear from everyone, even the other ghosts. In effect, Gryffindor and Slytherin House are both impressive and both command respect, but Slytherin is about exercising power in ways that are at times more imposing, even more exciting.

37. Rowling, *Chamber of Secrets*, 233.

38. Although the power of Slytherin is to bring about selective death while Gryffindor fights endlessly for life, the paradigm set up by Rowling is not so much that Gryffindor represents good and Slytherin evil, but that they represent the *regeneration* of good and evil respectively. Voldemort is virtually incapable of dying, even after he has been reduced almost to spirit by the spell that turned on its originator when he tried to kill Harry as an infant. The phoenix that contributed a tail feather for the wands of both Voldemort and Harry bursts periodically into flame, and rises again from the ashes.

39. Rowling, *Chamber of Secrets*, 245.

40. Rowling, *Philosopher's Stone*, 90.

41. Rowling almost never uses the word *children*, which is a distinctly respectful way of writing for them.

42. Rowling, *Philosopher's Stone*, 160.

43. Ibid., 221.

44. Ibid., 213. Later, in *Chamber of Secrets*, the memory of Tom Riddle, the teenaged Voldemort, attributes Ginny Weasley's peril to the fact that she trusted "an invisible stranger." Rowling, *Chamber of Secrets*, 288.

45. Rowling, *Prisoner of Azkaban*, 257–59.

46. Rowling, *Goblet of Fire*, 157.

47. C. S. Lewis, *The Screwtape Letters* (London: Centenary Press, 1950), 148.

48. Rowling, *Goblet of Fire*, 157.

49. Rowling, *Prisoner of Azkaban*, 202.

50. See ibid., 172 and 203, where Hermione threatens to tell Professor McGonagall about the map if Harry goes back to Hogsmeade. In response to her threat, Ron pretends she does not exist.

51. Rowling, *Chamber of Secrets*, 65.

52. Rowling, *Philosopher's Stone*, 85.

53. Rowling employs a device common in children's literature in the relationship between Harry and Ron, that an only child or orphan befriends a child from a large family. Prominent examples of such symbiosis are Anne Shirley and Diana Barry in Lucy M. Montgomery's *Anne of Green Gables* (1908) and Mary and Dickon in *The Secret Garden* (1911) by Frances Hodgson Burnett.

54. Rowling, *Philosopher's Stone*, 149.

55. Rowling, *Chamber of Secrets*, 8.

56. Rowling, *Prisoner of Azkaban*, 74. The home away from (and often superior to) home is at the heart of all school stories. Robert J. Kirkpatrick argues that the Harry Potter books "may belong on the fringes of the school story genre, but they are, consciously or otherwise, firmly rooted in its oldest, and most endearing, traditions." Robert J. Kirkpatrick, *The Encyclopedia of Boys' School Stories* (Aldershot, UK: Ashgate Press, 2000), 287. For further discussion of Rowling's connections to the public school story tradition, see Karen Manners Smith's chapter in this volume.

57. The Mirror of Erised presents a challenge to Harry as he is able to feel part of a family for the first time, and so almost loses the necessary drive to deal with the problem of figuring out the mystery of the Stone. Thinking about seeing his parents again, he almost forgets about Nicolas Flamel and the object that the three-headed dog is guarding. Rowling, *Philosopher's Stone*, 154.

58. Rowling, *Goblet of Fire*, 573.

5

Harry and Hierarchy: Book Banning as a Reaction to the Subversion of Authority

Rebecca Stephens

The controversies over the Harry Potter series are by now almost as much of an obligatory start to articles about the books as is the mention of their record-breaking sales and the passionate devotion they inspire in hordes of fans. For those who admire Harry's ability to inveigle kids to read and for those who simply enjoy the darn good stories in the four Potter books, it's easy to dismiss those who seek to ban the books with the labels familiar from many other recent book challenges: right-wing fanatics, Christian fundamentalists, and worse. These tags, however, are not at all productive for much of anything other than garnering media attention, as perhaps they have been designed to do. For those who seek to understand the books within their cultural context and for those who, as I do, teach young adult literature to future English teachers, trying to understand just what it is that drives certain parents to protest the books' use in schools is much more useful than merely labeling the protestors as some kind of lunatic fringe.

Despite the facts that the Harry Potter books are the creation of a British author and first published in the United Kingdom, attempts to ban the series are primarily an American phenomenon. In London, the *Evening Standard* commented on U.S. fundamentalists' objections and asserted that "[n]o such doubts were expressed in this country, where children's insatiable appetite for the Potter books meant they were universally welcomed."[1] While the statement is not strictly accurate today, attempts at censorship in the United Kingdom have been extremely rare: only two cases of religious objections were given much coverage by the British mainstream media. The first was an instance where the head of a Church of England primary school, Carol Rookwood, removed the Harry Potter books from her school's library and suggested that parents also prevent their children from reading the series at home.[2] The Dean of the

Gloucester Cathedral was also critiqued for allowing the filming of a portion of the Harry Potter movie in its cloisters.[3] These actions, however, were given little support by the national church authorities in England. In fact, Bishop Stephen Sykes, the chair of the Church of England's doctrine commission, responded to the school ban by saying that "The Church's position is that magic and sorcery are contrary to the Christian religion, Mrs. Rookwood is absolutely right ... [b]ut my feeling is that children are capable of interpreting what they read. Children who are capable of reading *Harry Potter* could be told not to take witchcraft seriously, or might even realize that for themselves."[4] Interestingly enough, most reporting in the British press of the censorship of Harry Potter focuses on the U.S. challenges in a generally uncomplimentary way; commentators seem to seek to create a psychic distance between the European view and that of the would-be censors in the States. As Roberta Harrington of the Scottish newspaper the *Sunday Herald* writes, "The Harry Potter controversy may seem bizarre, but it is hardly unexpected to those who watch such trends in the United States, a violent culture that is home to millions of fundamentalist Christians. In Europe, America is well known for prudery and prohibitionism."[5] Though there are many far-reaching historical reasons that might account for these cultural differences—the absence of a national church in the United States, a more democratic and explicitly secular educational system in this country, and the plurality of U.S. religions—the fact remains that when discussing the phenomenon of censoring the Harry Potter books, we are discussing a practice that is peculiarly American and dependent on certain factors within American social, political, and religious culture.

The reasons given for challenges to Rowling's novels in American schools from Michigan to South Carolina are a roster of the complaints often leveled at the books that regularly appear on the American Library Association's annual list of most-challenged titles.[6] The Harry Potter stories are too violent, present "occult activities" as fun, are anti-Bible, depict sorcery and magic, and open the door to "spiritual bondage." Most frequently cited is the depiction of witches and wizards, which, according to many of the books' detractors, is likely to desensitize children to the dangers of the dark supernatural world. My first reaction to reading of these claims was to think of C. S. Lewis' Narnia books, which are rife not only with wizards and witches but also with fauns, giants, centaurs, and virtually every other supernatural being in imaginative existence. This, of course, is a comparison noted by many others, but most significantly for this essay, is also made by the Potter series' detractors. For example, John Andrew Murray, a writer for the conservative Focus on the Family organization who is one of the most aggressive critics of the books, makes the comparison and concludes that the difference between Rowling's and Lewis's fantasies "hinges on the concept of authority." He asserts that what redeems the Narnia books from their basis in the supernatural is their Christian perspective.[7] This perspective, however, is much more elusive in the Narnia texts than Murray's matter-of-fact statement would suggest. Even though the Narnia books contain components of Christian mythology and have been widely read as Christian allegories, the perspective comes from interpreting these books rather than their explicit content. In fact, there is not a single mention of God in any of the Narnia books and the God/Christ-figure Aslan is literally a lion. The Rowling-Lewis comparison thus raises an interesting paradox: what makes one book depicting the supernatural "Christian" and the other somehow "dangerous"? The answer, I believe, lies in the way that authority is represented in each set of books and the way these representations lead to different understandings of the role of values within contemporary culture.

There seem to be two facets of the Narnia books that explain why certain groups accept Lewis's wizards and witches as part of a Christian cosmology while identifying Rowling's stories of similar characters as "occult," or even anti-biblical. Part of the positive reception of Lewis's work is certainly dependent on the perception of Lewis as a Christian apologetic fighting on the "right" side of a spiritual battle. He is not only widely known for his Christian beliefs and lay theological writings, but is actually "venerated as the great Christian intellectual of the twentieth century" by many evangelical Christians.[8] Because he is a figure whose beliefs are sanctioned and praised by conservatives across religious lines, there is doubtlessly a reassuring sense for many potential critics that Lewis's use of the supernatural is driven by sound convictions. For example, a Baptist minister who wrote two books on Lewis states that "C. S. Lewis is a household name all over the world and is easily the century's most trusted and read Christian writer."[9] Similarly, an article in the *National Catholic Register* explicitly links "authentic piety" to Lewis's children's series: "Children like the Narnia Chronicles because they evoke a fantasy wonderland populated by people like Digory, Polly, Lucy, Edmund and the great lion, Aslan. Catholic parents like them because they know Aslan is a Christ figure and the author, C. S. Lewis, wrote the books in part to evangelize readers."[10] By contrast, little is known about Rowling's religious beliefs, which leaves plenty of room for the unease of conservative Christian parents to grow, unassuaged by the sanctions that Lewis's religious credentials provide for the Narnia books.

The problem, however, in a wholesale recommending of Lewis's fiction as more Christian than the Harry Potter series is that the allegories are not readily apparent, especially to young readers—precisely the audience whom the protesters are directing to the Narnia books and away from Harry. I remember my own experience of rereading the Chronicles more times than I can count between the ages of nine and eighteen; it was only when I took a graduate seminar in Renaissance literature that I learned enough about Lewis's scholarship and beliefs to fully analyze the Narnia books for their metaphorical meanings. This experience would not in the least surprise Lewis, since he recommended not explaining the Christian symbolism in the Narnia series to children until they were older; he said, "they should be simply enjoyed as stories."[11]

There are, of course, some overt uses of Christian mythology throughout the Chronicles. For example, in *The Magician's Nephew* (1955), which tells the story of the start of the world of Narnia, Aslan sends the boy Digory Kirk to pick an apple from a tree in a valley reminiscent of the Garden of Eden; there, the evil Queen Jadis tempts Digory to eat one of the fruits.[12] Aslan's self-sacrifice and rise from death in *The Lion, the Witch, and the Wardrobe* (1950) is an obvious reference to Jesus' crucifixion and resurrection. Though there are many other such points in the Chronicles, the books are perhaps even more heavily weighted with magic and populated with characters from pagan mythology than is ever mentioned in the context of the Harry Potter debate. In fact, it would seem that reading the Narnia books might have become a self-fulfilling prophecy where Lewis's Christianity is taken so much for granted that the other perspectives are overlooked.

As Mervyn Nicholson has illustrated, Lewis's literary influences were not all Christian; the writers E. Nesbit, Bram Stoker, Rider Haggard, and H. G. Wells, among others who were either "hostile or indifferent to Christianity," formed a creative basis for many of the events in the Chronicles.[13] In addition, the series' cast of mythological characters includes not only characters from Greek mythology, such as Bacchus, but characters like the ancient Italian woodland deities, fauns, and tree spirits.[14] The use of such non-Christian figures derives, of course, from rituals for and beliefs about worshiping the natural world. Intriguingly, one of the attacks against *Harry Potter* that is frequently paired with its "anti-Christian" perspective is that the books are likely to lead children to the practice of Wicca. Since one of the primary tenets of the Wiccan religion is connection with the natural world, and such worship is never mentioned in Rowling's book, Lewis's repetitive use of Dryads and Naiads might seem much *more* likely to lead to the practices of paganism than Harry's mechanical spell-casting.

It is certainly worth speculating that there may also be some gender issues at work here. Given the long history of associating the practice of witchcraft exclusively with women, it is not surprising that conservative groups are more ready to buy into the idea that a woman—one who is also a single mother, an anathema to the "family values" advocated by many of these organizations—is actually advocating witchcraft as a religion than to attribute the same motives a male author who engages in similar depictions—especially a male author who is already allied in the popular mind with evangelical Christianity.

Attributing Christian allegory to the Narnia Chronicles is only one facet of the objectors' preference for Lewis's writing, however. More important to the construction of a perspective labeled "Christian" by the conservative challengers than the use of religious symbolism are the conception of authority and the boundaries of supernatural power in the books. One of the key differences between the two series is in the ordering of their worlds' relationship between the real and the supernatural. In Narnia, our recognizably ordinary world is clearly the "real" one until the narrative finale. Narnia, in Lewis's stories, serves a variety of functions that do not cross over into this "real" world, and parts of Narnia can never be brought back into our nonmagical reality. In *The*

Silver Chair (1953), for example, Narnia offers an escape for Jill and Eustace, who are fleeing from the school bullies at Experiment House when they pass through the wall into Aslan's country. When they return to the everyday world, they find themselves at the precise moment they left it. Though Aslan helps them to protect themselves and sits at the very border of the worlds, he cannot enter the world beyond his fantastic existence. Furthermore, the arms the children attain to fight the bullies are more physical and psychological than magical.[15] Thus, these characters visit Narnia with a set purpose, for a defined length of length of time, to fulfill a higher goal—a quest determined by Aslan in most cases—and the trappings of magic must remain firmly in Narnia. Likewise, in the earlier book, *The Voyage of the Dawn Treader* (1952), Eustace briefly becomes a dragon before exploring the eastern edge of the Narnian world, but what he returns home with is not magical: his former priggishness is left behind in Narnia along with the dragonish skin.[16] The imaginary world does not truly collide with the "real" world until the very end of the last book, *The Last Battle* (1956), where the worlds meet in life after death.[17] Through most of the series, however, characters who travel from Narnia to the nonmagical world lose their enchantment and fantastical powers when they cross the boundaries. Jadis, the sorceress who bewitched the dying world of Charn in *The Magician's Nephew*, is not able to exercise her powers to reduce humans and steel to rubble in England, even though she retains her extraordinary physical strength. Likewise, the apple Aslan gives Digory for his mother in the same story heals her, but no longer confers immortality. Literal movement between Narnia and our "real" world maintains this sense of clear-cut boundaries, usually in the shape of wardrobe doors, or metaphorically in the way-station of the Wood Between the Worlds or the great jarring thump of the train wreck in *The Last Battle*. The final effect is quite simply that the reader always knows where one world ends and the other begins.

In the Harry Potter tales, however, distinctions are more blurred. The world of wizards is a hidden world, just behind or below the surface of our own world. For example, the portkeys used for transport to the Quidditch World Cup in *Harry Potter and the Goblet of Fire* are objects Muggles would see and dismiss as mere litter, like a junk tire.[18] At the cup premises, wizards temporarily lodge themselves in a Muggle campground and, though their tents and fires ape the outward appearance of authentic campers, the exteriors hide magical interiors with features such as en-suite Jacuzzis.

More importantly, it is the magic itself that crosses over boundaries between worlds. Harry's friends, the practical-joking Weasley twins, can—even though they are not supposed to use magic during school vacations—feed magical toffees to Harry's repulsive and vengeful cousin Dudley. One effect of this traversal is to make Rowling's wizarding world seem closer. I certainly saw this in the people mobbing the King's Cross station in London during the summer of 2000, where platform nine and three-quarters just might have shown up for the release of *Goblet of Fire*. Though I doubt most of the participants truly believed this and dressed as Dumbledore and other characters merely for fun, this sense of flimsy boundaries perhaps explains some of the fear of true belief in wizardry that Rowling's detractors allege will result from reading the books.

An apprehension of ambiguous borders between fantasy and reality might be equally applied to the Narnia books, even with their physical boundaries—children do, after all, often search the backs of closets looking for entry into Narnia after reading *The Lion, the Witch, and the Wardrobe.* We must therefore take into account the issue these boundaries represent beyond physical geography. The key border between Aslan's world and ours is his will. The characters in the Chronicles travel to Narnia only at Aslan's desire, which is most explicitly stated in *The Silver Chair,* the only book in which the characters actually ask to come to Narnia seemingly on their own initiative. Behind their school gym, Jill and Eustace start a ritual to ask Aslan to let them go into his world, but it is only when they are interrupted and forced to abandon the ritual to run from "Them" that they find the door open to another world. Not only is the ritual aborted by the disruption, but also Aslan himself contradicts the notion that their request itself was of their own devising. "You would not have called to me unless I had been calling to you," he tells Jill when she mentions her and Eustace's previous request.[19] Furthermore, the reason the protagonists are allowed to enter Narnia is to serve Aslan's purpose, not their own need to escape their bullying peers. Aslan has called them to rescue King Rilian, the rightful but enchanted King of Narnia, and this is just one example of many that emphasize Aslan's ultimate control of all events. Ultimately, it is this paradigm of a single controlling authority figure that finally seems to be the underlying force in the repeated categorization of Narnia as Christian, and *Harry Potter* as non-Christian, and even anti-Christian.

Murray stresses this issue in voicing what he sees as the major difference between the two series: "Rowling's work invites children to a world where witchcraft is 'neutral' and where authority is determined solely by one's might or cleverness. Lewis invites them to a world where God's authority is not only recognized, but celebrated—a world that resounds with His goodness and care."[20] His and other critics' focus on authority suggests that the problem is truly more abstract than just witches and wizardry. What they actually seem to fear most about Rowling's books is their subversion of traditional hierarchical power structures, where there is a single "right" or "true" source of power. In Murray's words, "That's the nature of a legitimate power—it is granted and guided by authority." For him, of course, the only authority is Jesus. The critic's assertions suggest that the Christian perspective he claims as redeeming to Lewis's books is in fact the hierarchy of authority that is maintained throughout the Narnia series.

In other words, what is truly troubling to *Potter* detractors seems to be the lack of a single controlling authority in the books, not just the practice of magic. In Rowling's books, the headmaster of Hogwarts, Albus Dumbledore, might seem to be such an authority figure, but he, unlike Aslan, is far from omniscient. Dumbledore does not exercise total control over events or people in the way Aslan does. He certainly gives Harry guidance and works as a force for good, but Harry makes his own choices and usually must also suffer consequences from his mistakes without any *deus ex machina* manipulating what happens. In *Goblet of Fire*, the limitations of Dumbledore's power are made especially clear. Even though Dumbledore designed protection for Harry after his parents' death, "invok[ing] an ancient magic" to shield Harry as long as he remains under his relatives' guardianship,[21] Voldemort is able to remove Harry from the circle of the Dursleys' protection and that of Hogwarts itself by turning the Triwizard Cup into a portkey that transports Harry directly to Voldemort's location as soon as the young wizard touches it. Dumbledore does not know in advance about this spell, so he cannot rescue Harry or prevent Cedric Diggory's death at Voldemort's hands, nor does he know about the imposter who has inhabited Mad-Eye Moody's body throughout the entire school year, at least until it is almost too late. These are just a few of the instances that clearly indicate that Dumbledore, while indeed strongly on the side of good and invaluable in the fight against evil, is clearly no Aslan who calls characters across worlds and even determines their ability to enter the final kingdom. In fact, since Harry is the only person to have survived wand-to-wand combat against Voldemort, Harry himself is in many ways more powerful than Dumbledore or even his own godfather Sirius, who was unable to resist his own unjust incarceration in Azkaban.

In classic young adult literature fashion, Harry has literally been on his own since he was a baby, so despite the nominative (and punitive) guardianship of his aunt and uncle, he is the ultimate authority for himself. His absent parents and their surrogates—Dumbledore, Sirius, and even the Weasley family—help him make his way, but their distance makes him essentially self-responsible. The distance is exemplified in several ways: the Weasleys must listen to Dumbledore's and the Dursleys' restrictions on when Harry can visit them; aside from a couple of weeks in the summer, Mrs. Weasley can only act as a surrogate parent from afar by sending hand-knit sweaters and homemade treats to Harry at Hogwarts; Dumbledore must keep his headmasterlike professional distance unless a crisis occurs; because of his escaped-convict status, Sirius must stay geographically remote most of the time, and even when he can be physically close to Harry, he must remain disguised rather than assuming an overtly parentally protective role.

Interestingly, the nature of these relationships means that, like Harry, all of the forces of the good in the book are decentralized. There is no one individual or being that is the ultimate arbiter of goodness; instead, good forces are bureaucracies. Bureaucracy by definition might suggest hierarchy, but in Rowling's books this is not really the case. In the various ministries, power seems horizontal, spread throughout the various agencies. Although there is a minister in the Ministry of Magic (a position that Dumbledore was offered and declined), the ineffective Cornelius Fudge insures that the agencies' main task is to prevent the Muggles from realizing that "there's still witches an' wizards up an' down the country," rather than legislating good and bad.[22] Ultimately, no single figure unifies the various ministries. In fact, the only thing that seems to draw them together is Voldemort's return in each of the Potter books. Significantly, while the forces of good are nonhierarchical, the forces of evil have a central controlling figure in Voldemort.

The contrast between these forces leads us to one of the most important ideas embodied in the Harry Potter series and one of the keys to both its challenges and its phenomenal popularity. In Rowling's books, traditional power structures are actively subverted, as are paradigms of hierarchy and rule-centered behavior. Regulations created by authorities seem made to be broken. In *Harry Potter and the Sorcerer's Stone*, Dumbledore even provides an Invisibility Cloak to help Harry circumvent the school's curfew rules to pursue the stone.

Furthermore, it is the lack of unity, and not the absence or flouting of rules, that defeats evil in the stories. The singular power of the evildoer, Voldemort, always leads to his downfall. In each novel, Voldemort co-opts his followers and demands their absolute obedience, even to the point of inhabiting their bodies and literally possessing them. Harry is able to defeat Voldemort because his is always a group effort; he is not only helped in each confrontation by Dumbledore, but he is also aided by his friends. In *Sorcerer's Stone*, for example, Ron's chess abilities and Hermione's common sense in figuring out the potion riddle are essential to Harry's seizing the stone; in *Goblet of Fire*, the ghosts of those whom Voldemort has murdered, including Cedric Diggory and Harry's own parents, come out of his wand and to his aid. In this scene, even Harry's wand is dependent on Voldemort's because its power to vanquish lies in the fact that their two wands share the same core: both contain feathers from the tail of Dumbledore's phoenix.

That the evil force is the one with a single authority is in direct opposition to the Christian rightist belief that there is a divine design for good in the world and one true power source ordering it. The inverted depiction and the threat it poses to de-elevate hierarchies of power as the correct world order is perhaps the real menace of *Harry Potter*. Though the central antagonist might seem to play into a common misperception about the practice of witchcraft as an alliance with another singularly evil being, Satan—a misapprehension dating back in the United States to the Salem witch trials—and thus fuel fundamentalists' fears, a parallel anxiety exists: contemporary practitioners of witchcraft and other new neopagan movements essentially have "no unifying organization, written scripture, dogma, or defining ritual practice."[23]

Fears of an order deposed certainly seem to echo in the cries against "moral relativism" in the Harry Potter books, which also turn on the sense that absolutes and a fixed ordering of power have been lost. To understand why the loss of hierarchy might drive people to see a widely loved series of children's books as perilous, it is helpful to understand the protesters and the common paradigm that unites their objections. Though the challenges to the Harry Potter books have been brought to schools by concerned parents, these parents' comments echo the words of the religious right organizations that have criticized or condemned the books publicly. Focus on the Family, the group for whom Murray writes, is one assembly; Concerned Women for America is another (they also funded the widely publicized "Scopes II" textbook banning trial lawsuit in the 1980s).[24] Examining these organizations' goals and agendas can help us better understand some of the claims in the Harry Potter debate, particularly in relationship to understanding the pertinent views on hierarchy and authority.

Most evangelical belief systems initially seem antihierarchical in that they usually rely on a personal relationship with God rather than on a literal hierarchy of humans to sustain the order of the belief system. However, the sense of truth and order in the world for these groups does rely on hierarchy to make the world coherent. As Karen McCarthy Brown describes it, fundamentalism is the religion of people for whom the world is overwhelming. "Bitterly disappointed by the politics of rationalized bureaucracies, the limitations of science, and the perversions of industrialization, fundamentalists seek to reject the modern world while nevertheless holding onto its habits of mind: clarity, certitude, and control."[25] The certainty that God or Jesus is the source of absolute truth and the unquestionable agent of control is characterized in the language of these groups, especially voiced through narratives of conversion and the demands of being "born again." As one Pentecostal woman describes it, "Christians need to be equipped to have the answers to [moral relativism], to learn, to study the issues, to know God's word, to be bold and speak out and not be intimidated, and impact the culture. Because we have the truth."[26] Thus, an absolute acceptance of authority is inherent in the doctrines of most of those who publicly protest against Harry Potter.

Further, this hierarchy passes into ordering human relationships. We can see entrenched values of hierarchy clearly in the common stance of those who object to evolutionism, both on the grounds that it eliminates a belief in God as a single authoritarian creator, and on the principle that humans rank "higher" on the scale of beings because of our ability to reason. It is also quite evident within the patriarchal outlines often prescribed for family relationships, especially in the subordination of women in sects such as the Southern Baptists, and in the perceived threat to gender hierarchy from feminism's questioning of women's roles. This fear gets repeatedly voiced in labels like commentator Rush Limbaugh's infamous "femi-Nazi." The demand for a strictly ordered hierarchy of power within the family structure appears even more rigid in recommendations for interactions between parent and child. Parents in almost all religious right–based cases of school book censorship see themselves as the authority when it comes to what influences their children are exposed to. What makes this more heightened than many other parents' similar concerns is that it is accompanied by the sense that contemporary U.S. society is one that is overwhelmingly at odds with their values and is, in fact, overtly intending to undermine all Christian beliefs. Media that focus on these parents, in fact, commonly and overtly voice this theme: they are lone agents in fighting evil and the overwhelming forces of a contemporary lack of morals. Listeners to Laura Schlessinger's talk radio show, for example, are exhorted to be "Dr. Laura's Warriors" in protecting their children from exposure to values that are different than their own. That she also regularly excoriates the American Library Association for advocating "porn" by including a link to a health website on its teens' webpage is indicative of this attitude that sees threats to children everywhere.[27] This siege mentality reinforces the notion that a hierarchy of parental authority is the socially and morally correct order of things and to disturb this order is to put one's children and one's self in jeopardy. Perhaps this is one of the most goading of the potential concerns of the religious right: "[T]he most lethal threat to the family, in the judgement of the Evangelical Right, is neither the sexual revolution nor feminism, but the awful truth that the established institutions of American society have determined to keep parents from controlling the values of their adolescent children."[28] Thus, the lack of rules, and in particular the lack of parental authority in the Harry Potter series, is perceived not only as a threat, but also as an opportunity for moral beacons and "warriors" for the children to warn other parents who are so misguided as not to recognize the dangers inherent in contemporary culture.

To add fuel to this righteous fire that targets Rowling's books, not only are Harry's parents conspicuously absent while other authority figures abet the protagonist in his rule-breaking behavior, but Rowling's only model of the nonmagical traditional family, the Dursleys, is, essentially, a travesty. Harry's uncle, Vernon Dursley, is chiefly preoccupied by image and appearing normal in the eyes of the neighbors. He experiences complete humiliation by the postman's laughter at Mrs. Weasley's unorthodox letter-stamping (she's not familiar with the methods of Muggle mail service); his antipathy for Harry is based on the fact that his wizardly sister-in-law was a potential embarrassment to his ultra-normal life. Aunt Petunia is not only driven by maintaining this façade, but is virtually obsessed by her son, Dudley. She is a ludicrous parody of an overprotective mother whose attitude blinds her to her son's reality and serves only to corrupt him further. She responds to any criticism of Dudley by taking his side against all figures of authority that disagree with her vision of him, even refusing to recognize that his medically diagnosed obesity is more than just "puppy-fat."[29]

If we combine this satiric presentation of parental "sheltering" with the perceived persistent threats to authority in general, we can see why this book might seem to some conservative parents to be one more wave in an ever-growing tide determined to undermine their parental role. Rowling's writing disturbs the hierarchy essential not just to family harmony, but also to the values of their faith.

Examining the results of this combination of fears leads to the final piece of the censorship puzzle that most frequently eludes more liberal observers: why are these parents not content to merely censor their own children's reading materials? Why do they demand the books' complete removal from entire schools? The answer lies in a hierarchical ordering of the value of different belief systems. As mentioned above, many on the Christian right conclude that the main problem with contemporary thought—particularly the values of "secular humanism," which forms the basis of so many of the book challenges in schools—is the emphasis on moral relativism, rather than absolute values of what is right and what is wrong. Cries of moral relativism do also frequently accompany objections to the witchcraft in *Harry Potter* and are expressive of a hierarchical viewpoint where the one set of religious values are considered by believers to be more correct than another set. While the broad societal trend has been toward greater tolerance, for some fundamentalists this has meant a breakdown of the national fabric and the conviction that "Christians should be trying to change American society to better reflect God's will."[30] What follows logically, then, is the expectation that institutions such as schools must "return" to Christian values in order to save a whole society that is out of control. This assumed lack of control stems from the idea that our world is crumbling because the proper order of things—the hierarchy of power with God and Christians on top—has been disturbed. Shafer Parker, writing in the Canadian *Report/Newsmagazine* (Alberta Edition) about the link between Harry Potter's popularity and the "widespread interest in witchcraft without parallel in modern times," voices such a concern. Drawing parallels to 50 B.C.E., he states that "[t]hen as now, globalism created a rootless society, out of touch with the old verities that had provided a sense of security and place"; he concludes that "[t]he West now suffers from the same spiritual vacuum that characterized the Roman empire in the centuries immediately prior to the birth of Christ." It also means that "after the current fascination with esoteric religion has run its course, the West will again find its centre in a self-conscious decision to kneel alongside the shepherds and Wise Men, and worship the Babe in the manger."[31] In other words, only a return to a strict religious hierarchy with one "true" religion reinstated as the source of authority and order will stop the current cultural decline.

But if the decline of religious, institutional, and parental authority is the entire story of the objections to *Harry Potter*, why are the same groups not marching in the streets against Philip Pullman's trilogy, which is *much* more radical than Rowling's series? As Nicholas Tucker points out, there is much that is conventional in the Harry Potter series;[32] however, a good deal more controversy surrounds it than does Pullman's fantasies. The attack on religion and other established institutions of power is blatant in the *His Dark Materials* series: the Authority in the books, the "God" of many of the worlds' religions, is a man so doddering that he has forgotten his name and regressed to an infantile state. He is also revealed to be mortal when freed from his crystal cage.[33]

I would argue that the reason for the silence on Pullman while the Harry Potter series reaps tremendous protest lies in the very fact that the latter is a cultural phenomenon. If the mission of religious right protestors is to raise "counter-culture kids,"[34] then what better way to demonstrate and mark one's self as different than to swim against a tide of adoration, by *not* reading the book that "every Muggle in America has read"?[35] What better way to prove one's point than by returning to Lewis's books, which are reminiscent of a time where order, authority, and proper hierarchies of power prevailed?

But, of course, we cannot return to such an earlier time—if, indeed, such a time ever did exist—any more than Harry can return to Mugglehood after learning about his wizard's heritage. The Harry Potter series is a narrative for our age in a way that the Narnia books, as wonderful as they are, are not. The subversion of hierarchy in Rowling's series seems, in fact, to be one of the main factors that make these books so powerful for many children who are growing up in a world where traditional rules are not working. In October 2000, *USA Today* published the results of Scholastic's "How the Harry Potter Books Have Changed My Life" essay contest. The contest winners wrote movingly about how Harry's difficulties helped them through dilemmas in their own living situations, and most of these circumstances dealt with the absence of parents or other traditional family structures. One fourteen-year-old remarked on the "amazing parallels" between Harry's life and hers:

Here was a boy exactly my age who also didn't have a caring family. My mother's neglect put me in foster care for ten years. ... At one home I was beaten, forced to swallow hot sauce, run laps in the blistering sun, squat in awkward positions, and food was withheld. I didn't sleep under the stairs, but I did share a claustrophobic room with eight girls. When I was lonely and miserable, I dreamed about magical worlds and fantasized about being rescued by someone like Hagrid.[36]

Another girl wrote that while living with her mother in a homeless shelter, pretending "that all the other people in the shelter were Muggles and my Mom and I were wizards ... made me feel like I was a part of the books," which helped her to cope with this traumatic situation.[37] Obviously, both young readers found the upside-down world of authority in Harry Potter's life to be empowering for their own difficult and fragmented worlds. These are just a few of the many examples of how children reading the Potter books make connections with the practicalities of their own lives, and use Harry's strength, inventiveness, and loss of family as points of association because the books reflect the world as they know it.

Reality in the United States today *is* frequently without clear-cut traditions, space, families, and even homes. In Milwaukee alone, calls for homeless shelter beds doubled between 1998 and 2000 and the number of children filling those beds has increased by 47 percent over the same period.[38] Even in less extreme situations, there is a need for children to have imaginative sources and role models that help them contend with the fast-changing pace and diversity of our world.

So, where does all this leave us? With some sympathy, perhaps. After all, there is some emotional validity in the fear that the world is moving too rapidly. Who among us, even if we don't think the appropriate response is to impose more authority and moral absolutes, has not felt overwhelmed by the amount of choices, viewpoints, and information we are bombarded with daily? Who hasn't wished for a more simply ordered world? Who hasn't felt at least a twinge of isolation, or the sense that the world is composed of arguing factions that just cannot get along? For this reason, the Harry Potter debate is a microcosm of our cultural debates about how to live with diversity and change. Clearly we cannot afford to ban the Harry Potter books when they serve such an important function for so many, nor do most people, including the majority of Christians, want to. It is important to note that the major Christian publications *Christianity Today* and *Christian Century* have even endorsed Rowling's books.[39] But neither can we afford to dismiss Harry Potter's detractors as "laughably boneheaded."[40] Not only does doing so guarantee more furor down the road, as Rowling's well-publicized promise that the books will get darker can only mean more moves to ban them, but these labels simply reinforce the sense of isolation and willful misinterpretation which confirms the threat the protestors already feel. Dismissal, rather than attempts at understanding, is the most likely act to turn a skirmish into an all-out war, and walling ourselves off into factions only fragments our culture further. Ironically, one of the beauties of the Harry Potter books is that they have given people of different ages, ethnic identities, and nationalities a point of connection. As one ten-year-old said, "Harry Potter changed all of us. It brought us together and gave us a common link."[41] And perhaps it is this extraordinary feat by a modest children's book that is the ultimate reason for the phenomenon of Harry. Let us not undermine that feat with further divisiveness.

NOTES

1. Sarah Shannon, "Harry Potter Fails to Cast a Spell on U.S. Christians," *Evening Standard* (London), 1 October 1999, 18, LEXIS-NEXIS Academic Universe, http://web.lexis-nexis.com/universe (accessed 20 July 2001).

2. Paul Vallely, "Faith and Reason: Harry Potter and a Theology Lesson for Adults," *Independent*, 1 April 2000, 7, LEXIS-NEXIS Academic Universe, http://web.lexis-nexis.com/universe (accessed 20 July 2001).

3. R. Parsons, "Cathedral Shouldn't Welcome Harry Potter," *Western Daily Press/Bristol United Press*, 26 February 2001, 9, LEXIS-NEXIS Academic Universe, http://web.lexis-nexis.com/universe (accessed 20 July 2001).

4. Jenny Booth, "Friendly Witches Earn School Ban for Potter," *Scotsman*, 29 March 2000, 7, LEXIS-NEXIS Academic Universe, http://web.lexis-nexis.com/universe (accessed 20 July 2001).

5. Roberta Harrington, "Fundamentalists in a Frenzy over Power of the Occult," *Sunday Herald/Scottish Media Newspapers Ltd.*, 17 October 1999,10, LEXIS-NEXIS Academic Universe, http://web.lexis-nexis.com/universe (accessed 20 July 2001).

6. See the Center for Studies on New Religions (CESNUR) website on "Harry Potter—Culture and Religion" at http://www.cesnur.org/2001/potter/index.htm (accessed 21 May 2001) for an excellent compilation of articles related to the banning controversy. Beacham Publishing also provides a thorough bibliography of censorship articles at www.beachampublishing.com/home.htm. The American Library Association's yearly list of the most-challenged books is located at http://www.ala.org/bbooks/challeng.html (accessed 5 May 2001).

7. John Andrew Murray, "Harry Dilemma," Teachers in Focus: A Web Site of Focus on the Family, 2000, http://www.family.org/cforum/teachersmag/features/a0009439.html (accessed 20 May 2001).

8. Michael Joseph Gross, "Narnia Born Again," *Nation*, 1 February 1999, 28.

9. Perry Bramlett, quoted in Jay Copp, "A Touch of Narnia in Illinois," *Christian Science Monitor*, 23 March 1999, 18.

10. Joe Woodard, "De-Fanging C. S. Lewis," *U.S. Catholic News:The National Catholic Register*, http://www.catholic.net/us_catholic_news/ (accessed 10 August 2001).

11. Quoted in Virginia Byfield, "Narnia Fans, Meet Narnia's Creator," *Alberta Report/Newsmagazine*, 23 January 1995, 42. *Ebsco: Academic Search Elite*, http://www.ebsco.com (accessed 14 May 2001).

12. C. S. Lewis, *The Magician's Nephew* (New York: Collier Books, 1971).

13. Mervyn Nicholson, "C. S. Lewis and the Scholarship of Imagination in E. Nesbit and Rider Haggard," *Renascence* 51, no. 1 (1998): 41–62. *Humanities Full-Text WilsonWeb*, http://www.wilsonweb.com (accessed 10 May 2001).

14. Sir James G. Frazer, *The Golden Bough*, 1922 (New York: Macmillan, 1951), 126–56.

15. C. S. Lewis, *The Silver Chair* (New York: Collier Books, 1971).

16. C. S. Lewis, *The Voyage of the Dawn Treader* (New York: Collier Books, 1971).

17. C. S. Lewis, *The Last Battle* (New York: Collier Books, 1971).

18. J. K. Rowling, *Harry Potter and the Goblet of Fire* (London: Bloomsbury, 2000).

19. Lewis, *The Silver Chair*, 19.

20. Murray, "Harry Dilemma," n.p.

21. Rowling, *Goblet of Fire*, 570.

22. J. K. Rowling, *Harry Potter and the Sorcerer's Stone* (New York: Scholastic Press, 1997), 65.

23. Elizabeth Reis, "Introduction," in *Spellbound: Women and Witchcraft in America*, Elizabeth Reis, ed. (Wilmington, DE: Scholarly Resources, Inc., 1998), xx.

24. Stephen Bates, *Battleground: One Mother's Crusade, the Religious Right, and the Struggle for Control of Our Classrooms* (New York: Poseidon Press, 1993), 12.

25. Karen McCarthy Brown, "Fundamentalism and the Control of Women," in *Fundamentalism and Gender*, John Stratton Hawley, ed. (New York: Oxford University Press, 1994), 174–201, 174–75.

26. Quoted in Christian Smith, *American Evangelicalism: Embattled and Thriving* (Chicago: University of Chicago Press, 1998), 127.

27. The website is named after the frequently censored young adult book *Go Ask Alice*, a novel in diary form; in it, an anonymous teenager narrates the story of her descent into drug abuse and sexual activity. Since its publication in 1969, *Go Ask Alice* has been one of the most frequently challenged books, according to the ALA's Office of Intellectual Freedom.

The link on the ALA's web site that provoked the controversy was to a health site intended to provide straightforward answers to health questions, published by Columbia University. Because some of the site's information includes topics relating to sexuality, Laura Schlessinger and organizations like Concerned Women for America promoted a letter-writing campaign to the ALA and its corporate supporters of programs for children to demand the removal of the link from the ALA site. The campaign was unsuccessful and the link remains at http://www.ala.org/teenhoopla/health.html, along with the ALA's response to those who requested its removal. See http://www.ala.org/yalsa/askaliceq&a.html.

28. Grant Wacker, "Searching for Norman Rockwell," in *Piety and Politics: Evangelicals and Fundamentalists Confront the World*, John Neuhaus and Michael Cromartie, eds. (Washington, DC: Ethics and Public Policy Center, 1987), 343.

29. Rowling, *Goblet of Fire*, 29–30.

30. Smith, *American Evangelicalism*, 37.

31. Shafer Parker, "It's 50 B.C. All over Again," *Report/Newsmagazine* (Alberta Edition), 20 December 1999, 36. *Ebsco: Academic Search Elite*, http://www.ebsco.com (accessed 14 May 2001).

32. Nicholas Tucker, "The Rise and Rise of Harry Potter," *Children's Literature in Education* 30, no. 4 (1999): 221–34.

33. Philip Pullman, *The Amber Spyglass* (New York: Alfred A. Knopf, 2000), 410–11.

34. Lindy Beam, "What Shall We Do With Harry?" Plugged In: Focus on the Family, July 2000, http://www.family.org/pplace/pi/genl/A0008833.html (accessed 5 May 2001).

35. Troy Patterson, "The Entertainers 99: 6 J. K. Rowling" *Entertainment Weekly's* EW.com, 22 December 1999, http://www.ew.com/ew/archive/ (accessed 10 December 2001).

36. Ashley Marie Rhodes-Courter, quoted in Jacqueline Blais, "A Magical Breakfast of Potter Champions," *USA Today*, 9 October 2000, 8D.

37. Shelby Nicole Hill, quoted in Blais, "Magical Breakfast," 8D.

38. Meg Kissinger, "Home Is Just a Dream," *Milwaukee Journal Sentinel*, 20 May 2001, 12A.

39. See "Why We Like Harry Potter: A Christianity Today Editorial," *Christianity Today*, 10 January 2000, 37; also, "Wizard and Muggles," *Christian Century*, 1 December 1999, 1155.

40. Jacquielynn Floyd, "Most Folks Are Just Wild about Harry," *Dallas Morning News*, 4 December 1999, A37.

41. Nick Drews, quoted in Blais, "Magical Breakfast," 8D.

II

Literary Influences and Historical Contexts

6

Harry Potter's Schooldays:
J. K. Rowling and the British Boarding School Novel

Karen Manners Smith

American middle-school children being interviewed in 1999 for *We Love Harry Potter*, a book about J. K. Rowling's phenomenally popular Harry Potter series, reported that, in addition to loving the magic and wizardry of the books, they were fascinated by the fact that Harry and his friends went to a boarding school. Boarding schools are an educational experience familiar to only a few, mostly elite, American children, yet many of these young Potter fans expressed appreciation for the fact that English children could experience their adolescence at school, with their friends, instead of at home, with their parents.[1] British children are, of course, similarly intrigued.

The idea of a boarding school—the escape from at least parental authority, and the companionship of the dormitory—fascinates millions of children who realize that they have not the slightest chance of experiencing the reality and are thankful, with the more rational part of their minds, that they have not.[2]

J. K. Rowling herself, interviewed for the online magazine *Salon* in March 1999, commented on the "taboo allure" that the institution might hold for children:

No child wants to lose their parents, yet the idea of being removed from the expectations of parents is alluring. There is something liberating, too, about being transported into the kind of surrogate family which boarding school represents, where the relationships are less intense and the boundaries perhaps more clearly defined.[3]

In actuality, real boarding schools in Britain and in the United States separate children from their families for long stretches of time, enforce strict controls over every aspect of daily life, allow little privacy, and apply a great deal of pressure to succeed in both studies and sports. British sociologist Royston Lambert has called boarding school life "the hothouse society,"[4] alluding not only to the image of students as rare flowers, bred with great care, but also to the narrowly circumscribed arena for day-to-day interactions and the strain felt by these young people. In England today, only a minority of middle and high school students go to private boarding schools—about 3 to 6 percent of the total secondary school population—but these low numbers have not diminished the enduring appeal of the *idea* of boarding school or its popularity as subject matter for British writers of children's fiction and their readers. It may, in fact, be the comfortable predictability of the school story genre, rather than the appeal of actual boarding school attendance, that makes this branch of children's literature so popular. According to Australian critic Philip Hensher, British children know all about boarding school story conventions and enjoy seeing them repeated. "The world of prefects and detention, of masters in gowns, of school lacrosse matches, somehow filters down to children and they are reassured by the closed, certain world."[5]

J.K. Rowling, too, clearly knows all about the conventions of the boarding school story, though she claims that she never wanted to attend boarding school herself. She usually cites C.S. Lewis's Narnia books and the works of E. Nesbit, Noel Streatfield, Paul Gallico, and Elizabeth Goudge as the early influences that led her to write children's books;[6] however, it is reasonable to assume that a young English girl of her generation (b.1965), especially one who has read Streatfield, would also have read popular boarding school stories, since many were in print. Claire Armitstead, echoing Hensher, confirms the connection between Rowling and the school story tradition:

Look closer at this comic, gothic world [of the Harry Potter books], where pictures speak and every panel may hide a secret tunnel, and you find a classic boarding school fantasy, complete with dodgy food, sadistic teachers, bullies, and unshakable loyalties .... [I]t is so reassuringly familiar, ... fantastical on the one hand, but, on the other, quite conventionally domestic in its depiction of childhood experience.[7]

The Harry Potter books fit squarely into a school story tradition that stretches back to *Tom Brown's Schooldays* (1857), Thomas Hughes's semi-autobiographical novel about the Rugby School. According to some authorities, the tradition starts even earlier, dating back to mid-eighteenth century novels with school settings written by both male and female authors.[8] There are thousands of post–Tom Brown books in the school story genre, beginning with the earnest Christian didacticism of the Victorian practitioners, and moving on to the character- and competence-building themes that marked books of the Grand Era of the British Empire. The end of the nineteenth century brought volumes churned out by the cheap popular press—the so-called "penny dreadfuls"—and serialized stories in such popular boys' and girls' magazines as *Magnet*, *Gem*, *Boy's Own Paper*, and *Girl's Own Paper*. Throughout the middle years of the twentieth century, huge school story annuals—collections of stories, poems, serials, and artwork—were among the most popular children's birthday and Christmas gifts in Britain.

The boys' school story experienced its heyday from the 1890s to the inter-war years, flourishing under the aegis of Talbot Baines Reed and, somewhat later, Charles Hamilton, who wrote novels well into the 1970s under several pseudonyms, including the popular Greyfriars series by "Frank Richards." Anthony Buckeridge also kept the traditional genre alive until about 1970; his stories about the boy Jennings and his best friend Darbishire were serialized on the British radio program *Children's Hour* during the 1950s and 60s. Girls' school stories, a form that also enjoyed a wide readership until the 1960s, were written almost exclusively by women, most notably Angela Brazil, Elinor Brent-Dyer, Elsie Oxenham, Dorita Fairlie Bruce, and the prolific Enid Blyton.[9] Although the girls' school story may include subgenres not found in boys' stories—the ballet school story or the riding school story, for example[10]—overall (rather surprisingly, given the historic gender discrepancies and social inequalities of the culture in which school stories are based), traditional girls' school stories resemble boys' stories to a remarkable degree. Both sets concern themselves with athleticism, honor, friendship, and student-teacher interactions in similar ways. This robust, androgynous quality may help to explain their persistent popularity.

There are a few boys' school stories generally classed as "literary" rather than "popular," among them some of the works of Rudyard Kipling and P. G. Wodehouse. Kipling's *Stalkey and Co.* (1899), according to critic Robert Kirkpatrick, was "unique, in that it was the first to transcend the boundary between juvenile and adult fiction, while being so authentic that it attracted both criticism and praise in almost equal measure."[11] P. G. Wodehouse began writing school stories as a young man, publishing them as serials, but in his last book in this genre, *Mike* (1909), which details the adventures of Mike and his friend Psmith at Sedleigh School, he turned his gentle satire on the form. From this point, Wodehouse stopped writing school stories and began his career as a writer of adult comic fiction.

In addition to both popular and "literary" school stories for children, there is a subgenre of school novels written particularly for adults and dating back to the mid-nineteenth century. While some of these novels, such as H. A. Vachell's *The Hill* (1905), celebrate the boarding school experience, many are highly critical, beginning with E. M. Forster's *The Longest Journey* (1907), which attacked both the boarding school system and the British Empire. Another controversial novel from this period was Alec Waugh's *The Loom of Youth* (1917). Hugh Walpole explored his ambivalence about boarding school in two adult novels, *Mr. Perrin and Mr. Traill* (1911) and *Jeremy at Crale* (1927). William Golding's *Lord of the Flies* and John Knowles's *A Separate Peace*, both published in 1959, used the savagery of schoolboys to raise questions about human morality in the mid-twentieth century. David Benedictus's *The Fourth of June* (1962) was an indictment of sexualized relationships between boys at Eton College. School fiction written for adults is problematized both personally and politically in ways that would be foreign to the traditional school story, where conflicts tend to be about games and bounds breaking, peer pressure, and difficulties with friendships.

In addition to school story fiction written for adults, a number of school memoirs were published in the twentieth century—some by ex-servicemen and statesmen, and a number by well-known male British authors. Among the latter are H. G. Wells, *Experiment in Autobiography* (1934), Roald Dahl, *Boy* (1984), Robert Graves, *Goodbye to All That* (1931), C. Day-Lewis, *The Buried Day* (1969), and Graham Greene, *The Old School* (1934) and *A Sort of Life* (1971). Memoirs tend to stress negative aspects of the boarding school experience, such as homesickness, brawling, the cruelty and brutality of teachers, cold dormitories, and bad food. They usually contain confessions of personal problems, anecdotes about bullying or ostracism suffered at school, or explorations of feelings associated with adolescent sexuality and highly romanticized friendships between boys. Thus, though often self-serving when it comes to accuracy, the narratives tend to be unsanitized, and not written for children, even when penned by children's book authors, such as Dahl. Few memoirists view the boarding-school experience through the rose-colored glasses typically employed by novelists who write school stories for children.[12]

After World War II, interest in boarding school stories began to fade. Publicly funded coeducational secondary school had been mandated for all British schoolchildren, and librarians, educators, and literary critics interested in modernizing the curriculum and the reading habits of the young were generally contemptuous of a genre they considered irrelevant and outworn. But school stories have never entirely disappeared. Newer versions of the genre are set frequently in state-sponsored schools and deal with issues that confront today's youth, including race and ethnicity, family problems, adolescent sexuality, and drugs. Coeducational school stories and stories set in day schools—mostly written for children at what Americans would recognize as the elementary or middle school level—dominate contemporary publications in the genre and reflect the normative experience of British children in the late twentieth and early twenty-first centuries. Some examples of recent school stories include the works of Anne Digby, Phil Redmond—whose Grange Hill stories, set in a large comprehensive day school, were televised for the BBC—and Anthony Horowitz, whose *Groosham Grange* (1988) is a modern boarding-school story that successfully combines elements of horror and comedy. Diana Wynne Jones's *Witch Week* (1982) is set in a coeducational boarding school and, like the Potter series, deals with witchcraft and parallel universes.[13]

Historically, the large, traditional British boys' private boarding schools have been called "public" schools. Although there continues to be nothing "public" about these schools, the term originally meant that anyone who could afford the fees could send his son to one of them—hence, they were "public." Among the great public schools we would place Eton, Harrow, Charterhouse, Rugby, and Winchester. Some of these institutions trace their origins back hundreds of years; others were started by Victorian benefactors. Traditionally, such schools warehoused boys in Spartan dormitories and turned out athletic "gentlemen" schooled in the classics. Not all of these young men went on to Oxford and

Cambridge after graduating. Many led lives of monied leisure; others went straight into business, the professions, the civil service, or the officer corps.[14]

British public schools were, and are, expensive private schools with limited enrollment, catering to the ruling elite—gentry and aristocracy—and also to ambitious members of the middle classes. The Duke of Wellington conveyed the significance of the British public school most famously when he claimed that "The Battle of Waterloo was won on the playing fields of Eton." In the highly stratified society in which the schools were founded, equal access to education for all was undreamed of; even those who could afford it did not always seek education for their children. Up until fairly recently, few English people challenged this elite construction of the word "public" (though a Briton of any social class would have been able to explain it to a puzzled American).

Today, privately funded schools are most frequently called "independent" schools to distinguish them from state-sponsored or "maintained" schools. There are fewer than 250 of these independent "public" schools still operating in England, and each is identified by a top administrator who belongs to the National Headmasters Conference.[15] Public schools continue to charge high fees and vary widely in size, accommodating anywhere from under two hundred to over a thousand students. Only a third of these schools are exclusively for boarders; sixty are now reserved for boys only; the others are coeducational in some or all of the classes. The late twentieth century significantly altered the shape of the public school and its student and administrative bodies, most notably with the change of acceptance policy (now based on prior performance and competitive examinations)[16], the admission of female students, the hiring of women teachers, and the extension of scholarships to minorities.[17]

Almost all British school stories celebrate the culture of the public schools and other boarding schools, and they usually share common themes related to the virtues of chivalry, decency, honor, sportsmanship, and loyalty. Familiar features in the genre include competitive team sports in general (called "games" in England), and intramural—that is inter-dorm, inter-house, and inter-school—rivalry in athletics and other things in which points can be accumulated towards an annual championship. The books explore relationships between pupils and schoolmasters and schoolmistresses and frequently deal with the isolation experienced by the student who does not "fit in." School stories abound in moral dilemmas involving cheating, tattling, smoking, drinking, gambling, rule breaking, and unauthorized absences from school. Heroes and heroines and their friends frequently find themselves unjustly accused of misdemeanors and subjected to unjust punishments; often children have to deal detective-fashion with thefts or vandalism of school property or personal possessions. The protagonists typically find themselves promoted—willingly or reluctantly—to authority at some point, such as being made prefect, Head Boy or Girl, or games captain. In many of the narratives, the gradual reform of a hitherto unpleasant or incorrigible character takes place; often he or she is reformed by the main character. All the books centralize the schoolboy's (or schoolgirl's) code of honor: sticking together with one's peers and never telling tales.[18] Occasionally, school stories have ventured into other genres, especially mysteries and spy fiction, and sometimes fictional schoolboys save their schools or their nations from enemy action—especially in novels published and/or set in World War I and World War II. As might be expected, many of the plots feature the introduction of strangers or foreigners and consequent xenophobia or racism. In recent years, horror and fantasy have become entwined with the school story. The Harry Potter books utilize all of these traditional school story themes. What follows is an exploration of some of the key school story elements that can be found in the first four volumes of Rowling's series.

Traditional school stories feature the hero (or heroine) and his (or her) best friend. A third companion commonly joins them, corresponding to the "rule of three" policy that historically operated in many boarding schools. For girls, the rule of three policy was generally a matter of safety. Boys in public schools, however, were often required to travel in groups of three—especially off campus—partly for safety, and partly to discourage "unnatural" closeness. Boys' schools were constantly contending with the fear and the reality of homosexual experimentation in single-sex, boarding-school life. Most memoirists attest to a great deal of such experimentation in the schools they attended, though, historically, school staffs everywhere relentlessly attempted to root out and punish these "unnaturally" close relationships between boys. (Today's housemasters and headmasters may be more tolerant.)[19]

In *Tom Brown's Schooldays,* Tom Brown first makes friends with Harry East, and the two become inseparable. Later, they adopt the frail and saintly newcomer, George Arthur, who then helps, through his example, to transform the two prankish boys into young Christian gentlemen. There are a number of variations on the best-friends theme: in H. A. Vachell's *The Hill* (1905), two boys compete for the love and friendship of a third; in Enid Blyton's *First Term at Malory Towers* (1946), Darrell Rivers initially becomes best friends with the cliquish Alicia, later transferring her affections to a new best friend with a stronger character and adding other worthy chums to her circle.

Harry Potter and Ron Weasley become lifelong friends in *Harry Potter and the Sorcerer's Stone* after just ten minutes on the train to the Hogwarts School. Although Ron and Harry have many tastes, fears, and ideals in common, Ron's background is the opposite of Harry's in almost every possible way; he is therefore the perfect sidekick. Harry is orphaned, but his parents have left him enough money to attend the school. Ron comes from a large, loving family with impeccable wizarding bloodlines but little money. In the wizarding world, the Weasleys represent the traditional British upper middle class: people who have been considered the mainstay of British society since before the nineteenth century. Although they may be less than wealthy in the modern world, families of the Weasleys' class sacrifice luxuries and even comforts in order to ensure the proper boarding school education of their children. Theirs is a class that frequently makes its appearance in other school stories: most of the characters in Blyton's Malory Towers series, for example, seem to come from this class.[20]

Once Ron and Harry's friendship is established, Hermione Granger has to prove that she is more than a just a grind before the other two take her on to complete the triumvirate. Adding a girl to the classic boys' school friendship system is Rowling's innovation, as is her use of a coeducational school in what is essentially a boys' school series. By book IV, *Harry Potter and Goblet of Fire*,[21] the friendship between two boys and a girl has weathered a number of strains, and Rowling has begun to introduce additional complexity, as Hogwarts students start to pair off in heterosexual couples.

There is no viable reading of the relationship between Harry and Ron as homoerotic. Their uncomplicated friendship can be contrasted with a number of relationships in traditional boys' school stories, starting with F. W. Farrar's *Eric, or Little by Little* (1858), where the homoerotic subtext is very clear. In the early Harry Potter books, the Harry/Ron relationship is diluted by the presence of Hermione. By the end of book III,[22] Rowling has established Harry's heterosexuality through his attraction to the pretty Cho Chang (coincidentally, also establishing Harry's freedom from race prejudice), and, in book IV, the author has begun to hint at a future relationship between Ron and Hermione. While modernizing the traditional friendship theme of the school story by including a strong female third and intimations of future romance, Rowling constructs and maintains a classically intense schoolboy friendship for Harry and Ron, simultaneously freeing it from any traces of "unnatural" closeness.

In most of the traditional school stories, authors depict a bully (and his friends), and, frequently, a weakling in need of the hero's protection. The bully is often an older boy, like Harry Flashman in *Tom Brown's Schooldays*. The bully can also be a schoolmaster or a prefect. Some classic prefect bullies include Frank Richards's villainous Gerald Loder in the Greyfriars series and Talbot Baines Reed's jealous and insecure Edward Loman of *The Fifth Form at St. Dominic's* (1881), who makes life miserable for best friends Horace Wraysford and Oliver Greenfield. Harry Potter faces bullies on two levels. His supernatural rival is, of course, Voldemort, the Dark Lord, whom he battles because it is foreordained that he do so. In the school story that frames this epic conflict, Harry must also face his earthly rival, who is the school bully, Draco Malfoy. Accompanied by his two schoolboy goons, Crabbe and Goyle, Draco taunts adults and schoolchildren alike.

In *Tom Brown's Schooldays*, Tom Brown, Harry East, and George Arthur suffer merciless bullying at the hands of Flashman and his friends. Flashman and the other older boys also abuse the fagging system. Fagging, which was pervasive in boys' public schools until post–World War II reforms, involves the sanctioned use of younger boys as servants for older ones. "Fags" were required to perform menial or feminized tasks, such as boot blacking, errand running, or making tea and toast. Sometimes a fag would be ordered to pre-warm a "fag-master's" bed, functioning something like a human hot water bottle. The close and sometimes intimate relationships between fags and older boys is thought to have been sexualized in some cases, hence the twentieth century use of the term "fag" as a pejorative synonym for homosexual.[23] Fagging is completely absent from the Harry Potter books, as it is purported to be in modern British schools, although, even today, younger students in boarding schools commonly clean dormitories and studies and occasionally run errands for older boys.[24] At Hogwarts, mysterious and semi-invisible servants do all the domestic labor for the school, and older students do not have sanctioned opportunities for oppressing or abusing younger ones. Again, Rowling avoids any suggestion of homoerotic relationships at Hogwarts, making the wizard school conform to images of reformed boarding schools in Britain today.

Draco Malfoy and Harry Potter are the same age, so Draco's bullying is not age-related; rather, it is motivated by jealousy and snobbery. The Malfoy family represents those elite, aristocratic British families whose sons at boarding schools maintained class exclusivity despite the relatively democratic mixing of the schools themselves. Rowling cleverly gives Draco's family an ancient Norman French name meaning "bad faith," thereby conveying both the family's lineage and its baneful predispositions. There seems to be nobody else at Hogwarts of Draco's social milieu, so he must content himself with the friendship of Crabbe and Goyle, sons of his father's political, though not social, allies. Here Rowling is closely following the boarding school story tradition, in which class differences frequently provoke bigotry. In a number of girls' school stories, for example, the heroine and her friends must overcome the snobbery of schoolmates and learn to befriend working-class scholarship girls newly arrived at the school.

At Hogwarts, Draco uses his father's aristocratic status and influence to cause trouble for Harry (raised by stolid, middle-class relatives) and for Hagrid, the kind-hearted but unsophisticated Hogwarts gamekeeper.[25] On several occasions, Draco's active bullying goes beyond snobbery and epithets, most notably in book III, when he tries to make Harry fall off his flying broomstick from a height of fifty feet during a Quidditch match. Violence, vengefulness, and snobbery are only parts of Draco's character. His is also the schoolboy voice of racism and race purity in the Potter books. Reflexively, he hates Harry, who has mixed human and wizard blood; Hermione, the child of "Muggles," or ordinary nonmagical humans; and Hagrid, whose mother was a giant, virtually an untouchable caste in the wizarding world. Draco's bigotry, imbibed from his parents, is similar to the kinds of prejudice frequently presented in British school stories as a problem for the hero or heroine to deal with. In Richards's Greyfriars series, for instance, the popular clique, under the leadership of the hero, Harry Wharton, ultimately overcomes schoolboy prejudice to adopt as one of their own Hurree Jamset Ram Singh, an Indian student who is also a prince. In Enid Blyton's *Summer Term at St. Clare's,* the girls in the first form learn to love and admire Carlotta although she is half-Spanish and has been raised in a circus. Together the first-form girls foil the snooty Prudence's plot to discredit Carlotta and get her expelled. Through the bigotry of Draco Malfoy and his father, Lucius, J. K. Rowling presents both race and class as arenas for conflict and resolution. Problems surround these issues, and Harry must solve them with the help of Hermione, Ron, and Headmaster Dumbledore. Future Harry Potter books will have to tell us whether or not Draco learns, with help, to overcome his prejudices.

Bullies and bigots in the school story genre do not merely harass heroes. Frequently, schoolboy and schoolgirl heroes find themselves defending their weaker comrades from school bullies. Tom Brown's role at Rugby School involves his protection of the saintly and frail George Arthur; Darrell Rivers, in Enid Blyton's *First Term at Malory Towers*, must defend and encourage Sally Hope, who has trouble at home and is the subject of sneers at school. In fact, throughout the Malory Towers series, Darrell looks after a succession of troubled and friendless girls who are bullied or mistreated by their heartless and elitist schoolmates. Sally Hope, predictably, becomes one of Darrell's best friends.

Harry Potter's protégés, Neville Longbottom, Colin Creevy, and Ron's little sister, Ginny, need protection from themselves and from Draco Malfoy, and, sometimes, from Professor Snape, the classically hateful and perpetually unjust schoolmaster. (While Harry and Ron may rightly feel that Professor Snape, the Potions teacher and Master of Slytherin House, is unfair to them, he is not really a bully; neither is Percy Weasley, the ineffectual and pompous prefect—later Head Boy—who also happens to be one of Ron's older brothers.) It is up to Harry and Ron to protect Neville, Ginny, and Colin from the vicious jibes and plots of Malfoy and his crew, just as Tom Brown needs to support the sickly George Arthur against the taunts of rude boys who accuse him of being a sissy. Interestingly, the fact that Neville is from an aristocratic family neither endears him to Draco Malfoy nor saves him from the latter's scorn. Of course, in the additional dimension Rowling provides for her school stories, almost all of Hogwarts's characters—with the possible exception of Dumbledore, of whom Voldemort is said to be afraid—also need protection from the powerful, magical enemies of the Dark Side. Harry provides this essential shield, even in moments of fear. Rowling's central character, like those heroes in all conventional school stories, is thus—at least in part—measured by his compassion for underdogs.

Frequently found among the hero's friends in classic school stories is a pair of identical twins, often practical jokers whose activities provide both comic relief and confusion that gets sorted out at the end, usually by the hero.[26] The Harry Potter books have two sets of twins: the Patil sisters, who lack distinct characters, and Fred and George Weasley, two of Ron's other brothers. The entrepreneurial Weasley twins do not trade extensively on their interchangeability, as do twins in other stories. Rather, they make considerable contributions to the novels' plots, helping to humiliate Harry's piggish cousin, Dudley; assisting Harry's escape from his aunt and uncle in a flying car; and providing Harry with a map that allows him to spirit himself out of Hogwarts by a series of secret passages. (Proving that he really is a typical schoolboy at heart, in addition to being an epic hero, in book III Harry uses both the map and his Invisibility Cloak to make a forbidden excursion into the nearby village of Hogsmeade in search of sweets.)

Teachers and headmasters are indispensable adjuncts to the school story, often the only representatives of the adult world in this fiction, which is limited to school terms and only peripherally mentions parents. Form masters and mistresses may range from the comic to the cruel, the obtuse to the malevolent. Some are risible, such as Richards's Mr. Quelch in the Greyfriars series and almost every French mistress in the entire girls' school story genre. Just as many teachers are beloved and have become archetypes, James Hilton's kindly and inspiring Mr. Chips from *Goodbye Mr. Chips* (1934) being one of the most famous.

In the Harry Potter series, Professor Severus Snape is cast in the negative mold. He seems to delight in punishing Harry and Ron unfairly, and, at least in the first four books, Harry and his friends are never completely certain that the professor is not allied with the Dark Forces. Snape's hatred of Harry remains a mystery until we learn in *Harry Potter and the Prisoner of Azkaban* that Harry's father—Snape's arch rival—had once saved his life. Snape had never forgiven James Potter for this and carried the enmity over to the next generation. In contrast to Professor Snape, Minerva McGonagall, the classic spinster schoolmistress, is stern but fair. She is also clever, sharp-witted, and not easily hoodwinked. McGonagall is a whole lot smarter than the eponymous Scottish schoolmistress in Muriel Spark's novel *The Prime of Miss Jean Brodie* (1961), on whom she could well be modeled. Updating the genre once again, Rowling has made McGonagall an ardent sports fan; as the head of Gryffindor House, she presses Harry's Quidditch team to victory and fosters competitive spirit in her students.

With remarkably few exceptions, traditional school stories present wise, fair-minded, and inspiring headmasters and headmistresses. Within the hierarchical system of the public school, they are the final authorities, and, at least in the fiction, they seldom abuse this role. Usually they are exemplars of goodness and integrity, providing blueprints for the moral life. Author Thomas Hughes cast headmaster Thomas Arnold in a heroic mold in *Tom Brown's Schooldays*. Arnold, a character in the novel but also the real headmaster of the real Rugby School from 1827 to 1842, has been a template for nearly all the fictional headmasters that follow him: he is firm, all-knowing, and understanding, a molder of men. Arnold shapes Tom Brown's character as a Christian gentleman by weaning him away from obstreperousness and teaching him compassion and duty.[27]

Like Hughes's Arnold, J. K. Rowling's Albus Dumbledore is wiser, more powerful, and more influential than any mortal could possibly be. Dumbledore, however, is humanized by his comic sensibility and the rather fey eccentricity he sometime exhibits. It is Dumbledore's role to protect Harry Potter when he can, and to guide and shape him for his heroic destiny. In Dumbledore's words we hear Harry Potter's life lessons about courage, compassion, and integrity. In *Sorcerer's Stone*, Dumbledore urges Harry to continue to speak Voldemort's name and avoid letting the fear of the name increase the "fear of the thing itself." Gently administering a lesson about peer pressure towards the end of book I, Dumbledore tells the assembled students: "It takes a great deal of bravery to stand up to our enemies, but just as much to stand up to our friends."[28] Unlike the lessons that Thomas Arnold teaches Tom Brown, Dumbledore's messages are about character and morality without being specifically Christian. Rowling makes Dumbledore a sage adviser for the child reader of any belief system.

In addition to modeling virtue and wisdom, the headmasters of school fiction also use their authority to ignore the regulations when the main character is in trouble. Their actions facilitate both the boy's growth and his heroism. Headmaster Arnold punishes but forgives Tom Brown time and time again for his rule-breaking escapades because he thinks there is a fine character under the boyish defiance. In Harry Potter's case, Dumbledore repeatedly refuses to expel him for taking laudable and necessary actions that nevertheless contravene school codes or the directions of authority figures.

In all school stories, the hero or heroine possesses this rule-breaking spirit, and the best friend is usually complicit. Pranks, midnight parties, and unauthorized excursions off campus are all part of the protagonists' adventures. Occasional rule-breaking is in fact a test of the character, gumption, and originality that the hero will presumably need in order to be a success in life. The main character's escapades simultaneously demonstrate his normality: he must, after all, be "one of the boys," and never constantly abides by school dictums. Rebelliousness must apply to chums, as well. The only reason that Hermione can remain in the triumvirate with Harry and Ron is that her normal veneration for authority and regulations can be suppressed when circumstances require it. Though she continues to be cautious, she learns to go outside the bounds when the stakes are high and even to lie to teachers when her friends need support.

The conventional school story hero is not a habitual prankster, however, and only breaches serious rules when it is necessary for safety or a greater good; the chronic and unthinking rule-breaker, on the other hand, not only risks expulsion at all times, but may cause a great deal of chaos in the community. Thus Tom Brown, having secured his place in the community at Rugby School after a couple of terms, finally abandons rule-breaking under the combined influence of the headmaster and his saintly friend George Arthur, signaling the beginning of his maturation. In *Harry Potter and the Chamber of Secrets*, Harry and Ron win two hundred points each for Gryffindor after violating any number of school regulations; they have done so, however, in order to save Hogwarts's Muggle-born students from Tom Riddle and the basilisk.[29]

Harry Potter has many more opportunities to break the rules than most fictional schoolboys, and far more exigent reasons to do so since he has to save the world, but he and his friends also indulge in classic boarding school

rule-breaking: being out of the dormitory at unauthorized hours, sneaking off
to Hogsmeade without permission, interrupting teachers in class, and fighting
with schoolmates. For these transgressions, Harry and his friends receive de-
tentions and lose points for their house, which affects the inter-house rivalry
and earns them the temporary opprobrium of their Gryffindor housemates.
The reader knows that Harry is engaged in a heroic quest, but he is punished
like an ordinary schoolchild for simple rule-breaking. In school stories, punishments for infractions—lines, chores, demerits, and, in the older stories, canings
or floggings—are commonly delivered by teachers and by other students, sen-
iors, prefects, and the like, and provide the security of behavior limitations.[30]
The rule-structure, the punishments, the point system, and the ever-present
threat of expulsion in the Harry Potter books are absolutely typical of the traditional boarding school story. Rowling uses them to embed the fantasy elements of her books in a world children can comprehend and with which they
can identify.

School stories typically follow the trajectory of the school year, beginning
with the hero or heroine's departure from home and the journey to the school,
and ending just as the school breaks up for the long summer holiday. In all but
the largest story series, the hero moves up one class every book. In some series,
each book may cover a single term at the school. In series with a dozen or more
books, the hero and his friends never change classes at all. Jennings and Darbishire are endlessly ten years old, spending term after term at Linbury Court
Preparatory School and never growing any older. The Greyfriars boys show up
at school year after year through thirty-eight books, never graduating, never
aging. In contrast, J. K. Rowling has decided to complete her epic in the seven
books it will take Harry to graduate from Hogwarts. Each Harry Potter book
occupies a school year, and the children grow and develop over time.

Crucial establishing scenes for both fictional school stories and school memoirs deal with the departure from home and parents, the first trip to the new
school, and the arrival in a scary new place. Most of the public school memoirs
characterize these episodes as filled with dread and homesickness (many boys
were sent away to school as early as seven or eight), but the novels tend to displace these feelings onto secondary characters, leaving the hero to enjoy his adventure. This is certainly true of Tom Brown, initially a rather thoughtless boy,
a "robust and combative urchin" as the author describes him, who, unescorted
by any parents, travels to Rugby School in a stagecoach driven at a spanking
pace.[31] Darrell Rivers, the heroine of Blyton's Malory Towers series, is so well-
adjusted at age twelve that she has no qualms about leaving her parents and instantly bonds with a new best friend, Alicia, on the train to school; in striking
contrast, the spoiled Gwendolyn Mary sobs and sobs in her mother's arms,
nearly missing the same train. Walter Evson, the hero of F. W. Farrar's *St.
Winifred's, or The World of School* (1862), gets along very well on his first day
of school, but is up half the night comforting the smaller and more sensitive
new boy, Arthur Eden, who is homesick and has already been bullied by older

boys. The implication, in both boys' and girls' school stories, is that homesickness is a sign of weakness or excessive sensitivity; heroes and heroines either do not feel it or deal with it summarily and adjust with enthusiasm to new surroundings.

Harry Potter, of course, has every reason to hate the Dursleys, the cruel uncle and aunt who have adopted him after the death of his parents, so he is delighted to get away from them on the Hogwarts Express. And, of course, it is on the train that he meets his true friends, Ron Weasley and Hermione Granger. Rowling reverses the homesickness issue for Harry Potter, without making him seem oversensitive, as his home-life is truly horrible: Harry's unhappiness comes at the end of each school year, when he has to return to the Dursleys, so that, every summer, Harry is homesick for Hogwarts and the world of peers. Unlike Darrell Rivers, and, unlike his own friend, Ron, Harry is not allowed to be happy in both worlds.

Homesick or well adjusted, fictional students ensconced in their new schools rapidly discover that sports are a major aspect of boarding school life. All school stories feature sports, starting with the brutal football matches between the "School" and the "Schoolhouse" at Tom Brown's Rugby School, and carrying on through generations of boys' muddy football (soccer) matches and punishing games of girls' field hockey. Most authors of boarding school stories devote a lot of space to descriptions of these competitive sports. Many readers love these passages, but others describe them as boring. In this vein, critics such as Brooke Allen have labeled Rowling's passages about Quidditch—a combination of soccer and basketball played in the air on broomsticks—as monotonous.[32] Whether or not the assessment is accurate, Rowling is keeping faith with the school-story genre in spotlighting the significance of the sport for the school and for her hero. The difference between the Potter books and those more conventional narratives, however, lies in the fact that the modest, bespectacled Harry excels at the game. His skill, which seems almost genetic, is a marker of his heroic destiny. More commonly in school stories, whose main characters are destined for lives of ordinary success, the hero is not a great, but only a good athlete, and someone else, whom he admires intensely, is the stellar athlete. Tom Brown's sports heroes are two brothers named Brook, both prime athletes and leaders in the school.

Besides game and sport, food might be the most important—almost obsessive—part of boarding school life and stories. Memoirists write about being hungry most of the time at school. Many recall the lack of variety, the poor quality, the stinginess of the servings, and the special privations during wartime. Others remember being compelled to eat food that had spoiled, or food with worms or maggots in it. In all school stories, parcels from home assuage a desperate hunger—perhaps emotional and mental as much as physical—or students satisfy cravings with a trip into the nearby village to buy sweets at a tuck shop, where candy and sundries are sold. Tom Brown and East sometimes purchase sausages to grill over the fire in their study at night. Informal dining parties are standard fare in boarding school novels, and girls' stories in particular seem to abound in secret, giggly midnight feasts. Inevitably, the matron or prefect arrives and the girls have to hide the food under the floorboards. Clandestine repasts feature very peculiar food, including sardines, meat paste sandwiches, peanuts, cake, and pickles consumed all at the same time.

At Hogwarts, food magically appears upon golden plates in the dining hall, and it tastes exquisite, though it is, for the most part, recognizably British fare. English food is not a notable world cuisine, but it is cozy and familiar to Rowling's readers, and much of what she describes on the Hogwarts menu is what Americans would call "comfort food": mashed potatoes, roast beef, sausages, Yorkshire pudding and gravy, hot, sweet tea, cakes, and pastries. However, at a feast for ghosts—none of whom can eat anyway—Harry and his friends find themselves hungry and unsatisfied for one of the few times in the novel. They are offered rotting fish, burned cakes, moldy cheese, and dishes swarming with maggots. The pièce de résistance is a cake shaped like a tombstone.[33] Abundance and richness are contrasted with details of waste, putrefaction, and decay. Rowling reveals her particular delight in writing about food; in fact, it seems to bring out her sense of humor.

This humor surfaces in Rowling's creation of Hogsmeade delicacies as well. While in *Tom Brown's Schooldays,* boys of all ages regularly drink ale, a custom endorsed in most families of the period, Harry Potter and his friends—a century and a half later—drink iced pumpkin juice and, visiting the village tavern, consume nothing stronger than butterbeer (alcohol content unspecified). Best of all of Rowling's foods are the sweets Ron and his brothers buy in the village sweetshop: familiar candies like chocolates and peppermints, but also some wonderful innovations: cockroach clusters, black pepper imps, Droobles Best Blowing Gum, and Chocolate Frogs (a nod to Monty Python's Crunchy Frogs?), which contain trading cards. Bertie Botts Every Flavor Beans are jelly beans that taste, literally, like everything, from strawberries and lemons to spinach and earwax. Rowling's pleasure in inventing food both delicious and disgusting is reminiscent of Roald Dahl's children's fiction. Significantly, Dahl devotes a chapter of his memoir, *Boy,* to descriptions of the disgusting sweets he ingested in his school days—concoctions so vile and semipoisonous that they are no longer manufactured. Like Dahl, Rowling has tapped into children's ambivalence about food and their fascination with the gruesome and revolting.

Although Rowling's revision of the school story is highly respectful, she clearly parodies certain elements. In the creation of Percy Weasley, she captures the stuffy self-importance of prefects, who mediate between the school's adult authorities and the students but generally end up being very bossy to children who are otherwise their equals. Nor is Rowling averse to borrowing a great character from an earlier practitioner of the genre. It would not be at all surprising to hear that Harry's repellant cousin, Dudley Dursley, was modeled on Billy Bunter of Richards's Greyfriars series. Bunter is the sly, overweight, idle, lying, cowardly, snobbish, conceited, and greedy boy antihero of nearly two score popular novels. Though virtually unknown in the United States, this neg-ative archetype of the English schoolboy is an icon of British culture. Dudley is Bunter copied to a T, especially in the scene in book I where he parades his new school uniform—a maroon tailcoat, orange short pants, and a straw hat—for the family (Rowling here parodies elements of the uniform—especially tail-coats—still worn at Eton). In addition to the uniform, Rowling's Smeltings stu-dents carry canelike sticks "for hitting each other while the teachers weren't looking. This was supposed to be good training for later life."[34] Rowling not only skewers the Bunteresque Dudley, but questions what lessons are being taught at the prestigious academies that educate society's future leaders.

Beyond respectfully revisiting classic school story themes, and beyond humor and parody, Rowling also engages in political and cultural moderniza-tion of the school story genre. At Hogwarts, common experiences of modern adolescence are acknowledged and help to anchor the story in the readers' world: Hermione, for example, wears braces on her teeth; at the beginning of every school year there is a list of items forbidden on school grounds; in the fourth book, boys and girls bring dates to a school dance. Television, computers, and movies are included in Rowling's books as parts of the Muggle world, but are absent from the world of Hogwarts, Diagon Alley, and Hogsmeade, which has an alternate technology, magic.[35] Rowling seems especially concerned to ensure that a boarding school that exists in a parallel magical England within the real England of the 1990s and 2000s reflects some aspects of contemporary British life. Hence, not only are the school and the school's sports teams coedu-cational, but also there are students whose families are clearly Irish, Indian, West Indian, and Chinese, an amalgam of ethnicities resembling the population of modern-day, multicultural Britain. Further, the magical English world is also part of a magical planet earth, within which is a magical European Union that, among other things, promotes school exchanges.

Although Rowling has successfully adapted the school story genre to res-onate with modern readers, she has clung to an aspect of the traditional boys' boarding school story that seems particularly old-fashioned. Early in the twen-tieth century, when boys' public schools began to be regarded as training places for the administrators of the British Empire, school story fiction celebrated the manliness, athleticism, and ethnocentrism considered necessary qualities for the tribunes of Empire. While generally avoiding ethnocentrism, Rowling nev-ertheless perpetuates the imperial service tradition in her Hogwarts graduates: Ron Weasley's big brothers, Charlie and Bill, both work in the wizarding for-eign service, Charlie tagging dragons in Romania, and Bill in a branch of Gringotts bank in Egypt. Barty Crouch Jr., who appears in book IV, is similarly sent abroad after his graduation. Foreign service seems a predictable future for Hogwarts graduates, just as it was for graduates of British public schools at the turn of the twentieth century, although, unlike Hogwarts graduates, the real British administrators of Empire took a route through the university system before departing for far-off assignments.[36]

The British Empire has been gone for half a century; the British foreign service is a shadow of its former self, but Rowling, who has already created a set of wizarding cabinet ministries resembling the ministries of the contemporary British government, may need some kind of quasi-imperial structure for wizard warriors as her story globalizes—another gesture to the twenty-first century—in the last three books. Like the boy and girl heroes of World War II–era school stories, Hogwarts students may become involved in an escalating world war. Rowling's mature wizards (Hogwarts staff and graduates) will become guardians of the planet—a planet full of bungling Muggles and dangerous dark forces—much in the way that British civil servants, armed with education and zeal, once made it their mission to "protect" the indigenous inhabitants of their vast Empire from themselves and each other.

It is always fun to speculate about where Rowling will take Harry and his friends in the next books—in fact, contributors to Internet Harry Potter fan clubs are preoccupied with such predictions. If Rowling remains faithful to the school story genre, it is likely the following will happen: Draco Malfoy will have to become reformed, since this is what happens to many school-story bullies after the hero has gained sufficient moral maturity to effect their conversions. Draco may have to save Harry's life, or Harry will save his, and they will reach an understanding, if not a friendship. Similarly, Professor Snape will be better understood; by book IV, Rowling has already begun to hint that, unsavory as Snape is, he is a trusted lieutenant to Dumbledore. A sober, increasingly self-confident, and mature Ron Weasley—not Harry—will become Head boy, Hermione will be named Head girl, and Harry will be saved for captain of his house Quiddich team and possible international competition—if he can spare the time from his more epic concerns. These predictions are based solely on Rowling's observable adherence to the school story genre, saying nothing about magic or the escalating global contest between good and evil which is certain to dominate the remaining books in the series.

Writing in *The New Leader* in 1999, Brooke Allen claimed: "Witty, ironic, and self-referential, J. K. Rowling's books are the first post-modern school stories. But what makes them appealing is that they manage alongside this contemporary knowingness to maintain all the wholesome and innocent appeal of their predecessors."[37] As the mythic scope of the Harry Potter saga expands, Rowling will almost certainly continue to rely on the familiar tropes of the boarding school story to provide a comfortable zone in which the danger and magic of Harry Potter's world can be safely negotiated by children of many ages and many backgrounds in our world.

NOTES

1. Sharon A. Moore, *We Love Harry Potter* (New York: St. Martin's Griffin, 1999).

2. Geoffrey Trease, *Tales out of School* (1947), quoted in Robert J. Kirkpatrick, *The Encyclopedia of Boys' School Stories* (Aldershot, UK: Ashgate Press, 2000), 9.

3. Margaret Weir, "Of Magic and Single Motherhood," Salon Mothers Who Think, *Salon*, 31 March 1999, www.salon.com/mwt/feature/1999/03/cov_31featureb.html (accessed 15 October 2001).

4. Royston Lambert and Spencer Millham, *The Hothouse Society: An Exploration of Boarding-School Life through the Boys' and Girls' Own Writings* (London: Weidenfeld and Nicholson, 1968).

5. Philip Hensher, "Harry Potter and the Literary Hoax," *The Age*, 7 February 2000, www.theage.com.au/cgi-bin/printversion.pl?story=20000207/A3637-2000Feb7 (accessed 15 October 2001).

6. See Weir, "Of Magic and Single Motherhood"; an interview with J. K. Rowling in www.harrypotterbooks@bloomsbury.com; and Brooke Allen, "A World of Wizards," *The New Leader*, 82, no. 13 (1 November 1999), 13–14, 13.

7. Claire Armitstead, "Wizard but with a Touch of Brown," *Guardian Unlimited* Archive, 8 July 1999, http://books.guardian.co.uk/Print/0,3858,3881430,00.html (accessed 19 February 2003).

8. See, for example, Kirkpatrick, *Encyclopedia*, 1, and Peter Hunt, *Children's Literature* (Oxford: Blackwell, 2001), 299.

9. Brazil, Brent-Dyer, Oxenham, and Blyton fan clubs and journals persist to this day, with some of the books still in print. Brent-Dyer's Chalet School stories, written between 1925 and 1958, occupy a special niche: the series was the subject of a scholarly conference as recently as 1994. See the Chalet School website: http://users. netmatters.co.uk/ju90/csc.htm (accessed 18 October 2001).

10. Sue Sims and Hilary Claire, *The Encyclopedia of Girls' School Stories* (Aldershot, UK: Ashgate Press, 2000), 1–18.

11. Kirkpatrick, *Encyclopedia*, 207–09. See also the chapter on *Stalkey and Co.* in Geoffrey Richards, *Happiest Days: The Public Schools in English Fiction* (Manchester, Manchester University Press, 1988), 142–64.

12. Geoffrey Walford, *Life in Public Schools* (London: Methuen, 1986), 3.

13. Additional information on the history of the school story genre can be found in Isabel Quigley, *The Heirs of Tom Brown* (London: Chatto and Windus, 1982); P. W. Musgrave, *From Brown to Bunter: The Life and Death of the School Story* (London and Boston: Routledge and Kegan Paul, 1985); Jeffrey Richards, *Happiest Days: The Public Schools in English Fiction* (Manchester: Manchester UP, 1988); Mary Cadogan and Patricia Craig, *You're a Brick, Angela! A New Look at Girls' Fiction from 1839–1975* (London: Gollancz, 1976); Rosemary Auchmuty, *A World of Girls: The Appeal of the Girls' School Story* (London: Women's Press, 1992); and Beverly Lyon Clarke, *Regendering the School Story: Sassy Sissies and Tattling Tomboys* (New York: Garland, 1996).

14. Unlike in the United States, where all private boarding high schools are nicknamed "prep schools," traditional British preparatory schools are the middle schools that prepare their students to enter the British "public" schools. Usually they serve children in the eleven to fourteen age range.

15. There are seventy-five overseas schools with membership in the National Headmasters Conference, principally in British Commonwealth countries, and there are twenty state-sponsored schools in the United Kingdom with linked membership. See Lambert and Millham, *Hothouse Society*, 3; Walford, *Life in Public Schools*, 5–11; the

Headmasters Conference website at www.hmc.org.uk or visit www.rmplc.co.uk/orgs/hmc/brochure.html (accessed 18 October 2001).

16. See, for example, www.etoncollege.com. Additional information on the British public school may be found in: T. W. Bamford, *The Rise of the Public Schools: A Study of Boys' Public Boarding Schools in England and Wales from 1837 to the Present Day* (London: Nelson, 1967); George MacDonald Fraser, ed., *The World of the Public School* (London: Weidenfeld & Nicolson, 1977); Geoffrey Walford, ed., *British Public Schools, Policy and Practice* (Lewes U.K.: Falmer Press, 1984); Walford, *Life in Public Schools;* Jonathan Gathorne-Hardy, ed., *The Public School Phenomenon* (London: Hodder & Stoughton, 1977); Royston Lambert, *The Chance of a Lifetime? A Study of Boarding Education* (London: Weidenfeld & Nicolson, 1975); Lambert and Millham, *Hothouse Society;* Clive Griggs, *Private Education in Britain* (Lewes U.K.: Falmer Press, 1985); Rupert Wilkinson, *Gentlemanly Power: British Leadership and the Public School Tradition: A Comparative Study in the Making of Rulers* (London: Oxford UP, 1964); Simon Raven, *The Old School: A Study in the Oddities of the English Public School System* (London: Hamish Hamilton, 1986).

17. In addition to the all-boys and coeducational "public" schools, there are still, of course, independent all-girls schools, many with boarding facilities. These schools have a separate governing body: the Girls' Schools Association. Girls' boarding schools in England are primarily an invention of the late nineteenth century, since, prior to that time, none but the very wealthiest English girls were thought to need much education beyond the basics. After 1900, middle-class and elite families increasingly saw the boarding school education of daughters as a desirable preparation for marriage to elite men and adult lives of genteel social responsibility. Only a few families regarded girls' private secondary education as a stepping-stone to higher education and careers. Like the literature that celebrated them, girls' boarding schools were most popular in the mid-twentieth century, though a number of them survive today, and their graduates go on to college.

18. Kirkpatrick, *Encyclopedia,* 7–8.

19. Lambert and Millham, *Hothouse Society,* 317–41.

20. J. K. Rowling, *Harry Potter and the Sorcerer's Stone* (New York: Scholastic Press, 1999). See also Griggs, *Private Education,* 175–78.

21. J. K. Rowling, *Harry Potter and the Goblet of Fire* (New York: Scholastic Press, 2000).

22. J. K. Rowling, *Harry Potter and the Prisoner of Azkaban* (New York: Scholastic Press, 1999).

23. Dictionary sources generally equate the word "fag" with "drudge." Another possible derivation of the term fag may have had something to do with faggots of firewood the younger boy had to tote; he could also be beaten by an older boy using one of these faggots.

24. Walford, *Life in Public Schools,* 49–51, 226–28; Bamford, *Rise of the Public Schools,* 68–69; Richard E. Gross, *British Secondary Education* (London: Oxford UP, 1965), 135–36.

25. A gamekeeper at a boarding school? Perhaps the equivalent would be the groundskeeper, matron, or custodian who appears in most school stories.

26. Very rarely are the twins themselves the heroes or heroines of the stories. One notable exception: the main characters in several of Enid Blyton's St Clare's School stories are Pat and Isabel O'Sullivan, a pair of wild Irish twin girls.

27. The fictional Thomas Arnold is a seemingly perfect, one-dimensional character; the real man was a strict disciplinarian and a lot fonder of caning boys than Hughes lets on. Richards, *Happiest Days*, 23–46.

28. Rowling, *Sorcerer's Stone*, 298, 306.

29. J. K. Rowling, *Harry Potter and the Chamber of Secrets* (New York: Scholastic Press, 1999).

30. Usually the punishments for pranks and infractions of the rules are mild, though in the nineteenth-century school stories, corporal discipline predominates. Tom Brown is flogged for fishing in a privately owned stream and being rude to a local servant, but he and his friend East receive only a sorrowful lecture from Dr. Arnold and fifty lines of Homer to memorize for climbing the school tower and carving their names on the clock. Harry Flashman, the school bully, is judged unredeemable and eventually expelled from Rugby School for drunkenness.

31. Later stagecoaches carrying Tom and his friends callously run over pigs and narrowly avoid killing pedestrians.

32. Allen, "A World of Wizards," 13.

33. Rowling, *Chamber of Secrets*, 133.

34. Rowling, *Sorcerer's Stone*, 32.

35. See Margaret J. Oakes's chapter in this volume for further discussion of this topic. Interestingly, most modern boarding schools in the real world attempt to limit students' access to television and movies during the school year.

36. There is no wizarding university in the Harry Potter books; perhaps Rowling will have to invent one for Harry if the fans clamor for more school stories after he and his friends graduate from Hogwarts. Thomas Hughes sent Tom Brown to Oxford in a sequel to *Tom Brown's Schooldays*; Elinor Brent-Dyer followed many of her Chalet School graduates into stories of their marriages and adult careers. For further discussion of the topic of Empire, see Giselle Liza Anatol's chapter in this collection.

37. Allen, "A World of Wizards," 13.

7

Accepting Mudbloods: The Ambivalent Social Vision of J. K. Rowling's Fairy Tales

Elaine Ostry

One of my favorite details of the Harry Potter series is the talking mirror who tells Harry that he is fighting a losing battle with his unruly hair.[1] As we all remember the talking mirror of "Snow White," this incident is one of the many moments in the series when J. K. Rowling refers to fairy tales. She uses familiar motifs of the fairy-tale genre: the emphasis on transformation, the "outcast child" hero, the idea of a parallel world in which anything is possible, the battle between good and evil, the protection of the dead mother, wish-fulfillment, tasks, secret chambers, and a cast of fairy-tale characters such as giants, elves, ghosts, and mysterious helpers. With her inventiveness and sharp sense of humor, she updates these old motifs. Moreover, she includes her own social agenda. In doing so, she does what all fairy-tale tellers and writers do: change the tale to suit their interests.

Jack Zipes, among others, argues that the fairy tale should be viewed through a sociohistorical lens because the fantastic elements of the fairy tale are not disconnected from the real world. On the contrary, Zipes claims, "[fantasy] plays upon the imagination not to open it up to escape into a never-never land but to make greater contact with reality."[2] The fairy tale can skillfully criticize the world in the disguise of entertainment. Children's literature in general and the fairy tale in particular reflect this double agenda to amuse and instruct. As Marina Warner writes, the fairy tale is "all the better to speak to you with, my dear, all the better to persuade you with."[3]

So what is Rowling's social agenda? She uses the grand theme of fairy tales, the battle between good and evil, to combat two evils of our time: materialism and racism. The series enacts a great "race war," in which the heroes fight against those wizards who possess a vision of racial purity.[4] Rowling intends to teach children that what matters is one's character, not color, pedigree, or wealth. However, her radical presentation of social issues is hindered by "utter traditionalism."[5] This ideological doubleness mirrors the fairy tale, which is simultaneously radical and traditional. Because of Rowling's faithfulness to the fairy tale, she often contradicts herself. Just as the fairy tale's radical qualities are matched by traditional inflexibility, so is Rowling's antimaterialism matched by an awe of wealth, her antiracism foiled both by a reliance on "color blindness" and stock types, and her hero simultaneously ordinary and princely. Despite Rowling's intention to show the opposite, appearance and status are crucial to characters' success in the series. Rowling thus teaches two lessons at once—lessons at odds with each other. Like the fairy tale, children's literature in general seems to have a foot in both radical and traditional camps. By analyzing *Harry Potter* as a fairy tale, I hope to show this ambivalence as part of the innate tensions of children's literature. The popular response to *Harry Potter* seems to reflect a truth that we adults do not want to own up to: when it comes right down to it, we do not really know what we want from children's literature, comfort or change.

The Harry Potter series is positively soaked in an understanding of the fairy-tale form. Zipes states that metamorphosis is the "key theme" of fairy tales,[6] and there are many levels of transformation in these texts. In fairy tales, the poor orphan or neglected child often becomes king of a distant country, a transformative social advance usually ending in "happily ever after." Harry is a classic "outcast child" of fairy tale and myth, in the ranks of Cinderella, Snow White, Peau d'Âne, Oedipus, and Joseph.[7] Many of these children are orphans like Harry; others, like Cinderella, may as well be orphans since their fathers fail to defend them. Like Cinderella, Harry is mistreated by his family, given horrible ill-fitting clothes to wear, and is unable to go anywhere. He and other outcast children suffer poverty and abuse before achieving fame, wealth, and security through a combination of luck, beauty, and charm. Harry's salvation from this dreadful home life comes in the form of persistent letters from Hogwarts. When he finally goes to Hogwarts, he finds himself in a kind of fairyland. The fairy tale features a shift from the mimetic to the fantastic, or "faery." Faery is the concept of a parallel world, accessed only by magic, where the laws of the real world are suspended or reversed. Hogwarts is bewitched, hidden from Muggle eyes; anything is possible there. The Dursleys deflate.

The fairy tale is also marked by the transformation of physical form. Hogwarts exemplifies the concept of transformation as well as other-worldliness, as everything is in flux at this magical school. Staircases shift; whole rooms appear and disappear at random.[8] In the fairy tale, animals and humans often exchange forms, as we see in "The Frog Prince" and "The Beauty and the Beast." Rowling's wizards shift from human to animal form on a regular basis. Our very first sight of Professor McGonagall is as a cat consulting a map. The idea of the Animagus—a wizard who can transform him or herself into bird, beast, or bug at will—dominates the last third of *Harry Potter and the Prisoner of Azkaban*. Professor Lupin is a werewolf. To keep him company, his closest friends, including Harry's father, learned how to transform themselves into animals. Furthermore, the physical transformation that underlies the series is Lord Voldemort's long, strange journey back to human form.

Rowling uses fairy-tale motifs to criticize materialism, a theme that shows the doubleness of the genre. The fairy tale was originally told primarily by the peasantry, who dreamed of a better life. Unsurprisingly, then, poverty is exemplified as good, and the "modest choice" is a popular fairy-tale motif. The "modest choice" is when the protagonist chooses the natural over the artificial, the paltry over the sumptuous. For example, when Beauty asks her father for a rose, she makes the modest choice that distinguishes her from her sisters, greedy for gold. Greed is often (although not always) punished in the fairy tale.[9] Jeanne Murray Walker writes that "[f]antasy defies materialism by showing that there are, indeed, coherent communities formed around other values."[10] In Rowling's series, Draco Malfoy constantly taunts Ron for his poverty. He is the rich kid who wields his wealth as a weapon. Hermione points out that his reliance on social position underscores his own lack of ability: when Draco buys the Slytherin team Nimbus 2001 broomsticks and becomes their new Seeker, she says that none of the Gryffindor players "had to *buy* their way in."[11] By contrast, the Weasleys epitomize the poor yet happy family unit. Harry praises their home as the "best,"[12] and thereby, like Beauty and Cinderella, makes the modest choice that affirms his goodness.

However, as in the fairy tale, the attitude towards wealth in Rowling's books is conflicted. Fairy tales tend to end with the disenfranchised gaining power, and the poor becoming wealthy. The reward of the modest choice is always wealth, especially through marriage. Ironically, by being humble one gains power; by championing the simple life, one rises above it. Likewise, Harry is rewarded in *Harry Potter and the Philosopher's Stone* (published in the United States as *Harry Potter and the Sorcerer's Stone*) with the status of being Lily and James's son and with untold Galleons kept in Gringotts Bank. Max Lüthi comments that the fairy tale is fascinated with gold and silver;[13] similarly, Harry is agog at the sight of "mounds" of gold in his vault.[14] When he receives a Firebolt—a far superior broomstick to Draco's Nimbus 2001—from a mysterious donor, he hardly turns it down in the spirit of fair play. Hogwarts itself is a place of wealth, of rich feasts and medicinal chocolate. The emphasis on food resembles similar stress put on food in utopias like the edible land of Cockaigne, the dream of hungry peasants. Moderation in the food and decor is unheard of, and gluttony does not, as in "Hansel and Gretel," lead to punishment.

Rowling uses Harry's two sidekicks, Ron and Hermione, to argue against materialism and prejudice. Ron, while hailing from an indisputably pure wizarding family, is poor. He has status but no wealth. We can infer that Hermione, as the daughter of dentists, is well off, but as her parents are both Muggles, she has no status in the wizarding world. Harry, however, has both wealth and status at Hogwarts. Even though he cannot remember defeating Voldemort, he profits from his fame.

The attack on appearance based on wealth runs deeper with the complicated issue of race, and Rowling's presentation of this issue is similarly conflicted. The battle between multiculturalism and racism provides the framework for the series; it is the modern liberal version of the fairy-tale battle between good and evil. Race lies at the root of the two major conflicts in the series: tensions between Muggle-born and pure-blood wizards, and between human wizards and nonhuman magical creatures. Rowling strives to promote liberal values, yet we can see that she is ultimately trapped by the conservative nature of the fairy tale.

When Hermione mocks Draco for buying his way onto the Slytherin team, he calls her a "filthy little Mudblood."[15] Ron instantly starts fighting him in retaliation. Harry, like the reader, does not know what is going on and is educated by Ron and Hagrid. Ron explains that Mudblood is a "really foul" term for a Muggle-born (as opposed to "pure-blood") wizard.[16] It is, in short, the N-word for the wizarding world. Perhaps Rowling is aware that one of the worst insults leveled against African Americans is "mud people."[17] Rowling uses the fairy-tale form to protest racism, as the sympathetic characters insist that being a pure-blood wizard does not guarantee success or justify discrimination.

Although this incident occurs one-third of the way through the second book of the series, we see it coming from Harry's very first encounter with Draco Malfoy. One of Draco's first questions to Harry is whether his parents "were *our* kind," and Harry is uncertain what he means.[18] Draco continues that Muggle-born wizards should not be allowed to go to Hogwarts and scorns how many of them had not even known about its existence. Hogwarts, he says, should be reserved for "old wizarding families."[19] Wanting to know the pedigree of everyone he encounters, Draco is both a classist and a racist. Harry, like the "sort" Draco describes, has just found out about Hogwarts himself, and the irony of the scene is that although he fits the description of what Draco is castigating, he has greater status than Draco himself. In their second encounter, Draco tries to recruit Harry to his own circle and, by implication, to the Dark Side where purity of blood is valued. He offers to help him find the "right" wizards to be friends with, an offer Harry refuses.[20] Calling the Weasleys and Hagrid "riff-raff," Draco leaves, battle lines drawn.[21]

Draco's whole family is engaged in the battle between good pluralism and bad racism. Draco's father criticizes his son in *Harry Potter and the Chamber of Secrets* for being less successful than Hermione, the Muggle-born brain of the school.[22] The very name "Malfoy," French for "bad faith," illustrates the family's position. They demonstrate bad faith, being part of Hogwarts and yet rejecting its basic philosophy of inclusion. Hogwarts itself was founded in order to create a safe haven for wizards from the persecuting Muggles in the Middle Ages. However, the philosophy of exclusion and persecution persisted, as cofounder Salazar Slytherin wanted to keep Hogwarts restricted to "all-magic families."[23] Being of "bad faith" also implies that their philosophy, or faith, is evil.

Harry opposes the Slytherin philosophy, but just what is Muggle about Harry? How does he represent pluralism?[24] This is a surprisingly difficult question to answer. Hagrid tells him that he is not *"from* a Muggle family," and yet a few lines later refers to Harry's mother as coming from a "long line o' Muggles."[25] But if his mother came from Muggles, does not Harry? Are not Squibs considered racially wizard despite their lack of magical talent? Harry is part wizard and part Muggle, but it is easy to forget this, as he seems so thoroughly wizard. In *Harry Potter and the Goblet of Fire,* Hagrid says that he wants Harry to win the Triwizard Tournament to prove that "yeh don' have ter be pure-blood ter do it."[26] This statement gives the reader pause. On one hand, Hagrid is right, as Harry has mixed blood: his mother was from a Muggle family, his father a pure-blooded wizard, and he will defend pluralistic values. On the other hand, Harry is the elect of the wizarding world, the only one to defeat Voldemort. If Ron had been chosen for the task, the success of it would have been much less sure despite his pure wizarding blood. Harry holds the pedigree, through a mere freak of destiny. If Rowling means to point out Harry as, in the terms of the book, biracial, then she fails somewhat.

Indeed, Rowling's message about purity of blood seems somewhat contradictory. The whole point of the race war is to defend the Muggle-born wizards. However, wizards universally look down upon Muggles, and being a wizard means joining an elite world. Hagrid hates taking the slow subway and cannot understand how Muggles get on without magic.[27] The Dursleys—the only Muggles described in detail—are detestable in the fairy-tale tradition of abusive (step)parents. Hagrid qualifies his comments about Muggles by saying that "some o' the best" wizards were Muggle-born, but his initial reaction is a firm "[y]er not *from* a Muggle family. If he'd known who yeh *were*—,"[28] emphasizing Harry's status in the wizarding community. Rowling wants to have her cake and eat it, too: to have Harry the fairy-tale hero born to greatness, and yet promote a social vision in which only merit counts. This contradiction is found in the fairy tale itself, and Rowling has inherited it.

Rowling primarily depicts the battle between pluralism and racism in the magical terms of wizards and Muggles. However, readers are sure to notice how she teaches them a lesson about tolerance that can be applied to their own lives and history: they learn that they should judge people by their merits, actions, and morals rather than their race. In an October 2000 interview, Rowling described Voldemort as "someone who is incredibly power hungry. Racist, really."[29] David Colbert points out that Dumbledore defeated the dark wizard Grindelwald in 1945; the obvious parallel with Hitler fits with my reading of the series as a battle against racism.[30] At times, Rowling's social vision does refer specifically, if obliquely, back to the real world experiences of her readers, by including students of different races. But how effective is her use of race? Minorities are mentioned, but they are not heroes; all the major players are Anglo-Saxon. Angelina Johnson is a black member of the Quidditch team, and Lee Jordan wears dreadlocks. (Although of course whites can wear their hair in dreadlocks, it is a hairstyle chiefly associated with blacks.) Angelina's race is not noted until *Goblet of Fire;* perhaps this addition is an afterthought meant to emphasize Rowling's increasing attention to racial issues. Another minor character is called Parvati Patel. Harry has a crush on Cho Chang, the "very pretty"[31] (the phrase is constantly repeated) athlete of, presumably, Chinese descent. This is, however, all we know about her. The message that love crosses racial lines is perfectly sound, but I do question the way Rowling deals with different ethnicities in her texts. By not specifying exact cultural groups or doing more than casually mentioning race, she shows a color-blind attitude: race does not matter, so the differences should not be noticed, much less discussed. According to Michael Omri and Howard Winant, "[w]hites tend to locate racism in color consciousness and find its absence color blindness."[32] However, current multicultural theory views "color blindness" as naïve and unintentionally harmful, glossing over—or whitewashing—cultural differences instead of trying to understand and appreciate them. David Theo Goldberg posits this liberal humanist attitude as contradictory: "The more ideologically hegemonic liberal values seem and the more open to difference liberal modernity declares itself, the more dismissive of difference it becomes and the more closed it seeks to make the circle of acceptability."[33] Multiculturalism, many critics claim, should celebrate differences rather than ignore them.

Physical appearance, especially the difference between dark and fair, plays a great role in fairy tales. The fairy tale shows a contradictory approach to appearance, and Rowling has inherited this doubleness in her depiction of non-human magical creatures. In the fairy tale, characters are often tested by physical appearances. For example, a common motif is the fairy disguised as an ugly old woman, who rewards or punishes people according to how they treat her. Appearances, then, are deceiving. The "loathly lady" tale type shows the ugly woman to be truly beautiful if shown forbearance. Frogs turn into princes. Fairy-tale characters succeed if they distrust appearances, and if they can value someone regardless of how that person looks. Rowling would like her readers to learn this lesson, as her presentation of Hagrid as a gentle giant shows.

Yet the fairy tale—and Rowling's series—relies on physical stereotypes as a form of narrative shorthand. Especially important are the positive and negative associations with light and dark, an inherently racist tradition. The fairy-tale heroine is usually described as fair whereas the witch is dark-haired.[34] Blondeness connotes youth, beauty, light, goodness, innocence, fertility, and—like real gold—imperviousness and wealth.[35] Dark hair and swarthy skin are generally reserved for evil characters. Warner claims that "[b]londeness is less a descriptive term about hair pigmentation than a blazon in code, a piece of a value system that it is urgent to confront and analyse because its implications, in moral and social terms, are so dire and are still so unthinkingly embedded in the most ordinary, popular materials of the imagination."[36] Heroes and heroines tend to be lovely, and beauty is given moral value: Perrault claims that Cinderella is beautiful because she is good. In "Diamonds and Toads," diamonds and flowers fall out of the good girl's mouth when she speaks, whereas the bad girl coughs out toads and snakes.[37]

Rowling, despite her desire to teach tolerance, engages in the stereotypes of the fairy tale, as traditional European standards of beauty continue to be upheld in her work. Aside from the blonde Draco, her evil characters are dark and often misshapen. Voldemort is the "Dark Lord," master of the "Dark Arts," and Harry is determined not to go over to the "Dark Side." Dumbledore's first name, Albus, is Latin for "white."[38] Snape, as Joan Acocella remarks, resembles the stereotypical Jew with his "sallow skin" and hooked nose.[39] So do, perhaps, the goblins who run the bank, possessing pointed beards and "swarthy, clever" faces.[40]

Some good characters are swarthy; however, they are cast as humorous and inferior. Hagrid, the half-giant, has black hair and eyes, and Dobby (and presumably the other house-elves) has an "ugly brown face."[41] Hagrid is hairy and unkempt, with a "wild look" frequently in his eyes.[42] The house-elves have bat-like ears, saucer eyes, and huge toothy grins; Dobby looks "like a large and very ugly doll."[43] Hagrid and the house-elves cannot even dress themselves properly. Their appearances mark them as "lower" characters and even suggest a lack of self-control. Their behavior follows suit, as they sob easily. Hagrid needs to be saved by the trio of Harry, Ron, and Hermione again and again, and the elves likewise do not seem able to take care of themselves.

Rowling protests racial intolerance by showing how such creatures as giants (specifically half-giants), werewolves, and elves are treated. They are the underclass of the wizarding world and suffer from the stereotypes placed on them. Giants have a savage reputation, but Hagrid is tender-hearted. Likewise, the prejudice against werewolves has robbed Lupin of work even though his condition can be controlled. Both Hagrid and Lupin must conceal their true natures as much as possible. Similarly, Madame Maxime hides her giant heritage even when a fellow half-giant, Hagrid, guesses at it. Both of them are "passing," denying their racial heritage in order to avoid prejudice. "Passing" has a long troubled history in the real world, especially among African Americans. Unlike Madame Maxime, however, Hagrid is conflicted about his ability to pass, and tries to feel proud of his mixed racial identity. "I am what I am, an' I'm not ashamed," he says, moments after submitting his resignation when his identity is revealed.[44]

Such pride is not easy to express when most people believe tales of the savagery of giants. Draco Malfoy describes Hagrid as a "great hairy moron" and mimics his lower-class speech. However, his cruelty is not far removed from how the narrator and sympathetic characters themselves view the giant. Ron is the mouthpiece of common prejudices, and he immediately shrinks from both Hagrid and Lupin when he finds out their identities. Hagrid and Lupin are not ultimately dependable despite their good hearts. Hagrid does not have the brains to keep the secret of how to subdue Fluffy, the guard dog of the Philosopher's Stone. Lupin tries to attack the children when he forgets to take his medicine;

similarly, Hagrid resorts to violence, as when he nearly chokes Karkaroff in *Goblet of Fire*, and needs to be restrained.[45] Hagrid drinks. Hermione, although she disregards tales of giant cruelty and links them to prejudice towards were-wolves, condescends to him: "you've had enough to drink. . . ."[46] Both Hagrid and Lupin essentially lack self-control and therefore seem to deserve their lower status.

The hierarchy of magical races is further seen in the treatment of the house-elves and their quest for freedom. The elves are the slaves of the wizarding world, as Rowling painstakingly elaborates. The wonderful food and luxury of Hogwarts is, as Hermione reminds everyone, based on the "slave labour" of house-elves.[47] Unpaid, they receive neither benefits nor holidays. Again, Rowling uses the fairy-tale form to discuss problems in our own history, past and present. The situation of the house-elves unites the issues of race and class, and Rowling shows how even the liberal bastion of Hogwarts engages in racist / classist acts. Through Hermione, she protests economic slavery, implicating the class system in general. However, even sympathetic characters argue that the house-elves like their position: Ron says that Winky enjoys getting "bossed around."[48] This attitude is historically attributed to slaves. Even today, the image of happy slaves devoted to their masters, as they are in *Gone with the Wind*, persists in the popular imagination. Hermione's distress that *Hogwarts: A History* leaves out the house-elves recalls how contemporary textbooks still fail to tackle slavery adequately, if at all. The expression "[w]e've been working like house-elves here!"[49] mirrors the British saying "to work like a black." Hermione complains that the wizards are disrespectful to Winky by "calling her 'elf,'" an insult that reflects the terms "boy" and "gal" that whites have historically used to depersonalize and infantilize African Americans.[50]

With the above correlations between elves and slaves, Rowling means to help young readers understand the stereotypes about slaves when (or if) they learn about them in school. Rowling is particularly sophisticated in this aim with her depiction of elves distressed by the prospect of freedom, illustrating the depth of false consciousness in elf culture. An understanding of the psychologically complex idea of false consciousness can help children better comprehend the different ways in which people are enslaved. Once again, however, Rowling's social vision proves ambivalent. Only Hermione cares about the house-elves, and the other children—including Harry—mock her efforts to help the elves and raise social awareness all around. Harry gives Dobby, the house-elf who defies his master to help the boy, his freedom, but only incidentally. Furthermore, the house-elves, false consciousness aside, seem destined for lower status. Dobby is a hapless creature, unable to communicate properly with Harry, and nearly killing Harry when trying to save him. His slavish adoration of Harry is played for laughs and underscores his essential slave nature. Like Caliban, it seems he must serve someone. The other elves are even more pathetic.

Rowling makes an admirable attempt to broaden children's perspectives on social justice, and surely she would love for them to fight the good fight as

Hermione does. With her attack on materialism, she attacks the Thatcherite vision that profits are more important than people, and that a certain amount of social suffering is necessary for the economy to function properly. Yet for all her laudable motives, her presentation of race and class issues ultimately fails to convince, for there is a class system in the wizarding world based on race, even apart from the debates about Mudbloods.

Indeed, the wizarding world is founded on concepts of exclusivity even as most of its denizens champion pluralistic values. Hogwarts would not be exciting if we knew how to get there, and if everyone could go.[51] The feeling of exclusivity also attends the fairy tale, which depends on the special, "chosen" quality of its heroes and heroines. On one hand, the fairy tale challenges the social system, having the dirty servant girl sleeping by the cinders become a princess. Fairy tales have been used to champion any number of causes, from the fate of unpaid soldiers to marriages based on love rather than economics. On the other hand, once the heroes obtain high status at the end of the tale, they fail to alter the status quo that they themselves once challenged.

Although Harry grows up a bit, he is essentially a static character like the fairy-tale hero. He tells Hermione and Ron that he will never join the enemy, and we believe him. The books rest on the image of Harry as inherently virtuous. The kind of neglect he encountered at the Dursleys would realistically create an antisocial boy desperate to curry favor and win power for himself; instead, when he magically receives attention beyond his wildest dreams at Hogwarts, he instantly rejects this status. If only he were a little tempted. Harry vehemently rejects the notion that he should be in Slytherin even before the Sorting Hat suggests it; despite actually physically possessing some of Voldemort's qualities (as the Hat has seen), he is beyond temptation. In this sense he resembles effortlessly innocent fairy-tale characters like Snow White.

Despite his heritage, Harry is strongly characterized as an ordinary boy; Roni Natov calls him "Everychild."[52] Through Harry, we access the fairyland of Hogwarts and learn about the wizarding world. Harry is not particularly bright; Hermione constantly helps him with clues he must solve. He is brave, but then, so are Ron and Hermione. He is not exceptionally kind; the general fate of the house-elves does not bother him. When Hermione embraces him in *Philosopher's Stone* for showing friendship and courage,[53] the reader might be forgiven in wondering how deeply Harry has demonstrated these qualities by this point. He is not disciplined, either; even with the death-defying Triwizard contest, he leaves solving his clues to the last minute. He would never have been able to do it without helpers and luck, which generally attend the fairy-tale hero.

Ironically, the emphasis on Harry's ordinariness means that his heroism seems to depend on chance and inheritance. It does not matter that Ron is just as brave when he gets the chance, and Hermione brighter: Harry is the star. The ordinary quality of Harry and the image of him as the disadvantaged orphan clash with the status he has as the ultimate insider: son of James and Lily Potter, the spiritual heir to Dumbledore, and the wizard whom Voldemort could not kill—who is, in fact, part Voldemort. His status is as automatic and indelible as his tell-tale scar, as Harry realizes his first day at Hogwarts when everyone stares at him. He is, like the fairy-tale hero, simply fated for better things. Like the Grimms' Cinderella, he is magically protected by the love of his dead mother. There is no real doubt about Harry's fate, or about his character; while his friends develop, he is stuck in the role of fairy-tale hero. No wonder Ron is jealous.

My discussion of Rowling's presentation of materialism, racism, and her hero reveals an approach that wavers between protest and acquiescence. The latter is due in part to her reliance on the fairy tale. The fairy tale may contain radical elements, but it is also firmly conservative. Its values have been as much for social stability as for social advance; in other words, the peasants wanted to get a piece of the pie, not change the menu. Jack Zipes, Maria Tatar, and Ruth Bottigheimer, among others, have shown that its tellers and writers have been primarily interested in teaching children the status quo. It is hard to think of a fairy tale without the usual stereotypes, and tempting to imagine it impossible. Today, though, traditional fairy tales are often revised, challenging the fairy-tale genre. In "Princess Dalhi," by Tanith Lee, for example, the Cinderella figure happily dances in rags at the ball and rejects the prince despite his power.[54] But I agree with Zipes that Rowling is not writing a radical fairy tale.[55] Her use of fairy-tale elements seems to be traditional, and her vision is just as conservative as it is liberal.

The double nature of the fairy tale—traditional and radical—is echoed in children's literature at large. Peter Hollingdale writes that "all children's literature is inescapably didactic,"[56] an opinion held by a large number of critics. Unexpectedly, perhaps, this may be especially true of fantasy, as Walker calls fantasy a "didactic genre" that "gives order to chaos."[57] Hollingdale suggests that at times "the conscious surface ideology and the passive ideology of a novel are at odds with each other," and I claim that the Harry Potter series is a good example of this phenomenon.[58] Hollingdale goes on to say that the classics of children's literature are more radical than we give them credit for,[59] yet surely the reverse is true, too, and books that claim radicalism can possess a strong conservative streak.

This doubleness is part of Rowling's incredible success. As Claire Armitstead of the *Guardian* writes, readers crave the "reassuringly familiar," to be found in "conventionally domestic" writing.[60] The familiar fairy-tale motifs add to this cozy feeling, and the delight in seeing them is compounded by the (adult) reader recognizing the boarding school stories, and even *Star Wars*, of her youth. Hollingdale writes that "[a] large part of any book is written not by its author but by the world its author lives in,"[61] and hence Armitstead's label for the books—"[c]onservative tomes for conservative times"[62]—fits. Rowling is further bound by the conservative nature of the genres she draws from, especially the fairy tale. The result is half-wizard, half-Muggle, and wildly popular.

Perhaps what we really want from children's literature is something novel, but not too new.

NOTES

1. J.K. Rowling, *Harry Potter and the Prisoner of Azkaban* (London: Bloomsbury, 1999), 46.

2. Jack Zipes, *Breaking the Magic Spell: Radical Theories of Folk and Fairy Tales* (London: Heinemann Educational Books, 1979), 141.

3. Marina Warner, *From the Beast to the Blonde: On Fairy Tales and Their Tellers* (London: Chatto and Windus, 1994), 193.

4. Joan Acocella, "Under the Spell," *The New Yorker*, 31 July 2000, 74–78.

5. Ibid., p. 74.

6. Jack Zipes, *Spells of Enchantment: The Wondrous Fairy Tales of Western Culture* (Toronto: Penguin, 1991), xvi.

7. E. Sidney Hartland, "The Outcast Child," *Folk-lore Journal* 4 (1886), 308–49.

8. J.K. Rowling, *Harry Potter and the Philosopher's Stone* (London: Bloomsbury, 1997), 99.

9. The most obvious example is Jack in "Jack and the Beanstalk." Many tales begin with the premise of finding one's fortune.

10. Jeanne Murray Walker, "High Fantasy, Rites of Passage, and Cultural Values," in *Teaching Children's Literature: Issues, Pedagogy, Resources*, Glenn Edward Sadler, ed. (New York: The Modern Language Association of America, 1992), 109–20, 110.

11. J.K. Rowling, *Harry Potter and the Chamber of Secrets* (London: Bloomsbury, 1998), 86.

12. Ibid., 36.

13. Max Lüthi, *Once upon a Time: On the Nature of Fairy Tales*, Lee Chadeayne and Paul Gottwald, trans. (Bloomington: Indiana UP, 1970), 51.

14. Rowling, *Philosopher's Stone*, 58.

15. Rowling, *Chamber of Secrets*, 86.

16. Ibid., 89.

17. This term is part of the white supremacist Christian Identity doctrine, which holds that blacks descended from an unholy union between Eve and an apelike subhuman and concludes that blacks are essentially soulless animals.

18. Rowling, *Philosopher's Stone*, 61.

19. Ibid.

20. Ibid., 81.

21. Ibid.

22. Rowling, *Chamber of Secrets*, 44.

23. Rowling, *Philosopher's Stone*, 53.

24. Harry need not be "raced as other" to defend pluralism, of course; however, Rowling's depiction of Harry's "ethnicity" is contradictory, again suggesting that her liberalism is clouded by traditional representation, exemplified by the fairy tale.

25. Rowling, *Philosopher's Stone*, 61.

26. J.K. Rowling, *Harry Potter and the Goblet of Fire* (London: Bloomsbury, 2000), 396.

27. Rowling, *Philosopher's Stone*, 53.

28. Ibid., 61.

29. Rowling, "A Good Scare," *Time*, 20 October 2000, http//www.time.com/time /magazine/printout/0,8816, 58416, 00.html (accessed 19 February 2003).

30. David Colbert, *The Magical Worlds of Harry Potter: A Treasury of Myths, Legends and Fascinating Facts* (Toronto: McArthur and Company, 2001), 70.

31. Rowling, *Goblet of Fire*, 78.

32. Michael Omri and Howard Winant, *Racial Formations in the United States: From the 1960's to the 1990's*, 2d ed., (New York: Routledge, 1994), 71.

33. David Theo Goldberg, *Racist Culture: Philosophy and the Politics of Meaning* (Oxford: Blackwell, 1993), 6–7.

34. This motif has been much emphasized in fairy-tale films such as Disney's *Cinderella*.

35. Warner, *From the Beast*, 362–86.

36. Ibid., 364. Warner goes on to say that "[t]he Nazis' Aryan fantasies were partly rooted in this ancient, endearing colour code which cast gods as golden boys and girls and outsiders as swarthy."

37. There are many variants of this English fairy tale in other European cultures.

38. Colbert, *Magical Worlds*, 70.

39. Acocella, "Under the Spell," 77.

40. Rowling, *Philosopher's Stone*, 56.

41. Rowling, *Chamber of Secrets*, 249.

42. Ibid., 156.

43. Ibid., 16.

44. Rowling, *Goblet of Fire*, 396.

45. Ibid., 488.

46. Rowling, *Azkaban*, 92–93.

47. Rowling, *Goblet of Fire*, 162. For a further discussion of the antislavery theme in the series, see Brycchan Carey's chapter in this volume.

48. Rowling, *Goblet of Fire*, 112.

49. Ibid., 197.

50. Ibid., 125.

51. Such exclusivity is part of the school story genre itself, in which students are proud of their schools, and their houses and their status within the house seems to mark characters' social positions for life.

52. Roni Natov, "Harry Potter and the Extraordinariness of the Ordinary," *The Lion and the Unicorn* 25, no. 2 (2001): 310–27, 319.

53. Rowling, *Philosopher's Stone*, 204.

54. Tanith Lee, "Princess Dahli," in *The Outspoken Princess and the Gentle Knight: A Treasury of Modern Fairy Tales*, Jack Zipes, ed. (Toronto: Penguin, 1991), 59–73.

55. Jack Zipes, *Sticks and Stones: The Troublesome Success of Children's Literature from Slovenly Peter to Harry Potter* (New York: Routledge, 2001), 182.

56. Peter Hollingdale, "Ideology and the Children's Book," in *Literature for Children: Contemporary Criticism*, Peter Hunt, ed. (New York: Routledge, 1992), 18–40, 30.

57. Walker, "High Fantasy," 117–18.

58. Hollingdale, "Ideology," 31.

59. Ibid., 39.

60. Claire Armitstead, "Wizard, but with a Touch of Tom Brown," *Guardian*, 8 July 1999, http://books.guardian.co.uk/Print/0,3858,3881430,00.html (accessed 19 February 2003).

61. Hollingdale, "Ideology," 32.

62. Armitstead, "Wizard," n.p.

8

Hermione and the House-Elves: The Literary and Historical Contexts of J. K. Rowling's Antislavery Campaign

Brycchan Carey

Unfree—or, at least, unpaid—labor has always been central to children's literature, and slaves, whether as bonded humans or magical "helpers," appear regularly in both British and American writing for children. In particular, the development and, where practical, the mobilization of antislavery sentiment has long been an important part of a British literary education. In two of the first four Harry Potter novels, J. K. Rowling introduces an enslaved people, the house-elves, and uses their plight both as a commentary on the society and economy of the magical world she creates and as a way of demonstrating the opportunities for political activism available to young people in the real world. The responses of different characters to the issue suggest possible responses to social and political issues, but they also reflect actual political debates, participated in by both adults and young people, over the past two centuries. By drawing on an issue with a long and contested history, but also with a solid tradition in children's literature, Rowling creates resonances for the adult reader and opportunities for discovery and engagement for the younger reader. This essay will look at both the historical and literary tradition within which Rowling is working and at the opportunities and encouragement to political activism that she extends to her readers.

In *Harry Potter and the Chamber of Secrets*, the second of the Potter books, the reader encounters, in the form of house-elf Dobby, the enslaved house-elves for the first time. These creatures are vaguely anthropomorphic, but rather small with protruding eyes and ears.[1] Their speech is odd, characterized by pronoun and word-order mistakes, and is reminiscent of 1930s and 40s Hollywood misconceptions of African-American dialects: almost the only representation of African Americans commonly available to British audiences until surprisingly late in the twentieth century. Indeed, it seems clear that Rowling has tried to make connections between the house-elves and historical slaves, both in North America and in the British Caribbean colonies. The house-elves' patois, if unlike any dialect that has ever existed in the real world, sufficiently resembles a filmmaker's plantation fantasy to put adults in mind of the issue.[2] In addition to the dialect is the name, reflecting the division of labor on a plantation: we do not know if there are "field-elves" growing sugar and cotton, for example, but the implication is there.

The story of the house-elves, however, hints at a psychological enslavement deeper than mere fetters. As the story progresses, we find that the house-elves have been enslaved for so long that they have lost the ability to conceive of themselves as free. The Hogwarts kitchen house-elves, after hearing Dobby talk about his freedom, edge away from him as if he were infectious. Winky, the elf sacked by Bartemius Crouch, tells Harry and Hermione of her shame at her freedom.[3] Even when freed, or acting alone, the elves continue to follow their internalized logic of bondage, enslaved by what William Blake called "mind forg'd manacles."[4]

The strange self-punishing behavior of Dobby, Lucius Malfoy's house-elf, is the most memorable feature of our introduction to the house-elves, when Dobby appears unexpectedly in Harry's room at the Dursleys'. This is also Harry's first encounter with a house-elf, and for him it is a somewhat perplexing affair. Brought up by nonmagical Muggles, Harry is an outsider from the community of witches and wizards. He understands little of its economy and society and is more than usually naïve for an eleven-year-old about behaving appropriately towards others. However, despite his initial fear, Harry is polite and respectful towards this new species of magical creature. Once he realizes that Dobby poses no clear threat, he asks the house-elf to sit down, at which Dobby bursts into tears before punishing himself by banging his head against the window. Never before, we learn, has a wizard—even an apprentice like Harry—addressed Dobby as an equal. Moreover, Dobby gives Harry the extraordinary information he, like all house-elves, is a slave in eternal bondage.[5] Harry's response to this is remarkably practical. He wants to know if the elf is acting alone or at his family's request, and if Dobby is likely to get into trouble. But Harry is curiously untroubled by the implications of the house-elf's admission, an admission that suggests that the magical world into which Harry has recently moved is a good deal less egalitarian than the easy camaraderie of Hogwarts School would suggest. Harry's response is not political but, rather, that of a small boy confined to his room, a boy who has spent most of his childhood locked in a cramped cupboard by the tyrannical Dursleys.[6] Having himself suffered false imprisonment, Harry's engagement with the house-elves is essentially a sympathetic and personal one. Although he is later instrumental in Dobby's emancipation, this effectively happens behind closed doors, and the motivation is explicitly that of personally rewarding Dobby for his individual good behavior.[7]

Hermione Granger's assessment of the house-elf situation is rather different. On first seeing house-elves at the Quidditch World Cup, her comments are indignant and unfocused, but they soon develop into an overtly political state-ment. Bluntly calling the house-elves' condition "slavery," she demands action, without identifying who, exactly, is responsible. Ron Weasley, always keen to disagree with Hermione, protests that the house-elves are happy, but Hermione's retort is both pointed and, for the first time, apportions guilt: "it's people like *you*," she says, "who prop up rotten and unjust systems."[8] Unlike Harry, whose response to the problem was largely personal, Hermione sees the problem as a public one, requiring political engagement to reach public solu-tions. Moreover, her description of the magical world is accurate. The house-elves are indeed in slavery and slavery is, inherently, a "rotten and unjust" system. Shortly after the friends return to Hogwarts, Hermione founds the So-ciety for the Promotion of Elfish Welfare, better known to all by its unfortunate acronym: S.P.E.W. Hermione runs this society as a classic pressure group, with membership fees, committees, badges, and a consumer boycott. Although the issue is left unresolved by the end of *Goblet of Fire*, different personal and po-litical responses to the problem of slavery are thoroughly explored.

This is significant, as the Harry Potter novels are among the most politically engaged novels to have been written for children in recent years. Indeed, the central concept of the novels, Harry's personal struggle with the dark lord Voldemort, provides a site for discussion of a democratic society's response to elitism, totalitarianism, and racism. These evils are plainly illustrated by the be-havior of Lucius and Draco Malfoy and the support given by their Death-Eater friends for Voldemort's evil crusade. By contrast, the forces of good are less well defined. At school, teachers such as Severus Snape—and all the Defense Against the Dark Arts teachers—seem unreliable at best, sinister at worst. In public life, journalists, represented by Rita Skeeter, seem unconcerned with truth or justice. In government, the Ministry of Magic itself is not immune from blunder and overreaction, particularly from the complacent Cornelius Fudge and the zealous Barty Crouch (who with his Hitlerian toothbrush mous-tache resembles a dictator more than Voldemort himself). The problem for Harry, Dumbledore, and all right-thinking witches and wizards is not so much recognizing the forces of evil, but managing the forces of good. In Harry's world, for evil to triumph it is necessary only that good magicians fight amongst themselves.

The solutions to the problem of factionalism and in-fighting, the books seem to argue, are loyalty, teamwork, and eternal vigilance. Harry is loyal to his school, his house, and his friends, as are all the positive characters at Hogwarts. Although young and innocent, Harry still has recourse to magical maps, charms, and potions, fuelled by an insatiable curiosity, in his unending quest to find out the truth about his world. Yet Harry's political engagement comes down, in the end, to a personal battle with Voldemort. In contrast to Harry's personal struggle, Hermione's is a public one. She goes to the library and con-ducts research, she subscribes to newspapers and spars with their reporters, and she sets up campaign groups. Her loyalty, team spirit, and vigilance are as un-doubted as Harry's, but she plays the political game in another way. This is an important key to the Harry Potter novels. Clearly, a significant aspect of Rowling's project is the promotion of political participation for young people and, rather than be narrowly prescriptive, she instead offers a range of political models for young people to explore and emulate. Harry's team-playing spirit is one such political model as, less positively, is the bureaucratic sycophancy of Percy Weasley. Likewise, Harry's personal and mystical crusade against totalitarian evil is supported by Hermione's "rational" and public-minded contribution to the team. But in the end, for young people in the real world, denied the opportunity to do head-to-head battle with evil, the model of the political pressure group exemplified by S.P.E.W is the most promising route for an apprenticeship in politics.

This is the case despite Rowling's seeming ambivalence, both to Hermione and to the campaign. Ron Weasley and other students at Hogwarts might quickly weary of Hermione's enthusiasm while Hagrid might think that house-elves are born to servitude.[9] But on the other hand, Albus Dumbledore and Sirius Black, both in their small acts of kindness to elves and in their sharp evaluations of the institution, show that there is more to the issue than Ron's or Hagrid's cynicism suggests. Dumbledore may not yet be ready to emancipate the Hogwarts house-elves, but he does become the first wizard to employ elves as free wage-laborers.

Moreover, Hermione's tenacity and enthusiasm increasingly command a sort of grudging respect—itself a lot more positive than the open ridicule she received in earlier books in the series. Indeed, when asked to contribute to any sort of collaborative effort, Hermione invariably comes up with the goods, a clear endorsement of her studious and tenacious character. Even the off-putting acronym, S.P.E.W., which may seem to indicate authorial ambivalence towards, or even disgust with, the campaign, in fact marks an important phase in Hermione's political education. In her first foray into political life, she fails to think out the implications of the name for her campaign, a common enough mistake even for an experienced politician. Ron's mocking alternative, The House-Elf Liberation Front, brings to mind the British terrorist group calling itself the Animal Liberation Front, an organization familiar to British children with any interest in current affairs.[10] Hermione's polite emphasis on the house-elves' welfare, inherent in the title of S.P.E.W., explicitly rejects direct or terrorist action, but nonetheless leaves her open to ridicule and misinterpretation. By the end of Goblet of Fire, the issue of slavery is left unresolved, but Hermione's parallel problem, her misrepresentation by Daily Prophet reporter Rita Skeeter, concludes with Hermione firmly in control of the journalist.[11] Having the Animagus Skeeter locked up in a bottle while in the form of a bug marks Hermione's entry into the world of successful news management, a vital moment in any political apprenticeship. One imagines that, had this confrontation taken place earlier, S.P.E.W. might have been given a more media-friendly name. But one fact remains: Hermione's battle is not a personal one with an individually tailored nemesis; it is a political one. Although she has much to learn about her task, and although her campaign is initially ridiculed by her friends, it in fact provides a clear model for political action with which young people in the real world can identify and emulate.

If a generation of children are, we hope, to be spurred into political action by Hermione's example, it is important to examine Rowling's choice of slavery as the political issue significant enough to distract the young witch from the task of combating the evil Lord Voldemort. There can be no doubt, of course, that slavery is a wholly objectionable institution, opposed by all mainstream politicians in every democratic society. For this reason it has the advantage for a children's author of being largely uncontentious in party-political terms. Where slavery does exist in the modern world, it is supposed (if not always accurately) to be confined to distant locations and corrupt regimes: sex workers in South-East Asia, or domestic chattel slaves in Sudan. In Britain or the United States, no Labour or Tory politician, no Democrat or Republican, is going to find in Hermione's campaign a veiled critique on their party or government. But Rowling's choice of slavery as the issue that inspires Hermione to take action is not merely one of convenience. It is influenced, consciously or otherwise, by historical realities and literary precedent. The antislavery campaign was both the first mass political movement in British history and the event that introduced the campaigning techniques used by Hermione to British public life. Moreover, the campaign initiated a long relationship between slavery and children's literature. This relationship, which has not yet been made the subject of a detailed study, will be outlined here.

Slavery was experienced very differently in Britain and the United States. As a result, it has been discussed very differently in British and American literature and historiography. This extends to children's literature as well, and J. K. Rowling, as a British author, must be presumed to be writing from within a British rather than an American tradition. The causes, as well as the facts, of British slavery and abolition are the subject of a vigorously contested debate among historians, which need not be rehearsed here; the barest narrative, however, might be useful.[12] British involvement in the slave trade had its origins in the sixteenth century, but reached its peak with the growth of the British Atlantic empire of the eighteenth century. In the decade following American independence, a public pressure campaign to outlaw the slave trade to the remaining British colonies attracted widespread support from the British public, with a mass petitioning campaign, consumer boycott, and a powerful lobby of Parliament. Hundreds of publications opposing both slavery and the slave trade were printed and distributed between 1785 and 1795. The campaign was not immediately successful but, following a ten-year lull, the British slave trade was abolished by law in 1807. Historians are deeply divided on the causes of this campaign, variously arguing that there was a fundamental shift in popular sensibility, that the campaign was the flexing of the political muscle of the new middle classes, that the presumption of colonial mismanagement assumed a new importance following American independence, that slave resistance highlighted plantation brutality, or that it was merely realized that the institution of slavery was no longer profitable. Whatever the factor, or combination of factors, that led to abolition, another determined campaign in the 1820s and 1830s saw the abolition of slavery in British colonies, with the emancipation of slaves taking place by 1838. This "perfectly virtuous act," as it was described, rather smugly, by one Victorian historian, did not mean an end either to racism or imperial expansion.[13] But while British abhorrence of slavery in the age of empire may seem somewhat hypocritical and self-serving, it nonetheless received what appears to have been a genuine expression in literature for children, albeit an expression that does little to mask some of the more unpleasant racial attitudes prevalent in nineteenth and twentieth-century Britain.[14]

Discussion of slavery in children's literature takes two main forms. The first is the representation of enslaved human beings in realistic settings. These novels almost always convey a strong antislavery sentiment. The second form occurs in fantasy and fairy tales where various species of magical creatures are more or less explicitly described as slaves. In this literature, emancipation is often, but by no means always, a desired outcome. The first of these traditions has the earlier history. In Daniel Defoe's *Robinson Crusoe* (1719), which, if not actually written for children, is often given to children to read, slavery is integral almost from the start. Crusoe is on a voyage in the "Guinea trade"—a euphemism for the slave trade—when he is himself enslaved by the Turks. He makes an escape with the help of a fellow slave, Xury, whom he later sells, and thus, in the logic of the slave-owning society, makes a profit from trading stolen goods. On the island, Friday is effectively Crusoe's slave and, after his return to society, Crusoe establishes a Brazilian plantation that Defoe's readers would have understood could not be run without slave labor. In *Robinson Crusoe,* Defoe can hardly be described as opposed to slavery and, although he is prepared to allow Crusoe to lament his condition of captivity, the same luxury is granted neither to the African Xury or to the Carib Friday. Defoe, writing before the development of either a sustained campaign against slavery or a substantial literature for children, is not representative.

The later eighteenth century saw a pronounced shift in attitudes, both to slaves and children, which led to the formation of the abolition campaign at about the same time that authors and publishers started seriously to invest time and effort into children's literature. In many cases, the same people were involved. Authors such as William Roscoe, Anna Laetitia Barbauld, Hannah More, and Thomas Day all produced work for children at some point in their careers, and all wrote literature on an antislavery theme during the 1780s and 1790s. Of these, Thomas Day is the most significant. His poem *The Dying Negro,* jointly written with John Bicknell in 1773, is one of the first sustained literary critiques of slavery to appear.[15] When, ten years later, Day came to write his important children's novel *The History of Sandford and Merton,* it is not surprising that he should introduce slavery from the outset. When it appeared, in three installments between 1783 and 1789, *Sandford and Merton* was the most substantial children's novel then written. Although heavily indebted to Rousseau's *Émile,* Day claimed in his preface that the work was not "a treatise on education," that his main characters, two of whom were children, would "speak and behave according to the order of nature," and that the book was "intended to form and interest the minds of children; it is to them that I have written; it is from their applause alone I shall estimate my success."[16] This attention to the needs and interests of children was unusual in an age of heavy didacticism. Although children in later periods found the book preachy and humorless, the book must have proved a success with children of the eighteenth and early nineteenth centuries. It sold well and went through dozens of editions into the 1890s.

In effect, the book is a critique of slavery. It tells the story of Tommy Merton, the son of a rich slave-owner in Jamaica. Young Tommy has been grossly spoiled by wealth and the undue influence he has over the slaves who wait on him constantly. Sent to be educated, he is rescued from a poisonous snake by Harry Sandford, the stout and virtuous son of a "plain, honest farmer." The two become friends, and Tommy is introduced to Mr. Barlow, the local clergyman. Under his directions Tommy learns the virtue of patience, self-reliance, and respect for others, as well as how to read and write. The book is constructed as a series of instructive and entertaining tales, linked by this unifying narrative. Towards the end of the text, Tommy and Harry meet an unnamed "negro" who tells them the story of his past in Africa. After hearing this tale, Tommy, the slave-owner's son, "reflected, with shame and contempt, upon the ridiculous prejudices he had once entertained [and] he learned to consider all men as brethren and equals."[17] The novel, which is otherwise episodic, is thus clearly framed by an antislavery narrative in which Tommy's education indelibly transforms him from a self-absorbed slave-owner to a socially responsible abolitionist.

Day's egalitarian message may seem platitudinous now, but in 1789, the year of the French Revolution and the height of the British anti–slave trade campaign, it was both progressive and politically apposite. It also influenced several future generations of children's writers to believe that promoting the brotherhood of man and exposing the terrors of slavery was an important literary concern. For example, the novelist Maria Edgeworth (whose father, Richard, was a close friend of Thomas Day) included discussions of slavery in her writing for children. Her short piece "The Grateful Negro," which appeared in 1804 as part of her *Popular Tales,* tells the story of Caesar, a slave who, out of gratitude to a kind master, foils an insurrection. It is hard to determine if the narrative directly opposes slavery, but it clearly attacks those slave-owners who, like the story's Mr. Jefferies, "considered the negroes as an inferior species" and thus treated them "with the greatest severity."[18] In this context it belongs to the "ameliorationist" school of literature: a body of writing that urged better treatment for slaves without advocating emancipation. There are some parallels between this position and Hermione Granger's desire to promote elfish welfare without necessarily (in the title of her pressure group at least) advocating freedom for the elves. Moreover, Edgeworth's Caesar, with his refusal to betray his master, belongs at the head of a long line of literary slaves who display an apparent willingness to suffer the status quo rather than challenge the legal or supposed honor codes that maintained slavery. This line includes celebrated figures such as the eponymous Uncle Tom, but also Rowling's house-elf Winky. Winky's breakdown and drift into alcoholism (if butterbeer *is* alcoholic) are the outwards signs of the psychological difficulty she has adapting to her freedom. Her "mind forg'd manacles," and those of the other house-elves, are apparently the strongest barrier to Hermione's campaign.

Later in the nineteenth century, the topic of slavery was addressed by those writers who have become synonymous with the "dreams of adventure, deeds of empire" discussed by Martin Green in his book of that name. *Mr. Midshipman Easy*, Captain Frederick Marryat's sea novel of 1836, contains a striking portrait of Mesty, an African prince, sold into slavery in America, who stowed away to Britain after hearing "that there was no slavery in England."[19] More explicit in its antislavery message is R. M. Ballantyne's *Black Ivory*, which appeared in 1873. Ballantyne, in a preface, argues that "the horrible traffic in human beings is in all respects as bad at the present time on the east coast of Africa as it ever was on the west coast in the days of Wilberforce." He hopes that his book will "interest the young ... in a most momentous cause,—the total abolition of the African slave trade."[20] Humanity is not the only object of the book: British imperial ambitions are by no means thwarted by the desire to "restrain the murderous hands of the Arabs and half-caste Portuguese who for ages have blighted [Africa] with their pestilential presence!"[21]

In the twentieth century, the immediacy of the slavery issue may seem to have receded, but the topic nonetheless appears with regularity. Even ignoring historical novels such as Richard Hughes's 1931 *A High Wind in Jamaica* (which, in any case, deals with the post-emancipation period), slaves, almost always African in origin, are still fixtures in much children's literature. In Enid Blyton's 1949 vacation novel *The Mountain of Adventure*, for instance, the children discover that a gang of criminals is holding captives including Sam, a black man and former paratrooper, who was recruited in "some office in Mexico" and "offered a terrific sum of money" to "try some new kind of parachute jumping."[22] The parachute experiments turn out to be lethal and Sam, like the rest, does not see the money, nor is he allowed to leave the mountain in which he is imprisoned. He cannot be dismissed, however, as a simple victim of criminal activity. His ethnicity and his exaggerated Creole English clearly associate him with plantation slavery. His dialogue—"I poor nigger, little missy" is a representative sample—reflects the Hollywood stereotype of its era and foreshadows the house-elf dialect.[23] The manner of his recapture—pursued cross-country by dogs—is reminiscent of the manner in which escaped plantation slaves were recovered, both in British colonial plantations and in the American South. By including Sam, Blyton adds an exotic element to her adventure story.

Further, by showing the children as his emancipators, she taps into—and actually furthers—the tradition in British children's literature of representing slavery as villainous and antislavery campaigners as heroic. This project, however—as demonstrated in this case—is proud to display its humanitarian credentials but is plainly unconnected with any antiracist project.

Unlike the worlds of these realist novels, the world of the Harry Potter books is a magical one, obeying different physical laws and inhabited by a flora and fauna often only superficially resembling our own. Slavery in this world does not happen to people, in the strict sense of "people" as members of the species *Homo sapiens*, but to magical creatures. For this reason, the books' relationship with the slavery tradition in children's literature may seem unclear. However, the house-elves also belong to a long tradition of enslaved or enchanted magical helpers that take a variety of more-or-less human forms. The house-elves' distant ancestors are the elves and fairies of northern European mythology, invariably (and proverbially) free spirits, whose magical powers were as likely to harm as aid any human beings who strayed into their realm. Increasingly, however, these free spirits were found in bondage. In *The Tempest* (1612) Shakespeare famously portrays the magical Ariel, ethereal "spirit of the isle," as a slave no less than the earthly, semi-magical Caliban. This identification was not lost on Charles and Anne Lamb, whose children's version of *The Tempest* (1807), which appeared in the same year as the abolition of the slave trade, concludes with Ariel's emancipation.[24]

During the eighteenth—but more particularly the nineteenth—century, creatures of actual or invented folklore were increasingly found in children's literature where they provided a range of services to humans. One of the most celebrated is L. Frank Baum's *The Wizard of Oz*, an American book that was popular in Britain, particularly after Victor Fleming's 1939 film. Slavery appears throughout the novel. The first words the Munchkins say to Dorothy are: "[W]e are so grateful to you for having killed the Wicked Witch of the East, and for setting our people free from bondage."[25] The Wicked Witch of the West also keeps slaves, the Winkies, who were enslaved for her by the Flying Monkeys, themselves "three times the slaves of the owner of the Golden Cap, whomsoever he may be."[26] Ownership of this magic garment passes from the witch to Dorothy, thus conferring on her the role of slave-owner, a responsibility she passes in turn to the good witch Glinda, who uses the third of her wishes to grant the monkeys their freedom. Otherwise, Dorothy is pleased to emancipate both the Munchkins and the Winkies, and the latter, seeking a new form of government, submit cheerfully to the benevolent monarchy of the Tin Woodman.[27] References to slavery and emancipation thus permeate *The Wizard of Oz*, but this, perhaps, is unsurprising in a work for children written by a man whose childhood coincided with the American Civil War.[28]

In the writing of E. Nesbit, an author whom Rowling has frequently mentioned as a childhood favorite, slavery appears in a number of places, both as a historical reality and as a feature of magical creatures who exist to serve.[29] The

Psammead, or sand fairy, in *Five Children and It* and other books in the series, exists only to grant wishes for humans. This talent ensured the survival of the human race in prehistoric times. Later, sand fairies became an article of trade, especially amongst the Babylonians.[30] Both conventional antislavery sentiment and Nesbit's more focused brand of socialism appear in the novels. Indiscriminate wishing almost delivers one of the children, Robert, into a form of slavery himself when, temporarily swollen to a giant size, he is close to becoming indentured by a freak-show proprietor.[31] In a later series of adventures, the same children, again helped by the Psammead, are transported to ancient Egypt where a misunderstanding with Pharaoh over a magic trick causes further exploitation of the nation's slaves and captivity for the children.[32] Nesbit's writing is by no means related to the staunchly abolitionist or the heavily didactic literature of the eighteenth and early nineteenth centuries, but slavery—and opposition to slavery—remains a constant, if minor, theme throughout.

The relationship between slavery and imaginary peoples continues in children's literature into the latter part of the twentieth century. In Roald Dahl's 1964 novel *Charlie and the Chocolate Factory*, the factory is staffed by a group of people who can be closely identified with plantation slaves. These Oompa-Loompas are "pygmies ... imported direct from Africa"; they work not for cash wages, but for cacao beans, and "love dancing and music." Their situation as chattel is immediately grasped by the spoiled child Veruca Salt who demands that her father buy her an Oompa-Loompa.[33] In a noted essay written in 1973, Eleanor Cameron argued that the Oompa-Loompas had never "been given the opportunity to protest the possibility of being used like squirrels," which had been trained in the novel to open nuts. She reproved "Willy Wonka's unfeeling attitude toward the Oompa-Loompas, their role as conveniences and devices to be used for Wonka's purposes, their being brought over from Africa for enforced servitude."[34] In response, Dahl revised the book and the African pygmies became, in the words of Dahl's biographer, "dwarfish hippies with long 'golden brown hair' and 'rosy-white skin.'"[35] However, although the new Oompa-Loompas were no longer black, they were still slaves. Dahl's seemingly pragmatic and accepting attitude to a form of slavery had brought the issue back to the point where it started in literature for children, in the writing of Daniel Defoe.

While one can readily observe that Rowling's treatment of the slavery issue is informed by more than two centuries of children's literature (to say nothing of treatment of the issue in adult literature and other media), it is clear that the Harry Potter books also approach the theme in a way that addresses the concerns of a modern readership. Of course, slavery exists in the modern world in a number of forms, but, despite the best efforts of organizations such as Anti-Slavery International, few British or American citizens, adult or otherwise, have a high level of awareness of the issue. At the same time, the history of slavery and abolition, which the English National Curriculum now suggests as a topic for eleven- to fourteen-year-old students, could not be said to form a major part of that curriculum or, indeed, a very frequent topic of conversation for children of that age group. However, the issues of race and culture are very much alive in British society, forming the subject of debate in all forums from the playground to Parliament. For many children, the relationship between race and slavery may not be clear, but it is a relationship they will inevitably learn about as they grow older. Moreover, Rowling's decision to place the slavery issue in such close proximity to other questions of race in the novels is one that allows children to develop their own understanding of the problem, to form connections and reach conclusions that may not be obvious on a first reading. One such conclusion that may be reached is that, in the magical world, the possible enslavement of one species of magical creature by another implies that witches and wizards—humans—have imposed a systematic hierarchy with themselves at the top. Another conclusion that might be drawn, as the historical and literary tradition of slavery and abolition becomes clearer to young readers, is that people in the real world are just as capable of such enormities.

The relationship between race and slavery in the novels cannot be seen as accidental. Readers discover that giants, one of many nonhuman sentient species, have become the subject of what Hermione bluntly describes as "bigotry." For instance, Rita Skeeter's assessments unsurprisingly focus on the inherently violent nature of giants, as well as their alleged support for Voldemort.[36] This bigotry has been institutionalized by the ever-present Ministry of Magic: in what amounts to a magical version of apartheid, we learn that a clause in the regulations governing the use of wands stipulates that *"no non-human creature is permitted to carry or use a wand."*[37] In other words, the privilege—and the power—of magic is confined to humans despite the very evident fact that sentience is more widely dispersed.

Despite this interspecies bigotry, we are given to believe that Hogwarts is a multicultural and ethnically diverse institution, reflecting modern British society, if only because the students' names are drawn from those of a number of different ethnic groups. Rowling casts racists, in the form of Muggle-hating Death Eaters, as her chief villains. And, despite the problematic exclusion of Muggles from the magical world (no nonmagical child—doomed in the real world to grow up in a dull West Midlands suburban town, such as Dudley Dursley—can ever aspire to grow into a witch or wizard), one of the central messages of the books is that discrimination, particularly racial discrimination of any sort, is a characteristic of evil.

In the meantime, in the midst of all the struggles for world domination, there are still the house-elves. By the end of *Goblet of Fire*, they are still held in bondage—and still, as we have seen, seemingly glad to be in that condition. It is plain that their story will be expanded in future installments of the series, and this narrative expansion may well include a resolution. At the end of the fourth Harry Potter book, however, Rowling has clearly established that the house-elves are enslaved in a world that makes judgments on the basis of race. These clues, and the proximity of the slavery and race issues in the books, provide an approach to the problems of bigotry and discrimination that allows young people to grasp a truth on first reading and later learn how that truth has been applied or abused in the historical world. Once this has been understood, and the fact that racism, intolerance, and even slavery are part of the modern world has been understood as well, young people are implicitly invited to follow Hermione's lead, unpopular though it might initially seem to be, and take political action against prejudice. In bringing together the two main types of slavery to be found in children's novels, the realistic and the magical, Rowling's achievement has been to translate abolitionist sentiment into the magical world. In this context, it is plain that her novels grow from a long tradition, recast for a new generation.

NOTES

1. J.K. Rowling, *Harry Potter and the Chamber of Secrets* (London: Bloomsbury, 1998), 15.

2. Children, perhaps, are more likely to think of the character of Yoda in George Lucas's *Star Wars* films.

3. J.K. Rowling, *Harry Potter and the Goblet of Fire* (London: Bloomsbury, 2000), 330–31.

4. William Blake, "London," in *Songs of Innocence and Experience* (London: 1794).

5. Rowling, *Chamber of Secrets*, 16.

6. J.K. Rowling, *Harry Potter and the Philosopher's Stone* (London: Bloomsbury, 1997), 20 [published in the United States as *Harry Potter and the Sorcerer's Stone* (New York: Scholastic Press, 1997)].

7. Rowling, *Chamber of Secrets*, 248–49. The name of the chapter is "Dobby's Reward."

8. Rowling, *Goblet of Fire*, 112. Rowling's emphasis.

9. Ibid., 233.

10. Ibid., 327.

11. Ibid., 630–32.

12. For recent and useful studies of British slavery, slave trade, and abolition, see, respectively: Robin Blackburn, *The Making of New World Slavery: From the Baroque to the Modern, 1492–1800* (London: Verso, 1997); Hugh Thomas, *The Slave Trade: The History of the Atlantic Slave Trade 1440–1870* (London: Picador, 1997), and Robin Blackburn, *The Overthrow of Colonial Slavery 1776–1848* (London: Verso, 1988).

13. W.E.H. Lecky, *History of European Morals from Augustus to Charlemagne*, 2 vols. (London: Longmans, Green, & Co., 1869), I, 169.

14. The relationship between children's literature and empire is explored in Martin B. Green, *Dreams of Adventure, Deeds of Empire* (New York: Basic Books, 1979) and M. Daphne Kutzer, *Empire's Children: Empire and Imperialism in Classic British Children's Books* (New York and London: Garland Publishing, 2000). See also Giselle Liza Anatol's chapter on neocolonialism in this volume.

15. Thomas Day and John Bicknell, *The Dying Negro, A Poetical Epistle, Supposed to be written by a Black (Who lately shot himself on board a vessel in the river Thames;) to his intended Wife* (London: W. Flexney, 1773).

16. Thomas Day, *The History of Sandford and Merton, A Work Intended for the Use of Children*, 6th ed., 3 vols., (London: John Stockdale, 1791), I, iii–x.

17. Ibid., III, 297.

18. Maria Edgeworth, "The Grateful Negro" in *Popular Tales*, 3 vols. (London: J. Johnson, 1804), III, 191–240, 193.

19. Captain Frederick Marryat, *Mr. Midshipman Easy*, 3 vols. (London: Sanders and Otley, 1836), I, 128.

20. R. M. Ballantyne, *Black Ivory: A Tale of Adventure among the Slavers of East Africa* (London: James Nisbet and Co., 1873), iv.

21. Ibid., 177.

22. Enid Blyton, *The Mountain of Adventure* (London: Macmillan, 1949), 185.

23. Ibid., 136.

24. Charles and Anne Lamb, *Tales from Shakespear.* [*sic*] *Designed for the use of Young Persons*, 2 vols. (London: Thomas Hodgkins, 1807), I, 20.

25. L. Frank Baum, *The Annotated Wizard of Oz: Centennial Edition*, Michael Patrick Hearn, ed. (London and New York: W. W. Norton, 2000), 36.

26. Ibid., 251.

27. Ibid., 236 and 349.

28. Although remote from that particular conflict, Rowling seems to have had *The Wizard of Oz* and the Winkies in mind while writing *Goblet of Fire*. Winky is, of course, the name of Barty Crouch's house-elf, an allusion which is surely deliberate.

29. For example, see the interviews with Rowling on her U.S. publisher's website: "Harry Potter: Meet J. K. Rowling," http://www.scholastic.com/harrypotter/author/index.htm (accessed 14 August 2001).

30. E. Nesbit, *Five Children and It* (London: T. Fisher Unwin, 1902), 18.

31. Ibid., 223.

32. When finally freed, Cyril (denied the benefits of a Hogwarts education) laments the limitations of his knowledge and wishes that "people would teach you magic at school like they do sums—or instead of." E. Nesbit, *The Story of the Amulet* (London: T. Fisher Unwin, 1906), 294.

33. Roald Dahl, *Charlie and the Chocolate Factory* (London: George Allen and Unwin, 1967), 61–62.

34. The article, "McLuhan, Youth, and Literature," along with Dahl's reply and Cameron's reply to Dahl, are reprinted in Paul Heins, ed., *Crosscurrents of Criticism: "Horn Book" Essays, 1968–1977* (Boston: The Horn Book, 1977), 97–125.

35. Jeremy Treglown, *Roald Dahl: A Biography* (London and Boston: Faber and Faber, 1994), 188.

36. *Goblet of Fire*, 377, 381.

37. Ibid., 119, Rowling's emphasis.

9

Flying Cars, Floo Powder, and Flaming Torches: The Hi-Tech, Low-Tech World of Wizardry

Margaret J. Oakes

When considering the limits and dangers of human technology, many people think of HAL, the sentient computer of *2001: A Space Odyssey*, which—or perhaps I should say who—was a creation of electronic technology, but tried to cross over into the realm of human consciousness and decision-making. Like a digital Mr. Spock, HAL attempted to assimilate contradictory ways of making decisions and taking actions. However, HAL became confused; the technology was not capable of understanding the variability and irrationality of human thought processes. The hi-tech, orderly processing of information in electronic form ran afoul of the low-tech changeability that characterizes biological life.

In a similar fashion, the digital logic of our Muggle world, with its PDAs, DVDs, JPEGs, and RAM, seems incompatible in many ways with the idiosyncratic, particularized wizarding world of J.K. Rowling's Harry Potter series. Even before Ben Franklin went out in the rain with his kite, human control over natural forces had been the key to our ability to function more quickly, efficiently, and safely, but also with greater consequences for our existence. Since Franklin's discovery, uses of electricity, petroleum, and solar and nuclear energy have blown the roof off of the human limitations we assumed just a decade ago. From space exploration by robot, satellite navigation systems for airplanes, and dialysis machines, to baby monitors and in-home theaters, every aspect of human life has been touched—and usually improved—by technological advances. While we cannot yet "apparate" instantly from one location to another or communicate with seemingly alien creatures with batlike ears wearing pillowcases,[1] we do have black wands that instantly change images on a screen, humming boxes that cook food in seconds, and palm-sized devices that transmit volumes of information literally to our fingertips.

The parallel universe of the wizarding world, on the other hand, is a sort of Looking-Glass Land; similar, but not-so-similar, partner to our electronically advanced society: it is a contradictory combination of advancements worthy of the most far-reaching science fiction, and an everyday life so antiquated as to be almost medieval. Wizards can become invisible, change into animals, create light at their fingertips, and mend broken—or, in Harry's case in book II, inadvertently removed—bones within hours. However, they also still light torches, draw bed curtains to avoid nighttime chills in their drafty, ancient castles, and communicate largely by handwritten letters, composed with quill and ink and delivered by trained birds.

It is obvious that if we compare Muggle and wizard technological development, our two worlds parallel each other exactly, up to a point. This idea is one that has long preceded Harry Potter. Citing Lynn Thorndike's eight-volume work of the early part of this century, *A History of Magic and Experimental Science*, Alan Jacobs asserts that "both magic and experimental science are means of controlling and directing our natural environment."[2] C. S. Lewis, an author who clearly thought a great deal about the relationship between our world and others, noted that the parallel objectives of magic and science were even acknowledged by their practitioners:

For magic and applied science alike the problem is how to subdue reality to the wishes of men: the solution is a technique. ... [Sir Francis Bacon, the first experimental scientist,] rejects magic because it does not work, but his goal is that of the magician.[3]

I unfortunately do not have access to reference works on wizarding history such as *A History of Magic* by Bathilda Bagshot (mentioned by Rowling in her recent release of one of Harry's school reference works, *Fantastic Beasts and Where to Find Them*), a lack which prohibits me from pinpointing the exact historical moment at which our worlds parted ways. However, it is clear that our two existences share some essential abilities and limitations, partly due to our common habitation of this globe with its particular gravity, atmosphere, and biological evolutionary processes. For the most part, we look alike; our bodies behave in similar ways and have comparable needs for sustenance and upkeep. We share some technological achievements such as the wheel, optics, and basic engineering principles. With the added ability to control their world through magic, however, Rowling's wizards have opted out of advancing through science. Their powers over natural forces outstrip ours in many areas, yet they have chosen in others to retain the old ways, which require time and effort and which inflict a fair degree of discomfort or ineffectiveness. The question remains: why do they prefer this combination of the antiquated and the advanced?

We may best be able to explore this issue by shifting our attention back to our own Muggle world. The answer may lay in the price that we pay for our technological advances. In the twenty-first century, keeping up with rapidly advancing technology is a major factor in being able to function in an ordinary, nonmagical society. Rowling critiques this idea in one way by stressing the stupidity of the detestable Dursleys, Harry's adoptive family, in their desire to keep up, because they only do it for the sake of appearances. For cousin Dudley's birthday, Uncle Vernon and Aunt Petunia give him the latest computer and a racing bicycle, even though he does not need a new computer and he is too enormously fat to ride the bike. They have replaced their traditional fireplace with an electric one, but not in order to save the time and physical effort of messing about with heavy logs and messy ashes: the Dursleys' renovation seems tied simply to their ability to buy the most fashionable model.[4] But the Muggle desire for technological toys as proof of material gain is not the most important difference between Muggle technology and wizarding magic. A more fundamental distinction between our worlds is in the quite different capabilities of Muggles and wizards to first master, and then to manage, the knowledge required to make the technology or the magic work. Alan Jacobs writes that, in Rowling's world, magic "works as reliably in the hands of a trained wizard, as the technology that makes airplanes fly and refrigerators chill the air—those products of applied science being, by the way, sufficiently inscrutable to the people who use them that they might as well be the products of wizardry."[5] In the Muggle world, whether we are talking about electronic technology, nuclear reactors, solar energy, or combustion engines, our lives are controlled by machinery magically complex to many users: the vast majority of us do not understand how it works and only know the most superficial of its operations.

An unfortunate by-product of burgeoning technology of any kind—and in this sense "technology" can include magic—is an increasing level of knowledge required to understand it, coupled with a decreased level of knowledge required to use it. In other words, as our technology becomes more "user-friendly," the knowledge gap increases exponentially. The WYSIWYG (What You See Is What You Get) approach to designing objects, which simplifies the use of items such as electronic devices, cars, air conditioning systems, and food processors, often eliminates the need for any greater skill or talent than touching a button. I consider myself an experienced and proficient cook, but I cannot perform many manual food preparation tasks because I have devices that have eliminated the need for me to master them. During South Carolina summers, if the worst should happen and my air conditioning break down, I could not remember from my childhood all of my mother and grandmother's tricks with opened windows, strategically drawn curtains, and carefully placed fans to keep the interior of the house cool. We have all experienced the feeling of helplessness when the computers go down as we approach the checkout line of the grocery store, or when mysterious lights start flashing randomly on our car dashboards. Advanced technology can, paradoxically, make us inept, unprepared, or, at worst, stupid.

A consequence to this problem of replacing information with technology is the fact that since we do not know how machines work, our dependence upon

them is doubly dangerous. I cannot run outside and fix that broken air condi-
tioner, and I am forced to take my car to a mechanic who explains the flashing
lights to me in words that mean nothing to me. This is not to say that we might
not be able to learn how the contraptions of our automated lives work, but the
reality is that no twenty-first century human being has the intellectual capacity or the time to learn enough about all the devices we use to be able to operate, manage, or repair them without experts.

That is, no twenty-first century Muggle human being. Wizards, trained for
seven years in the magical arts at Hogwarts, Durmstrang, Beauxbatons, or the
other wizarding schools apparently dotting the globe, have taken a different
approach to harnessing nature for their own purposes. Jacobs has noted that
any trained wizard can personally manage magic much more complex than our
most advanced technology. Where we have created devices external to our beings that accomplish tasks for us, witches and wizards learn to control certain
forces with their own minds and talent, and thus accomplish similar tasks. We
flip a switch on a flashlight; illumination springs from a wizard's wand at the
sound of "Lumos!" We turn a key in a car; they throw green powder into a fireplace and shout out their destination (a much faster but somewhat less comfortable mode of transportation). We mend damaged bodies with new organs,
but at this point in our medical technology we still largely have to borrow them
from existing bodies, and we have little to aid the deeply comatose; Rowling's
characters can renew body parts and even bring petrified people (and a cat) back
to life with the application of the proper combination of botanical and animal
substances.[6] All of these wizarding achievements, as well as the lesser ones
learned by Harry and his Hogwarts schoolmates and the greater ones taken on
by Harry to fight Lord Voldemort and his forces, involve individual talent sup-
plemented or sharpened by training. Any average witch or wizard has powers
within his or her own knowledge and control that outstrip those of even the
cleverest, most McGyver-like Muggle, without relying on electricity, nuclear
power, digital technology, or even a pocket lighter.

We may assume that the potential scope of a wizard's magical abilities would
bestow unlimited and universal powers, but Rowling has not resorted to that
easy way out. For instance, witches and wizards apparently choose not to exercise complete magical control over their environments. After a big meal Molly
Weasley waves her wand at the dirty dishes, but instead of becoming instantly
clean, they quietly begin to wash themselves in the sink.[7] The Hogwarts faculty
members do not quell the icy storm that drenches the arriving students and
frightens the first years in book III.[8] Some wizards are wealthier than others
(the rich and haughty Malfoys versus the poor but good-hearted Weasleys, for
example), and they seem to choose not to create gold out of thin air, despite the
occasional creation of a Philosopher's Stone. The Malfoys are "old money,"
complete with a large family estate, but Rowling does not allow her wizards the
Faustian luxury of conjuring up lottery-scale riches; Arthur Weasley works for
wages at the Ministry of Magic to support his large family. The handling of

their wealth is not what we might expect either. One of Harry's first exposures to the magical world in book I is his visit with Hagrid to Gringotts Bank, a rather Dickensian looking establishment staffed by goblins so nasty they even intimidate Hagrid. While we might expect wizards merely to render their money invisible for safekeeping, or enchant it to electrocute anyone trying to steal it, these notions are passed over in favor of an institutional setting organized vaguely along the lines of Muggle banks, but with special features: Gringotts sits above enchanted passages hundreds of miles beneath London, reached by a goblin driving a sort of miner's cart, with dragons guarding the most precious vaults.[9] Thus, magic provides abilities that can vastly outstrip our Muggle ones, but Rowling's characters—at least the majority who practice "white" or good magic—have defined distinct limits that they wish to place upon their powers.

Furthermore, there seem to be some absolute limitations on the magical control that witches and wizards can exert. Magical creatures must be handled with care, as they cannot necessarily be controlled with spells or charms, and Hogwarts students must read and study actual books on magic rather than snap their fingers to transmit information into their heads. Even the Dark Lord Voldemort, with his immense powers, is physically dependent upon other beings after he is almost mortally injured during his various encounters with Harry and requires years of healing to be able to operate again.[10] All of these examples indicate that there is a discernable, consciously created structure to the practice of magic in Harry Potter's world. Alan Jacobs notes that for writers such as J. R. R. Tolkien and J. K. Rowling, "the sine qua non of such mythopoeia [the creation of other worlds in fiction] is the making of a world that resembles ours but is not ours, a world that possesses internal logic and self-consistency to the same degree that ours does—but not the same logic: it must have its own rules, rules that are peculiar to it and that generate consequences also peculiar to it."[11] These contradictions and limitations as well as others peculiar to Rowling's world raise the question: what sort of rules seem to apply in the development of "technology" in her mythopoeic world?

While Rowling is free to exercise the authorial prerogative of making and breaking her own rules in the world she creates, a logic of the metastructure of magic can be identified in the series. That magic is sufficient for their needs seems to be one rule which controls the use of magic for her wizards. Magic makes things easier, but it does not go beyond what is necessary into the frivolous. Their "technology" appears to have stopped at the point of development where ample control is achieved. Thus, wizards light torches, which are a perfectly adequate (and aesthetically pleasing) source of light, and quite reliable if one has no fear of the fire getting out of control. The best example of magic that stops at a sufficient level of use, however, is Rowling's elegant and versatile system of communication technology—owls. The list of supplies for Hogwarts permits each of the entering students to bring an owl to school. Whether students keep their own owls or borrow them from the school owlery, the birds are the major means of communication for all wizards. Operating under simple oral instructions from their owners, owls carry letters and packages back and forth between wizards, anytime, anywhere. Period. It is not a procedure as sophisticated or instantaneous as e-mail, but those of us who have had e-mails returned with mysterious error messages, received e-mails without necessary attachments, or found out that the time elapsed between messages sent and received was days rather than seconds, may yearn for the simplicity and directness of which Harry can be assured when he says, "Hedwig, take this to Hagrid." For that matter, anyone who has had a package vanish without a trace somewhere in transit or has been suspended in the limbo of "hold" on the telephone may wish for the face-to-face nature of this form of communication. Even if it is human-to-owl face, it still provides witches and wizards with the links to living beings of which we are often deprived in our existence overflowing with e-mail, pager, and voicemail messages that we leave and retrieve without ever actually engaging in direct conversation.

A rule related to the sufficiency of magical control is the fact that magic is practical. I mentioned earlier that Molly Weasley uses magic to wash her dishes; in contrast, the dishes at the huge banquets for students and staff at Hogwarts are made instantly clean,[12] a more logical approach in terms of the quantity of work and time involved. Further, Rowling does not adopt the stereotype that witches and wizards commonly travel by broomstick. Similar to bicycles in our culture, they are used more for recreation and sport, as the practicality of travel by both of these methods is severely restricted because of their potentially unpleasant exposure to the elements and unwieldiness for large group travel. The solutions here fit the situations: Floo powder, the fireplace-to-fireplace mode, is quick, direct, and well suited to family groups; the Knight Bus provides emergency travel for wizards; and the Hogwarts Express seems to operate just like an ordinary Muggle train, aside from the fact that it has a platform invisible to most of the travelers at London's King's Cross station. This last point indicates another practical advantage of these modes of transportation: they are not detectable by Muggles, thus avoiding the necessity of applying "memory" charms to those baffled nonmagical humans who would obviously be able to see people flitting about on broomsticks.

The practicality of magic is also indicated by the points at which it resembles, but improves upon, Muggle technology. Gringotts Bank, with its goblins and dragons, provides completely adequate protection for its customers' wealth without requiring security cameras or advanced identification systems. And, while I assume that dragons need to be fed occasionally, the safety of the bank's vaults does not depend upon electricity that could fail, security codes that could be broken, or even locks that could be picked. An even closer resemblance is in wizard photographs: they look like ours, and it is implied that a similar sort of device is used to take them. But the subjects of wizard photographs also seem actually to be in the photographs, existing in some form simultaneously with their real existence outside the photograph. While witches and wizards cannot speak from photographs, they can acknowledge that they are being looked at by communicating by winks and waves with their viewers, and they seem to have some life outside the frame of the photograph (e.g., some of the numerous photographs of Professor Gilderoy Lockhart apparently go somewhere to curl their hair when they think no one will be viewing them, and they run from the frames when they are caught sleeping in hairnets).[13] This makes wizard photographs a sort of cross between Muggle still photos and videotape, giving movement and personality to wizard vacation photos and collectible cards. We may raise the questions "why don't they make them talk—use them for communication—televideoing?"—but these are not the appropriate questions here. The photographs serve their own purpose, communication being already addressed neatly and efficiently in another fashion. Magic does not repeat itself unnecessarily.

Magic is also respected for its complex nature, and wizards are not allowed to cast spells willy-nilly to any purpose. Magic must be formally taught: students spend seven academic years in boarding school and are taught increasingly sophisticated levels and kinds of magic beginning with simple levitation spells and wand-lighting charms. Untrained witches and wizards are restricted in the exercise of their powers: Hogwarts students are not allowed to practice magic during the summer vacation, and "apparition," the ability to disappear from one place and reappear somewhere else, is only permitted after testing and licensing, similar to a Muggle driver's license. Upper-level Hogwarts students such as Percy Weasley, Ron's older brother, may have such permission, but it is not easy to achieve—the puckish Weasley twins, Fred and George, take great delight in reminding everyone that even their brilliant brother Charlie, who studies dragons in Romania, had to take the test twice.[14] As with nonmagical human technology, greater power is only achieved through more in-depth instruction and the mastery of more difficult skills.

The flip side of managing these powerful forces is the possibility that they will be used for harmful ends. Rowling fully acknowledges the dark side of magic and places clear controls on its misuse. The fact that students are taught "Defense Against the Dark Arts" from the outset of their Hogwarts education and the efforts of the Ministry of Magic to detect and stamp out the exercise of dark magic testify to a degree of anxiety over the abuse of magic for malicious purposes. Although some of these rules can be broken, most of the wizarding world has agreed on certain appropriate and inappropriate uses for particular spells and for magic in general. Throughout the books, Lord Voldemort misuses his powers in several ways: as far as we can tell after four books, he wants to gain control over much of the wizarding world, but also is obsessed with obliterating, in Holocaust fashion, all of those wizards with wholly or partially Muggle backgrounds (including Hermione Granger, of completely Muggle birth, and Harry, whose grandparents on one side were Muggle). It is even intimated that Voldemort desires to destroy harmless Muggles.[15] Certainly the near-torture of the defenseless Muggle family in book IV who have been diligently (and unknowingly) assisting the wizard campers at the Quidditch World Cup finals is among the most frightening scenes in any of the books (at least to us Muggle readers).[16]

These examples of the complexity and potential abuse of magic bring us back to the question about the combination of the old and new in the lives of Rowling's wizards and raise another about the ways that people in both worlds manage their progress over controlling their environments, whether that progress be scientific or magical. We know that dealing with the fruits of our technology—not just supercomputers or hi-tech military weapons, but also the devices that affect our everyday lives—will increasingly depend on a limited number of people who can develop, use, and maintain them. Greater and greater levels of advanced education are required just to keep up, whether on a minimal level of knowing how to operate household machines, or on a higher level of designing objects that are capable of more and more humanlike (or superhuman) tasks. It is true that in our world, as in the magical world, some people are smarter than others: some of us are naturally more gifted with talents for understanding and creating advanced technology; some of them are more skilled witches and wizards. But, as I have noted, very few of us have mastery over a great deal of technology, whereas any normally-schooled witch or wizard—inducted into training at the age of eleven and carrying on for seven years—has a control over natural forces with which it would take a whole fleet of Muggle scientists with years of advanced postgraduate education and experience to compete.

Part of this difference is caused by the fact that witches and wizards have an inherent competency for most magic—nature, rather than nurture, gives one the ability to use the "technology" once taught. Thus, witches may be born into Muggle families, but Muggles cannot be trained to be witches. If a child of wizards is not a Squib—one born sans magical ability, as is the case with Argus Filch, the Hogwarts caretaker—his or her magic is biologically given knowledge. It compares with the "knowledge" that ordinary humans have of the mechanisms of breathing and blinking, rather than the information and skills wholly attained from schooling. The purpose of wizarding school is to hone and train those natural capabilities, but it cannot create magical abilities that are not there. This education does not resemble our extensive, lifelong training in the use of technological devices, whether formally in a computer class or informally in reading our microwave oven manuals. Wizarding education is necessary to learn how to manage correctly abilities that will inevitably be manifested in the individual. Even Neville Longbottom, the most maladroit wizard in Harry's class at Hogwarts, has the capacity to use his magical skills; Neville's problem is in the degree of control he has over himself and his abilities, not his lack of knowledge of a device outside of himself. Harry can recall times even before he was notified of his birthright in which he had unknowingly used magical powers, especially when he was put in an uncomfortable situation. Once a cast-off sweater of Dudley's inexplicably shrinks so Harry cannot wear it; Harry ends up safely perched atop one of the chimneys of the school kitchen after being chased by Dudley's gang.[17] These consequences were a product of Harry's own desires and abilities, even if he did not know it at the time. Thus, even a below-average or uneducated witch or wizard is capable of magical achievements that are still out of reach of the most highly educated and technologically advanced Muggle individual.

This sense of biological connection that witches and wizards have with their talent significantly humanizes the process of engaging in magic in lieu of technology. Especially in first world countries highly developed in and dependent upon technology, people can spend disproportionate amounts of time with computers, vehicles, or whatever machines they use, and begin to think of this equipment as having a consciousness to which they can relate. Familiarity can breed a sense that we are interacting with objects of technology: we converse with them, learn the idiosyncrasies of their workings, curse them for perversely inexplicable actions, and cherish or disdain them according to their cooperation with our needs. In some measure, we may try to inject life into them. However, in the magical world, functioning life is almost always present in the objects of magic. The characters in the Harry Potter series exhibit a constant awareness that they are working with living things. This notion of consciousness can take many forms. The Mirror of Erised in book I can penetrate the mind of its on-looker and reflect deep desires of which the individual may only be vaguely aware.[18] The fat lady in the portrait that guards the entrance to Gryffindor Tower must be verbally addressed to enter the dormitory; furthermore, she can be frightened by an intruder and flee her picture frame, preventing the students from passing into the common room.[19] For amusement, Harry and Ron play "wizard chess," a game which is just like Muggle chess except for the minor fact that the pieces can talk and move, causing Harry great confusion because of the conflicting advice his chessmen keep hollering at him.[20] Hogwarts students receiving letters of reprimand from home do not have the privilege of dropping the missives into the nearest wastebasket and forgetting about them. In book II, a red envelope delivered by Ron's owl causes him great consternation. It is a "Howler," a dreaded scolding from his mother that cannot be ignored. Mrs. Weasley's voice booms out a hundredfold louder than usual, filling the Hogwarts Great Hall and finishing up with, "IT'S ENTIRELY YOUR FAULT AND IF YOU PUT ANOTHER TOE OUT OF LINE WE'LL BRING YOU STRAIGHT BACK HOME."[21] As if to emphasize Molly's anger at her son, the missive then bursts into flame. The envelope becomes an integral, participating part of the punishment rather than just a conveyance for information. It can even escalate the punishment by increasing the volume of the sender's voice the longer it is left unopened. Thus while Muggles may impose an imagined consciousness on some of the more advanced items in our world, the wizarding inhabitants must face real consciousness and volition in almost every ordinary object.

Of course, Muggles also work with living things that are sometimes unpredictable. We care for animals that want to do one thing when we want them to do something else, and we plant gardens that may bloom or not, depending on many factors. However, the students at Hogwarts quickly learn that plants and animals can possess an anthropomorphic sensibility that is absent in their Muggle world counterparts. In one of the funniest subplots in the series, Herbology teacher Professor Sprout is fairly tortured by the crop of mandrakes, a common antidote ingredient, which—or perhaps I should say "whom"—she is trying to raise. Looking remarkably like tiny, green babies with plants growing out of their heads, the mandrakes must literally be "raised" as if they are children. They demand much attention when very young, screaming and squirming when handled, and they go through an adolescence which involves gloomy teenage angst and the throwing of wild parties; Professor Sprout reports proudly that "The moment their acne clears up, they'll be ready for repotting again."[22] The unsuccessful attempts of Harry's friend Dean Thomas to turn a pincushion into a hedgehog in their Transfiguration class leave Dean with a pincushion that curls up defensively if someone tries to stick a pin in it.[23] These examples tell us that both the animate creatures and inanimate objects that magical beings encounter can have a heightened sense of consciousness: almost any living thing or object can be considered something which must almost be treated as an equal, a partner, or an adversary in some way. When Harry encounters the Marauder's Map in book III, which shows not only the entire mazelike layout of Hogwarts but also the location, movements, and conversations of all its inhabitants, he recalls something Mr. Weasley had said to Ginny about Tom Riddle's diary in the previous book: "Never trust anything that can think for itself, if you can't see where it keeps its brain."[24] Arthur Weasley assumes something that Rowling emphasizes throughout the series—respect must be shown to every single thing, whether or not it is "living" in the way we traditionally define it. The implication here is that, unlike the periodic crash of my computer or the blinking "Check Engine" light in my car that appears just after it has been serviced, the unpredictable, unreliable nature of objects in the magical world is caused by the actions and reactions of consciousness, not by electronic signals taking the wrong path or loose nuts or bolts in an engine. Witches and wizards interact with natural life, while we interact with materials dependent on forces that are of nature but which have no volition, despite our inclinations to anthropomorphize them. I remarked earlier that the wizarding world seems much less advanced than ours in some ways, but these examples also show that both the naturally and the humanly created "beings" in it make it a more complex place than ours in its own fashion.

Perhaps the desire to give life to the devices with which we come into contact each day can tell us something about ourselves and also suggest an answer to the question of why Rowling's universe is portrayed as it is. Technology gives us increasing powers over information, time, and distance. But the price we pay is not just in terms of the financial costs of our ever more complex gadgets. It is also commonplace in this era of increasing technology that we lose a physical sense of community, the warmth of human personality, and the skills of direct communication. Commuters travel alone, sealed in their cars; more and more people telecommute from home; television provides us with all the entertainment we need without ever venturing out of our living rooms. This is true even with the advances that involve real time communication such as telephones, e-mail, and chat rooms. We can exchange masses of words, dizzying numbers of pictures, and exhausting amounts of information, but never be in the same room with another human being. In the world of Harry Potter, social contact with sentient beings is not decreased as magical powers increase, but is in fact a fundamental part of the operation of magic. Hi-tech rational thinking and low-tech attention paid to the needs and desires of those beings around them work together for wizards instead of being at odds with one another. C. S. Lewis once commented that "It is not the greatest of modern scientists who feel most sure that the object, stripped of its qualitative properties ... is wholly real."[25] Rowling always reminds us of the qualitative properties, and the potential for good use, of nearly every creature and thing that wizards encounter. The feisty mandrakes, for instance, can kill with their unearthly screams but are also vital ingredients in healing potions. Perhaps we can, with an awareness of the intricacy and potential power of the life around us that Rowling provides, understand HAL's desires to participate in human life. As HAL is being destroyed, he tries to explain his actions to the human user who dismantles him: "I am putting myself to the fullest possible use, which is all I can think that any conscious entity can ever hope to do."[26] Despite the disastrous consequences, his initial desire was the same as our own—to have an influence over his environment. Rowling's world is full of individuals whose effects on their surroundings are recognized and respected by wizards. Perhaps we may find our own use of technology enriched by maintaining a respect for the qualitative value of the creatures and things in our world, too.

NOTES

My great thanks to my colleagues Christopher Douglas and Melinda Menzer for reviewing this essay, and to my fourth-grader, Jack, for checking my accuracy with the texts.

1. J. K. Rowling, *Harry Potter and the Chamber of Secrets* (New York: Scholastic Inc., 1998), 12.

2. Alan Jacobs, "Harry Potter's Magic," *First Things: A Monthly Journal of Religion and Public Life* (January 2000): 35–38, 37.

3. C. S. Lewis, *The Abolition of Man* (New York: Macmillan Press, 1947), 48.

4. J. K. Rowling, *Harry Potter and the Sorcerer's Stone* (New York: Scholastic Inc., 1997), 19–20; J. K. Rowling, *Harry Potter and the Goblet of Fire* (New York: Scholastic Inc., 2000), 42–43.

5. Jacobs, "Potter's Magic," 36.

6. Rowling, *Chamber of Secrets*, 144, 285

7. Ibid., 34.

8. J. K. Rowling, *Harry Potter and the Prisoner of Azkaban* (New York: Scholastic Inc., 1999).

9. Rowling, *Sorcerer's Stone*, 64.

10. Rowling, *Sorcerer's Stone*, 293, and *Goblet of Fire*, 9, 654–57.

11. Jacobs, "Potter's Magic," 36.

12. Rowling, *Sorcerer's Stone*, 124.

13. Wizard paintings differ in their abilities, however. The fat lady who guards the Gryffindor tower, Lord Cadogan, and others who inhabit the paintings at Hogwarts can chat freely with their spectators, and can move about from picture to picture, visiting one another.

14. Rowling, *Goblet of Fire*, 67.

15. Ibid., 143.

16. Ibid., 120.

17. Rowling, *Sorcerer's Stone*, 32, 33.

18. Ibid., 213.

19. Rowling, *Prisoner of Azkaban*, 160–61.

20. Rowling, *Sorcerer's Stone*, 199.

21. Rowling, *Chamber of Secrets*, 88.

22. Ibid., 234.

23. Rowling, *Goblet of Fire*, 233.

24. Rowling, *Prisoner of Azkaban*, 194.

25. Lewis, *Abolition*, 44.

26. *2001: A Space Odyssey*, dir. Stanley Kubrick, perf., Kier Dullea, Gary Lockwood, Douglas Rain, MGM, 1968.

III

Morality and Social Values: Issues of Power

10

Cruel Heroes and Treacherous Texts: Educating the Reader in Moral Complexity and Critical Reading in J. K. Rowling's Harry Potter Books

Veronica L. Schanoes

In this essay, I will explore two sites of ambiguity that have informed the structure of J.K. Rowling's Harry Potter novels: the construction of good and evil, and the representation of written narratives. I suggest not only that these two areas are inextricably intertwined, but also that they present Rowling's reader with an intricate set of cues calling the reliability of her own written project into question. In other words, Rowling's articulation of a uniquely complex understanding of morality is both dependent on and integral to the duplicitous nature of writing in her books.

A key scene in the first novel, *Harry Potter and the Sorcerer's Stone,* embodies this relationship between the ambiguous status of good and evil and the untrustworthiness of written narratives. Harry, having made his way past the various protections set up by the Hogwarts faculty to guard the stone, finds that Lord Voldemort is being aided not by Professor Snape, as he had assumed based on Snape's cruel and hostile behavior, but by the inept Professor Quirrell. Upon Harry's discovery, Quirrell's laughter becomes "chill and sharp." He sneers: "So useful to have [Snape] swooping around like an overgrown bat. Next to him, who would suspect p-p-poor, st-stuttering P-Professor Quirrell?"[1] This climactic episode turns on an explicit recognition of the relationship between writing and morality. The moment is not only thrilling; it carries great implications for the reader's comprehension of the possibilities for virtue and depravity in the world of Harry Potter and for the narrator's reliability. Quirrell mocks Harry, and, by extension, Rowling mocks her reader for being taken in by a particularly sly combination of her own writing and her use of genre conventions. Using Quirrell's voice, the author underscores our dependence on her narration for our understanding of events at Hogwarts and revels in her ability to manipulate that dependence.

In order to do so, Rowling gives us the character of Severus Snape, who, despite saving Harry's life on the Quidditch field, is not a cranky curmudgeon with a heart of gold. Snape is an oily, petty, nasty, vindictive man with a heart of pure malice. He relentlessly mocks Harry, attacks the young wizard's dead father, cruelly insults Hermione, does his very best to get Harry expelled or at least suspended, constantly berates Neville Longbottom, and forces Ron to chop up Draco Malfoy's daisy roots. Snape and Harry's father were enemies from youth. He does indeed "[swoop] around like an overgrown bat" with the dark looks of a gothic villain.[2] By all conventional narrative cues, Snape's nastiness should indicate that he is a villain of the deepest dye. But Snape is not evil. Snape is a good guy who protects Harry on several occasions and risks his own life in the fight against Voldemort.

In the described scene, then, Rowling forces her reader to distinguish between nastiness and wickedness, between subjective hatred and objective evil. She forces her reader to think beyond herself and her private identification with Harry to develop an awareness of the alliances necessary in order to do the right thing. This kind of distinction is one that few texts produced for adult consumption make; Shakespeare may remind us that a man may smile and smile and yet be a villain, but there is no corresponding line noting that a man may go out of his way to humiliate us and yet be a hero.[3]

The complexity of Snape's character both necessitates and relies upon Rowling's manipulation of written narrative. Snape is quite cruel, and Rowling uses his nastiness to cast suspicion on him time and time again. When Harry overhears Snape and Quirrell arguing in the Forbidden Forest, he, and the reader as well, assume that Snape must be on the side of evil, while Quirrell is assumed to be good *because he is opposing Snape*. As the story unfolds, Rowling reveals that Quirrell is indeed opposing Snape, but for exactly the opposite reason: Snape quite correctly suspects Quirrell of wrong-doing. Harry misinterprets the encounter because of his personal animosity toward Snape; he *misreads* the situation.

Rowling creates a similar opposition between Snape and Moody in the fourth book in the series, *Harry Potter and the Goblet of Fire*. Snape's obvious fear and avoidance of Mad-Eye Moody is one more reason for Harry and the reader to be well disposed toward the ex-Auror and to yet again suspect Snape of wrong-doing.[4] This observation comes directly after Moody has been firmly established as a positive character through the very narrative conventions that Snape subverts—he punishes Malfoy for unfairly attacking Harry by transforming him into a ferret—and in light of the resurgence of the Death Eaters. This passage thus reveals the same kind of narrative manipulation and unreliability described above. The opposition between Snape and Moody is accurate; the reading we are encouraged to make of it is not.

Even after book I, in which Snape is revealed to be loyal to Dumbledore and to have saved Harry's life *despite* their mutual hatred, the power of conventional narrative cues is so strong that he continues to be a figure of questionable morality for the children and possibly for the reader. In the third book, *Harry Potter and the Prisoner of Azkaban*, Rowling manipulates the plot to suggest that Snape's inherent nastiness might well drive him to evil actions: as the Potions master stares at Professor Lupin, "the expression twisting his ... face ... was beyond anger: it was loathing."[5]

Having established that Snape's hatred for Lupin is beyond even his formidable, normal standard, the narrator goes on some fifty pages later to intimate that this animosity might drive Snape to murder. Harry witnesses Snape bringing a potently smoking goblet to Lupin, who downs it with absolute trust. Rowling's narration makes us privy to Harry's visceral suspicions, making them our own.[6] In this passage, Harry's confusion of personal hatred with evil is so complete that even after Lupin explains the situation entirely accurately— he has been feeling "a bit off-color," and Snape's potion, which very few wizards are skilled enough to concoct, is "the only thing that helps"[7]—the protagonist still insists on Snape's evil: he agrees with those who imagine that Snape would try "anything" to procure the position of Defense Against the Dark Arts teacher.[8] These are just a few of many instances when Harry, and possibly the reader, misinterpret Snape's behavior because they confuse unpleasantness with depravity.

Harry continues to misread Snape's actions despite being proven wrong time and time again. Rowling encourages this same confusion on the part of her reader. The last line of chapter 18 in book III reveals that Snape has been hiding in a room, listening to Harry, Hermione, Ron, Professor Lupin, and Sirius Black. The very next chapter is entitled "The Servant of Lord Voldemort"[9] and its first four pages are devoted to a dramatic confrontation between Snape and the others. How can the reader resist suspecting Snape for a few minutes?

It is a testament to the strength of both Snape's nastiness and narrative convention that Rowling is able to provide the reader with a sporting chance to draw the distinction about evil so important to Snape's character without tipping her hand. As early as book I, Hermione argues for Snape's innocence: she admits that "he's not very nice" but asserts that he wouldn't betray Dumbledore.[10] By separating Snape's lack of "nice-ness" from his behavior in a larger conflict between good and evil, Hermione offers the reader the opportunity to do the same.

Ron easily brushes her off in book I before Quirrell is revealed to be the villain. In book IV, Hermione once again rises to Snape's defense. She reminds Ron, Harry, and the reader that even though they had suspected Snape before, his suspicious activity had in fact been a way of saving Harry's life. Harry, though, is not convinced: he recalls that even though Snape saved his life once, "Snape definitely loathed him. ... " Hermione calls on Dumbledore's authority to bolster her reading of Snape. She reminds us of the headmaster's perceptive understanding of character despite popular disapproval in the cases of Hagrid and Lupin, "'so why shouldn't he be right about Snape, even if Snape is a bit—' '—evil,' said Ron promptly."[11] This exchange pinpoints the matter exactly. Snape is not evil. But even while allowing Hermione to make an incisive distinction, Rowling, by presenting Harry's doubts about Snape via his thoughts about Snape's animosity, manipulates her reader into making Ron's mistake and equating Snape's nastiness with evil. Harry is ultimately more convincing than Hermione for a number of reasons that have nothing to do with any actual evil on Snape's part. Whereas Hermione speaks in direct dialogue, the reader is made privy to Harry's thoughts via free indirect discourse, a form of narration that entices us into equating Harry's thoughts with our own. This seduction is especially effective given the reader's (and Harry's) *desire* for Snape to be evil. Snape is the character we love to hate; if he were evil our ill-will would be not only justified, but righteous. If Snape were evil, the reader could count on revenge being visited upon him by the end of the series with the triumph of good. Rowling's construction of Hermione's character also undermines the smart girl's words; Hermione is routinely mocked for being a goody-goody, and Harry, Ron, and the reader may be tempted to write off her support of Snape as mere unwillingness to doubt hierarchy rather than accept her argument as evidence of moral sophistication. Hermione is correct, however. Snape seems to be second only to Professor McGonagall as Albus Dumbledore's right hand, and the headmaster's trust in Snape never once wavers. To understand why this should be, let us reconsider Snape's actions in light of all of the plot revelations through book IV, *Goblet of Fire.*

In book I, Snape saves Harry's life despite their mutual hatred and injures himself trying to stop Quirrell from aiding Voldemort. Snape does not play a very large role in Book II, *Harry Potter and the Chamber of Secrets,* but in book III, Snape's complexity of character becomes quite clear in retrospect. Snape works very hard to brew a potion ("particularly complex") in order to help a man for whom he holds a lifelong hatred and who currently occupies the position he wants. Snape's fateful appearance at the Shrieking Shack in the final chapters of book III occurs because Lupin forgets to take his Wolfsbane potion and Snape is bringing him his needed dose. And Snape really does seem to believe that he is again saving Harry's life by trying to capture Lupin and Sirius Black. Finally, in book IV, Snape and McGonagall aid Dumbledore in saving Harry's life, and Rowling implies that Snape may well be returning to his previous, extraordinarily dangerous role as a spy in Voldemort's circle. Whatever his assignment is, he is carrying it out despite being terrified.[12]

In book II, Dumbledore tells Harry that the essence of one's character is defined by what one chooses to do rather than by any inherent ability,[13] and in book IV, the headmaster chastises Cornelius Fudge for not realizing that how someone develops is far more important than what he or she is born as.[14] Harry, guided by his empathy and kind instincts, makes brave and good choices throughout the series. He has lost his family to Voldemort; it is natural for him to choose the side of good. But Snape is, at heart, mean-spirited. His schoolfriends all became Death Eaters, and presumably they are all dead, in Azkaban, or the Malfoys. His being on the side of the angels is a distinct choice, one that he consistently makes despite loathing his allies. By Dumbledore's standards, is he not an even greater hero than Harry? Snape's ambiguous moral status not only allows Rowling to emphasize the unreliability of the conventions of writing and her own narrative technique, as described earlier, but it also forces her readers to rethink their definitions of integrity and heroism.

Severus Snape is not the only character whose morally equivocal stance relates to the reliability of the written word. Sirius Black doubles for Snape in some interesting ways that highlight Black's own ambiguous position when it comes to ethics. Despite being revealed as a largely benevolent figure by the end of the book III, Black commits a number of truly callous and heinous acts that suggest that he has a capacity for ruthless cruelty similar to Snape's.

We are initially made aware of Sirius Black's presence at Hogwarts when the students find that the Fat Lady's home canvas has been viciously attacked and destroyed.[15] In a rage when denied access to Gryffindor Tower, Black has attacked the Fat Lady. His actions are frightening; whereas Snape can exercise enough self-control to help those he hates, Black assaults a minor nonhuman character out of sheer frustration. His destruction is not limited to portrait canvas, however. In his attempt to find and kill Peter Pettigrew/Scabbers the Rat, Black, in animal form, seizes Ron and drags him through the secret passage under the Whomping Willow. As Ron hooks one of his legs around the tree's roots to prevent his descent, the bone snaps and "a horrible crack cut the air like a gunshot."[16] After Lupin appears and is about to vouch for him, Black, now in human form, attempts to grab Scabbers once more and, in his fervor, falls upon Ron's broken leg, causing the young wizard to scream in pain. Black's later benevolence cannot erase these acts of violence committed against a thirteen-year-old boy. They do not represent the behavior of a conventional hero.

Black's ability to single-mindedly pursue Pettigrew at such costs is not morally pure, but it is in character. As Snape reminds Dumbledore, Black demonstrated he was capable of murder at the age of sixteen by playing an extremely dangerous prank on Snape.[17] While Harry, and the reader, may be inclined to dismiss this accusation because of Snape's unpleasantness (and indeed, one can sympathize with Black's youthful actions), the reckless way Black endangered Snape's life in the past coincides perfectly with his treatment of Ron. Black, while benevolent, nonetheless maintains a capacity for ruthlessness allying him with Snape. Perhaps he partially embodies in book III the kind of ruthlessness and cruelty he describes in book IV: certain wizards like Bartemius Crouch developed these traits to fight Voldemort.[18] Of course, in his transfigured state, Black is the worst possible omen of wizardly death: the Grim.

Both Black and Snape complicate a black and white moral schema. Where Snape forces the reader to accept a bad person who chooses the side of good, Black forces us to acknowledge the potential for violence and ruthlessness that can exist in a good person. Despite their mutual revulsion for each other, the two characters have more in common than either would like to admit. When Harry notices that Snape at the end of book III has developed a tic in his fingers as if "itching to place them around Harry's throat,"[19] the reader may well be reminded of Sirius Black during the fight in the Shrieking Shack: his free hand finds "Harry's throat. ... The fingers tightened, Harry choked. ... "[20]

Both Black's and Snape's moral complexity ties them to the written word. Black's escape from Azkaban is triggered by a newspaper story on the Weasleys' trip to Egypt—the same newspaper that promises to promulgate an unreliable version of the events in the final chapter of book III. By arranging the theft of Neville's list of passwords, Black emphasizes the potential of the written word for betrayal. He is one of the originators of one of the most marvelous and duplicitous written artifacts in the series: the Marauder's Map. Like Black, the map reflects a rather conflicted moral valiance. It is explicitly made for mischief.[21] The parchment functions as a vehicle for merriment rather than for actual evil in book III, allowing Harry to take unsupervised trips into Hogsmeade and producing text to insult Snape as he threatens to inflict punishments upon Harry. The map thus seems to enact a similar distinction between badness and evil as does the character of Snape: in the same way that the Potions master is nasty but not morally corrupt, the map is a tool of misbehavior and disobedience, but not of actual evil.[22]

However, just after the map becomes a *text*-based document, it becomes the basis for a very serious chastising of Harry. Lupin rescues Harry from Snape's unrighteous retribution and then confiscates the map, telling Harry that the mapmakers would have found it infinitely amusing to have lured him out of school. He forces Harry to take greater responsibility for the possible consequences of his actions, reminding the young wizard that his parents forfeited their lives to keep their son alive: "A poor way to repay them—gambling their sacrifice for ... magic tricks." As he walks away, Harry is left feeling "worse by far" than at any point in Snape's office.[23] Thus a deceptively innocent-seeming document becomes the catalyst for a very serious consideration of not only potential danger and evil, but also Harry's own choices.

Violence, cruelty, and thoughtlessness are not the only ways that a good character can be compromised. Ginny Weasley's loneliness and shyness cause her to turn to writing for comfort—writing that turns her into a vessel for evil at Hogwarts. Her solitude and literacy render her both vulnerable and dangerous. The same feelings that initially drive her to the diary also prevent her from confessing her suspicions of herself to Harry, Ron, and Hermione. Eventually she puts too much of herself into her self-created text, and this writing becomes a surrender of her identity and her life. Ginny wrote too much of her life; consequently, she is not able to go on living it. How does Ginny's situation complicate the structure of good and evil in the series? Her susceptibility to evil and unwilling complicity emphasize the potential of unimpeachably good and kind characters for evil—a moral ambiguity that enters the series through comforting but ultimately treacherous writing.[24]

My discussion thus far has focused on the vague moral status of Rowling's characters who all fall, more or less, on the side of good. Before moving on to discuss the author's representation of the written word in more depth, I would like to examine the character of one of the villains in the series, the fake Mad-Eye Moody. Just as Black's general benevolence does not prevent him from breaking Ron's leg and Snape's allegiance to the side of good does not mitigate his vileness, the false Moody's thoroughgoing evil does not erase his sympathetic actions.[25]

Moody's finest moment may well be the aforementioned transfiguration of Draco Malfoy into a bouncing ferret. No other teacher has been able to give Malfoy his comeuppance; this is the most viscerally satisfying scene in the entire series. It is Moody's first major interaction with students after his introduction at the feast, and it is the one whereby he duplicitously wins both Harry's and the reader's sympathies. The incident comes as the result of the first news publication by Rita Skeeter printed for us in the book. While Moody is not responsible for the article, Skeeter's treacherously slippery writing allows him to perform goodness. Malfoy picks a fight with Harry and Ron by "brandishing a copy" of the *Daily Prophet* and reading out loud the piece written by Skeeter in order to insult Ron's parents. After Harry rises to the defense of his best friend's family and then Malfoy attacks Harry while his back is turned, readers have the pleasure of seeing Moody publicly transfigure the repellant Malfoy into a ferret and bounce him from the floor to the ceiling. It is this passage which establishes the evil Moody as a trustworthy ally. Significantly, the way in which Skeeter's writing indirectly allows evil into Harry's world prefigures the way in which her texts will allow evil to gain a foothold in the larger wizarding world at the end of book IV.

While it may be a carefully calculated piece of theater, the triumph of seeing Malfoy as a bouncing ferret is not undermined by the ending of the book. Moody's act has an unforeseen positive consequence: Hagrid, usually at a loss for how to deal with Malfoy's constant challenges to his authority, finds inspiration in Moody: if Malfoy continues to misbehave, Hagrid threatens that he will "be takin' a leaf outta Professor Moody's book. ... I hear yeh made a good ferret. ... "[26] Hagrid is not typically associated with writing: even his textbook, *The Monster Book of Monsters,* is more a wild animal than a written text. His affinity with nature receives great emphasis and he never finished his schooling; for Hagrid to be positively associated with the written word is quite rare. Moody has helped Hagrid resist demoralization by Malfoy's jibes, and Hagrid acknowledges his inspiration with a pledge to take "a leaf outta Professor Moody's book." A notable reference to writing marks Hagrid's debt to an evil character.

Moody does more than vicariously allow us to give Malfoy what he deserves. He also performs a genuine kindness. Can his subsequently revealed evil nature undo the comfort he offers Neville Longbottom? After his meeting with Moody, Neville expresses a kind of self-confidence that Harry and the reader almost never hear from him.[27] Moody has taken the opportunity to present Neville with a book he hopes will bring Harry into Voldemort's clutches, again associating his treachery and its positive results as well as its evil with the written word. Furthermore, Moody provides Harry with help and support when he most needs it throughout book IV, in a way that no professor—with the possible exception of Lupin—has. Nonetheless, he is as treacherous as the scrap of paper with Harry's name inscribed upon it, the text with which he triggers the young wizard's participation in the Triwizard Tournament and his eventual transportation to the hands of Lord Voldemort. Moody's duplicitous moral status is reflected well by that piece of parchment. The paper with Harry's name on it allows the protagonist to achieve yet more fame and glory, but it also places him in mortal danger. Writing in Rowling's work often carries this double valiance, and therefore affects the reader's understanding of the author's own written project.

Certain passages regarding writing in the books seem to explicitly indicate a textual metaconsciousness, as they comment almost directly on the phenomenon that the Harry Potter series has become. The most prominent of these passages occurs in the first chapter of the first book, presumably before Rowling could have known the popularity her work was to enjoy. Professor McGonagall, contemplating Harry's future, predicts that the boy will become a legend: "[T]here will be books written about Harry—every [wizarding] child ... will know his name."[28] Dumbledore's response firmly highlights the *dangers* such fame pose to the boy's moral character. This danger is exemplified by books as well as by the term "legend," from Latin, meaning "that which must be read."

A similar passage occurs in book IV as Hermione encourages Harry to write to Sirius with information about the Triwizard Tournament. Hermione reminds Harry of his literary fame, saying "You're already in half the books about You-Know-Who," and convinces him that Sirius would far rather receive a personal communication than read about his godson in the newspaper.[29] Of course, Harry Potter *is* famous and he is in *every* book written thus far about Voldemort. Not only does Hermione, like Dumbledore, emphasize Harry's fame, but she also emphasizes the inadequacy of official written narratives, such as newspaper articles, to convey an accurate understanding of significant events. This inadequacy is emphasized throughout book IV. Hermione finds bias even in her most cherished resource, *Hogwarts, A History*.[30]

Rita Skeeter's newspaper articles are infinitely more notorious for their distortion of facts. In all cases, however, official narratives, despite a pretense of accuracy, objectivity, and coherence, are revealed to be made of unreliable, arguable assumptions and manipulative misinterpretations. In contrast, personal written communication, the dominant mode of communication over long distances in the wizarding world, maintains its integrity.[31] Rowling thus creates an opposition between health, happiness, and genuine emotion on the one hand, and official, widely read written narratives on the other. These passages of metaconsciousness openly force the reader to reflect upon the potential dangers and instability of the very text she holds in her hands.

The same is true for the ongoing ambivalent representation of writing and writers in the series, and thus, by implication, Rowling herself as a writer. The most consistent representation of reading and writing in the series is that of studying. The initial ridicule to which Hermione is subjected in the first book trails off in the second volume and is virtually absent by the fourth. While she is made to disparage the value of her intellectual skill at the end of book I,[32] the knowledge she gains from her work always plays a vital part in solving the problems presented in each book. Furthermore, Harry and his friends continually repair to the library to research a solution to their troubles. One of the many ways the narrator conveys scorn for the Dursleys is to note that in Dudley's second bedroom, books are the only unmangled things lying about; they look like they've never been touched.[33]

While studying itself is generally a positive activity, inordinate amounts of writing are cast as suspicious. One of the mysteries of book II is what Percy Weasley might be up to. In chapter 3, the boisterous George Weasley comments on his brother's behavior, noting that Percy has been behaving very strangely, as evidenced by excessive letter-writing.[34] This observation comes less than a page after the Weasleys' discussion of Lucius Malfoy's support for Voldemort. That context combines with George's tone to cast a very suspicious light on Percy. Percy's writerly activity brings on these misgivings. A similar pattern emerges in book IV regarding the Weasley twins themselves. Uncharacteristically private about their activities, Fred and George spend an unusual amount of time writing letters. Ron and Harry note their behavior a few times, and when they run into the twins in the Hogwarts Owlery sending a letter, their secretive manner and suggestive conversation provoke Ron to tell Harry that their recent obsession with money might lead them into serious trouble from which they might not be able to extricate themselves. Excessive writing becomes a reason for worried discussion about a possible turn for the worse in the twins' characters. Thus, while studying is generally portrayed as a positive activity, immoderate writing—extracurricular writing, perhaps—is worthy of immense distrust. While these passages may not have as great implications for the legitimacy of Rowling's writing as do some of the passages I examine below, they establish an interesting set of parameters.

The most direct confluence of evil and the written word occurs in book II. Ron warns Harry about the dangers posed by enchanted books. Books might "[burn] your eyes out." A book of poetry could force you to speak "in limericks for the rest of [your] life." Or you just might run across a book that you "could *never stop reading!*"[35] Ron's warnings can be read as Rowling's tongue-in-cheek response to accusations of the alleged dangers of her books. The language of a much-read book does indeed infiltrate the language of the reader, and the Potter novels are addictive for many; it is extraordinarily difficult to stop reading them when one first picks them up.

The passage also prefigures what we will later find has happened to Ginny. A source of evil, Tom Riddle's diary exerts power through its victim's writing and reading, and eventually takes over her life. The diary also invokes the potential of writing for betrayal. When Draco Malfoy grabs Riddle's diary, thinking it belongs to Harry, he threatens Harry while Ginny looks on, terrified.[36] Malfoy thinks that he is threatening to reveal Harry's secrets, but Ginny is fearful that Harry has already read her secrets, that her writing will betray her. Of course, it does, though not in the way Malfoy threatens.

The way the diary communicates to its readers/writers is quite suggestive of its treachery. As Harry writes a greeting onto the first page of the book, the words temporarily radiate on the page and then sink "without trace." Then, "[oozing from] the page, in his very own ink, came words Harry had never written."[37] The diary takes in Harry's writing and gives it back as its own, almost literally twisting his words. When communicating with Harry, the first thing to which Riddle's journal alludes is the instability of the written word, despite its reputation for permanence: "Lucky that I recorded my memories in some more lasting way than ink."[38] It does not, however, alert Harry to the perils of an unreliable narrator, and for good reason.

Tom Riddle takes Harry into his memory of events at Hogwarts fifty years previous—the last time the Chamber of Secrets was opened. The memory is about truth and secrets and it is accurate, but Riddle's "narration" suggests a false interpretation of the story. The diary sucks Harry into its world, and the protagonist accepts the narrator's position of objective authority without question, despite the example he has before him of Gilderoy Lockhart, whose books, tales, and published adventures were not his own. Like the naïve reader Harry plays in book I, when he and the reader allow themselves to be manipulated by personal animosity and narrative convention, Harry is bamboozled by an unreliable narrator due to his personal sympathies. Harry identifies strongly with Riddle's position as an orphan facing the prospect of going to a terrible home, so he automatically believes Riddle's version of events. The ease with which a seemingly clear narration of history can influence one's conclusions might well cause *Harry Potter* readers to pause and consider their own dependence on Rowling's lucid recital of particular details.

For just as Harry is preserved for us in the hundreds of pages we have so far, so is Riddle preserved in the pages of a diary.[39] Indeed, this protection is both the *purpose* of the enchanted diary—intentionally left behind, thus safeguarding Riddle's "sixteen-year-old self in its pages"[40]—and a classic aim of writing, to save the essence of oneself in a monument more lasting than bronze. As the diary steadily consumes Ginny and *becomes* Riddle, writing becomes a threatening entity all of its own, with its own motives, loyal only to itself.

Riddle's diary is not the only example of narcissistic, deceptive narration in book II. Gilderoy Lockhart, while not evil, is so arrogant and self-involved that he makes Snape look appealing. Lockhart is a hero in the wizarding world thanks to his self-aggrandizing series of texts, culminating in an autobiography entitled *Magical Me*. His relentless self-promotion causes Ron to doubt him early on. When Harry argues that Lockhart has no idea about how to go about Dark Arts defense, Hermione responds, "Rubbish. . . . You've read his books—look at all those amazing things he's done." Ron, in turn, mutters: "He *says* he's done,"[41] and turns out to be correct. Lockhart's character emphasizes the po-

tential for the written word to be manipulated for personal ends and the un-
earned trust passionate readers like Hermione often place in the text. Rowling
emphasizes Lockhart's good looks as a reason for Hermione's belief in him, but
the young witch is also the character most heavily invested in books and the
knowledge to be found in them. While Hermione, due to her intelligence and
clear-sightedness, can often accurately read the situations she and her friends
find themselves in—her incisive understanding of Snape's character, for example—she is without such insight within the world of *her* books. While books are
the source and medium of her intellectual strength, they also form the bedrock
of her knowledge, with the result that she has an extremely difficult time questioning the validity of the books themselves. It is partially her strict adherence
to the letters of the law and of instruction that cause her peers in the book to
mock her and mistrust her judgment. Lockhart, then, emerges as a figure who
creates confusion between the written word and the real world—confusion that
endangers the children's lives.

Harry and Ron finally confront Lockhart and force him to reveal his writing
as lies. He informs the boys and the reader that "[b]ooks can be misleading,"
and his would not have been at all successful "if people didn't think *I'd* done all
those things. No one wants to read about some ugly old Armenian warlock,
even if he did save a village. . . . He'd look dreadful on the front cover."[42] Lockhart's explanation that one cannot trust what one reads might point the alert
reader to the diary, the other prominent book in book II.

Rowling uses Lockhart to underscore the untrustworthiness of the written
word, just as the encounter with Quirrell described at the beginning of this
essay emphasizes the misleading possibilities of literary conventions. Rowling,
however, like Lockhart, is the writer of an immensely popular series. And
Harry, also like Lockhart, is a wizard with many books written about his gripping adventures. Through this egotistical figure, therefore, Rowling calls the legitimacy and trustworthiness of her own project into question. Like Lockhart's
readers, we have only the books to verify the "truth."

Rowling creates another character who does considerable damage to life at
Hogwarts by irresponsible manipulation of the written word: Rita Skeeter. As
discussed above, Moody's treacherous career as Harry's ally begins as the result
of a student scuffle brought on by Skeeter's article, but her writings have darker
consequences of their own as well. Skeeter's first piece about Harry causes him
great embarrassment as she manipulates his life story to suit her own ends.
When Skeeter's first article on him appears, Harry feels humiliated at the quo-
tations she has manufactured.[43] Skeeter's writing is established as manipulative
and untruthful, but for different ends than Lockhart's. Skeeter does not write
for personal gain or self-aggrandizement—although she might work to advance
in her career, her subject matter does not have anything to do with her own
achievements. Rather, she serves the needs of the writing itself. As Harry notes
in chapter 22 of book IV, Skeeter cannot continue to write about him as the
"tragic little hero," or she'll bore her readers.[44] Not loyal to any particular

person, Skeeter caters to popular writing in and of itself. Her desire to fulfill the agenda of the writing itself links her to Tom Riddle's diary. She becomes an agent of the writing, letting its needs dictate her actions, almost as if it were a being of its own.

As Harry notes, Skeeter's writing has its own agenda and makes its own demands that have little or nothing to do with reality, but her writings *create* a reality of their own. Her article is the excuse Cornelius Fudge needs to avoid believing in Voldemort's rise. Fudge refuses to trust Harry's account of Voldemort's reappearance. His suspicions of Harry are incomprehensible until Harry turns to him and charges him with reading Rita Skeeter.[45] The reporter's loyalty to the amoral (as opposed to evil) demands of writing may do as much harm as an openly evil writer; she allows Fudge to discount the testimony of a boy he had previously believed to be a hero. The *Daily Prophet* journalist thus creates a three-point moral scheme: good, evil, and writing. But while her writing seems to be outside both good and evil in the wizarding world, to answer only to its own needs, the objectivity and accuracy popularly attributed to it consistently open the door to evil. Not only does the publication of the first article in book IV allow Moody to perform goodness, as discussed earlier, but at the novel's end, her writings provide the excuse for the Minister of Magic to refuse to take action against Voldemort. Thus, the amorality of a writing loyal only to itself becomes a vehicle for evil.

Rowling's representation of writing and the writer is one that emphasizes the untrustworthiness of the written word and the power of writing to undermine belief in reality. But isn't Rita Skeeter's path exactly the one that Rowling, as a writer of fiction, must take? She must obey the demands of her narrative arcs, just as we are compelled to rely on her narration, perhaps made more alert by the education in narrative manipulation we have received over the course of the books. I began this essay with a consideration of the way Rowling uses the character of Snape to force her readers to understand the difference between subjective hatred and objective evil; I have gone on to demonstrate the ways Rowling uses representations of reading and writing to complicate and undermine any easy assumption of objectivity. However, I do not think that the author's work ultimately supports the abandonment of the idea of objectivity. Certain assignments remain unshakably stable: Lord Voldemort is bad, Albus Dumbledore is good, Professor McGonagall is good, and dementors are bad. The texts allow no room for debate on these judgments. Rowling explicitly disavows a completely relativist argument by placing it in the mouth of Professor Quirrell, who is ultimately destroyed by his alliance with evil. Quirrell claims he has learned from Voldemort that "There is no good and evil, . . . only power, and those too weak to seek it."[46] Rowling's writing explores the possible intersections, alliances, and complications between good and evil, but she is not interested in overturning the categories of good and evil themselves. The Harry Potter books thus provide their reader with an education in the importance of alert, questioning reading.

Rowling's books have come under attack from various groups whose insistence on particular standards of purity in thought, word, and deed make Hermione look like a rebel.[47] While an objection to the books' magical themes constitutes the bulk of such groups' outrage, they have also objected to the books' portrayal of resourceful children who disobey rules when they feel that circumstances demand it or in order to thoroughly enjoy themselves. Rowling does indeed present her readers with a world in which children must be astute, rebellious, and suspicious readers in order to survive and triumph. They must make alliances with truly despicable people and escape from others who initially seem to be friends. But most importantly, they must not rely complacently on the written word—magazine advertisements, comic strips, history books, diaries, or newspaper articles—especially when it purports to tell the truth. The benefits of reading in Rowling's wizarding world lie in the reader's ability to understand the machinations of text and author, to understand how writing works. Rowling's deceptively plain narration and direct plots contain an extensive education in careful reading; her work might even provide a gripping introduction to literary analysis.

Rowling complicates her reader's trust in her narrative project both by making the unreliability of written narrative an overt theme in her work and by enacting that unreliability in the nuanced moral profiles of her characters, which undermine conventional literary cues of good and evil. Just as the treacherous status of writing depends upon the complex moral system of Rowling's characters for its illustration and efficacy, so too does the ambiguous representation of writing work to unsettle our ability to make easy judgments about whether a given character is good or evil. But one form of writing is absent from Rowling's catalog of treacherous texts: fiction. Novels, plays, and short stories have not yet appeared in her fictional world. What might it mean that the only kind of text remaining uninterrogated in Rowling's work is that with which her reader is engaged?

The distinction Rowling seems to draw lies between authoritative narratives that purport to tell the truth, and personal, intimate narratives that establish reciprocity between writer and reader, such as letters. Fiction does not rely on an allegedly objective authority and does not demand blind acceptance; rather, the success of an unequivocally fictional narrative depends on a complicity between writer and reader, a willing suspension of disbelief. Perhaps the collusion between writer and reader required by fiction renders it harmless in Rowling's schema. Much of the damage done by writing in Rowling's novels comes when the boundary between the world of the text and the world of the reader becomes blurred and permeable: Harry enters Riddle's diary; Lockhart destroys real memories in order to maintain his literary image; Skeeter's distortions are reacted to as if they reflect reality. In these examples, the reader loses agency as he or she is required to accept the text's version of reality; perhaps the balance of power between writer and reader that enables fiction precludes these kinds of threats.

Rowling's representation of writing is ambivalent and the moral architecture of her written world is unusually complex. The novels provide an education in the variable meanings and interpretations of texts claiming to contain truth; readers of Harry Potter novels must continually hone their skills of literary criticism in order to grapple with the difficult moral structure of those novels. Rowling's novels offer her readers, child and adult, important object lessons in how and why we read critically.

NOTES

This essay is dedicated to Jenna Felice.

I would like to thank Anna Ivy for her suggestions, her incisive reading, and for sharing a wholly unaccountable affection for Severus Snape.

1. J.K. Rowling, *Harry Potter and the Sorcerer's Stone* (New York: Scholastic Press, 1998), 288.

2. Ibid., 288, 126.

3. William Shakespeare, *Hamlet*, G.R. Hibbard, ed. (Oxford: Oxford University Press, 1987), 1.5.6.

4. J.K. Rowling, *Harry Potter and the Goblet of Fire* (New York: Scholastic Press, 2000), 209–10.

5. J.K. Rowling, *Harry Potter and the Prisoner of Azkaban* (New York: Scholastic Press, 1999), 93.

6. Ibid., 156.

7. Ibid., 156–57.

8. Ibid., 157.

9. Ibid., 358.

10. Rowling, *Sorcerer's Stone*, 183.

11. Rowling, *Goblet of Fire*, 480–81.

12. Ibid., 713.

13. J.K. Rowling, *Harry Potter and the Chamber of Secrets* (New York: Scholastic Press, 1999), 333.

14. Rowling, *Goblet of Fire*, 708.

15. Rowling, *Prisoner of Azkaban*, 160.

16. Ibid., 335.

17. Ibid., 391.

18. Rowling, *Goblet of Fire*, 527.

19. Rowling, *Prisoner of Azkaban*, 430.

20. Ibid., 340.

21. Ibid., 192.

22. The map later falls into the hands of the false Mad-Eye Moody and he uses it to murder Bartemius Crouch Sr., but the map's status as an inanimate tool does not, I think, contribute greatly to its status as a written document bearing moral complexity within the series.

23. Rowling, *Prisoner of Azkaban*, 290.

24. The situation of Remus Lupin is similar. While undoubtedly one of the most sympathetic and heroic characters Rowling has written, he has little to no control over the deep capacity for violence and danger that is released in his wolf-state. Despite his kindness and bravery, he still has the potential to become a monster if he forgets to take his Wolfsbane.

25. While the character is eventually revealed to be Bartemius Crouch Jr. disguised as Mad-Eye Moody, I will refer to him as "Moody" in this essay so as to remain consistent with the text.

26. Rowling, *Goblet of Fire*, 234.

27. Ibid., 220.

28. Rowling, *Sorcerer's Stone*, 13.

29. Rowling, *Goblet of Fire*, 291.

30. Ibid., 238.

31. At least, in measured amounts. As I discuss later, too much letter-writing becomes cause for suspicion.

32. Rowling, *Sorcerer's Stone*, 287.

33. Ibid., 38.

34. Rowling, *Chamber of Secrets*, 30.

35. Ibid., 230–31.

36. Ibid., 238–39.

37. Ibid., 240.

38. Ibid.

39. Ibid., 308.

40. Ibid., 312.

41. Ibid., 103.

42. Ibid., 297.

43. Rowling, *Goblet of Fire*, 314.

44. Ibid., 390.

45. Ibid., 705.

46. Rowling, *Sorcerer's Stone*, 291.

47. See for example the following pieces: Lindy Beam, "What Shall We Do With Harry?," Family.org—Plugged In, July 2000, http://www.family.org/pplace/pi/genl/A0008833.html (accessed 15 August 2001); "The Christian Guide to Fantasy—Talking Potter," 30 December 2000, http://www.christianfantasy.net/harrypotter.html (accessed 15 August 2001); Deirdre Donahue, "Some Want Harry to Vanish for Awhile," 15 June 2000, http://www.usatoday.com/life/enter/books/book717.htm (accessed 15 August 2001).

11

Harry Potter and the Rule of Law: The Central Weakness of Legal Concepts in the Wizard World

Susan Hall

A prevailing theme in the Harry Potter novels by J. K. Rowling is justice[1]. This is not unusual in children's literature, where conventions dictate that evil is vanquished and right prevails. Unusually, however, Rowling is preoccupied not simply with justice, but with legality: the mechanical and social infrastructure through which justice is achieved. In Rowling's work, two separate legal systems, wizard and Muggle,[2] are presented in considerable detail and contrasted: the contrast, while subtle, shows the wizard system as deficient in adequately acknowledging the rule of law. The wizard world as a whole is weakened as a result.

According to the classical formulation by A. V. Dicey, writing in 1908, a society that acknowledges the rule of law is one that provides that (1) punitive measures are applied against individuals only for breaches of previously promulgated laws, such breaches being properly proved by even-handed judicial processes; (2) the law applies equally to all individuals within that society; and (3) the constitutional norms applicable to that society are developed by the application of the law to individual cases by the courts.[3] A society that allows those in authority wide or arbitrary discretion in their exercise of power over others, or a society that allows for *lettres de cachet* or for the *code duello,* is not one governed by the rule of law.

The wizard world depicted by Rowling is (as yet) neither an anarchy nor a dictatorship and appears at first glance considerably more attractive than the Muggle world. However, one finds that it does not recognize the rule of law in the Dicey sense at all. This absence of an understanding of the rule of law represents a fault line in the terrain of the wizard world on which the forces of chaos can apply maximum pressure.

In the four books so far published, Harry Potter and his friends Hermione Granger and Ron Weasley have rescued their society and individuals within it from various disasters. They act effectively because Harry and Hermione, having been brought up in the Muggle system, can bring rule of law–based thinking to problem solving. They function as touchstones against which previously unquestioned assumptions of the wizard world are measured and often achieve "the right answer" by means that other wizards overlook. For example, in *Harry Potter and the Philosopher's Stone* (published in the United States as *Harry Potter and the Sorcerer's Stone*), Hermione notes that one of the obstacles to pursuit of the stone is not "magic," but rather a logic puzzle, and since many of the world's best wizards do not possess "an ounce of logic, they'd be stuck" at the task forever.[4]

However, the value of the synergy between Harry and Hermione's wizard talents and their Muggle experience is rendered less effective because of the wizard world's prejudice against Muggles. Similar prejudice is applied to other beings who possess magical powers without being "pure" wizards, and whose valuable skills are shunned rather than celebrated by the wizard authorities. Furthermore, the Ministry of Magic, which rules the wizard world, does so by means of the exercise of wide discretionary powers, which are not subject to review by any legal process. Ministry officials enjoy a high level of immunity from being called to account for their actions. All these factors create dangerous instability, which few of those who are officially entrusted with governing wizard society are capable of recognizing, let alone quelling. Major plot points illustrating these themes include: the imprisonment of Rubeus Hagrid in Azkaban, the wizard prison, on suspicion of his involvement in the attacks on Hogwarts students in *Harry Potter and the Chamber of Secrets;* the trial, appeal, and order for the execution of Buckbeak, a hippogriff, for wounding Draco Malfoy in *Harry Potter and the Prisoner of Azkaban;* the granting of permission by the Ministry of Magic to perform the Dementor's Kiss on Sirius Black, also in *Prisoner of Azkaban;* the investigation by Muggle authorities of Frank Bryce for the murder of the elder Tom Riddle and his parents in *Harry Potter and the Goblet of Fire;* the revelation that Sirius Black had been imprisoned without trial, and the details from other trials around the time of the first Voldemort ascendancy as revealed by the Pensieve in *Goblet of Fire;* the circumstances surrounding the prison escape of the younger Barty Crouch with the connivance of his father in *Goblet of Fire;* and the legal status of house-elves, giants, and werewolves. Furthermore, the importance and frequency of such issues is steadily growing as Voldemort rises to power once more.[5] The weakness of the rule of law within the wizard world creates a vacuum, which Voldemort—who offers a perverted, dictatorial version of order—exploits.

By contrast with Rowling's structured vision, comparable works of fantasy look to the restoration of a king as a sole source of arbitrary but benevolent justice. Consider *The Return of the King* (1955), the culmination of *The Lord of the Rings* by J. R. R. Tolkien, and, even more so, Ursula K. Le Guin's *The Far-*

thest Shore (1973), the third book of the *Earthsea* sequence, in which the last act of Ged as Archmage is to bring "the young king to his kingdom."[6] The *Earthsea* books present a world in which magic and the teaching of magic are subject to their own natural laws, akin to the laws of physics, which is markedly different from the treatment of magic in the Harry Potter series. Outside this, however, the society depicted by Le Guin is an essentially lawless one. *Tehanu* (1990), the fourth and final book, deals with an attempt by certain wizards to hold onto political power against the efforts of King Lebannen to restore a form of order. The order imposed is based upon one man's personal power and prestige, not upon the rule of law.

THE LEGAL AND ADMINISTRATIVE STRUCTURE WITHIN WHICH ROWLING WORKS

Both the wizard and the Muggle legal systems discussed here are applicable in the United Kingdom (and, where the distinction is relevant, in England and Wales) during the last decade of the twentieth century. While both wizard and Muggle law draw heavily upon international conventions there is, in each case, a distinct body of purely national law. This chapter concentrates primarily on criminal law because Rowling has given us few clues as to how wizard civil law works.

The legislative, executive, and judicial functions within the wizard world are all concentrated in the Ministry of Magic, whose senior representative, the minister of magic, is Cornelius Fudge. The ministry has seven departments, the largest being Magical Law Enforcement, to which the other six, with the possible exception of the Department of Mysteries, are all answerable in some degree.[7] The other departments include the Department for the Regulation and Control of Magical Creatures, the Department of International Magical Cooperation, and the Department of Magical Games and Sports.

The ministry is the principal domestic lawmaking body for U.K. witches and wizards. It appears that the ministry represents the United Kingdom's interests in relation to the International Confederation of Wizards and carries out a principal role in drafting and negotiating international statutes. An analogous relationship might be that between the European Commission and the U.K. Parliament or, possibly, between the Council of Ministers and the U.K. Parliament in relation to the European Convention on Human Rights. However, Rowling's ministry's lawmaking role does not seem subject to any form of democratic scrutiny: Arthur Weasley, for example, is able to draft the law against enchanting Muggle artifacts with a loophole to allow him to pursue his own hobby unchecked.

The minister of magic liaises directly, and apparently upon equal terms, with the Muggle prime minister when emergencies (such as the escape of Sirius Black from Azkaban) warrant it. During the first Voldemort ascendancy, the ministry served as the official organ of opposition to Voldemort, giving wide powers to its operatives including the power to kill rather than capture, permission to use the Unspeakable Curses against his supporters,[8] and sanctioning imprisonment without trial.

The ministry is also the final judicial body, with senior ministers not only conducting trials as chief prosecutor but also acting as judge in the same trials, as seen in *Goblet of Fire*. Although juries are used in trials—such as the jury that acquits Ludo Bagman against Bartemius Crouch Sr.'s wishes—Crouch, the ministry representative, appears to act both as chief prosecutor and judge. He "reviews" Karkaroff's case, and proposes the sentences in the other cases brought before him. No defense representatives are in evidence. And in a clear case of conflict of interest, Crouch acts at least in a quasi-judicial capacity in the trial in which his son is one of the principal accused.

HARRY, RON, AND HERMIONE: DIFFERENT PERSPECTIVES ON WIZARD INSTITUTIONS

Our impression of the wizard world's institutions is seen from the perspectives of the three main child characters, each of whom represents a different wizard/Muggle combination. The interaction among their three distinctly different points of view, sometimes leading to conflict about what is or is not "right" or "just," is a principal means of highlighting rule of law issues.

Harry Potter himself is the son of a wizard of pure wizard ancestry and a witch with Muggle parents and has been brought up as a Muggle by the unspeakable Dursleys. Hermione Granger is an ultra-bright trainee witch, the daughter of two Muggles, both dentists. Ron Weasley is a member of a pure wizard family whose contact with the Muggle world is so slight that Ron himself does not know how to use a telephone, and his father, a ministry official, collects electrical plugs as fascinating novelties.

Furthermore, Hermione and Harry's Muggle backgrounds are themselves contrasted. The Dursleys are anti-intellectual and heavily materialistic in their attitudes. Vernon Dursley's newspaper of choice, the *Daily Mail*, is a middle-brow tabloid with characteristically Conservative views, particularly on social issues. Although his son, Dudley, owns some books, he rarely reads, and his ability at simple arithmetic at age eleven is markedly substandard.[9] Nonetheless, his parents appear unworried by this inadequacy. The Dursleys are supporters both of capital and corporal punishment and have a horror of "abnormality," which expresses itself in their treatment of Harry and his wizard friends. In spite of their potential bad influence, and also in spite of the mistreatment that becomes a regular part of Harry's childhood, the protagonist values justice and fairness when it comes to Muggles and magical creatures alike. While we see much less of Hermione's parents, they visit Diagon Alley to meet her friends in *Chamber of Secrets* and have clearly encouraged her in intellectual interests. Hermione's sympathetic reaction to her discovery that

Lupin is a werewolf in *Prisoner of Azkaban* and to the house-elf question in *Goblet of Fire* suggests that her family is liberal in its approach to social issues and politically active.

LEGAL COMPLICATIONS IN THE WIZARD WORLD

It is worth drawing attention at the outset to a number of specific complications in operating a legal system in the wizard world. These include tense relations between wizards and Muggles; fraught relations between wizards and other magical beings; and peculiarities in law enforcement resulting from use of magic.

Wizard/Muggle Relations

The principal role of the Ministry of Magic, the primary regulatory agency and source of law in the wizard world, is to conceal from Muggles the existence of witches and wizards, together with the magical beasts and beings with which they are familiar. This obligation is imposed by the International Statute of Wizarding Secrecy 1692 (as amended), a statute apparently passed by the International Council of Warlocks (referred to elsewhere in the Harry Potter books as the International Confederation of Wizards). Rowling has informed us so far in the series that Section 13 creates an offense of carrying out magical activity that risks notice by members of the nonmagical community;[10] Section 73 imposes an obligation on the relevant ministries for the concealment, care, and control of magical beasts, beings, and spirits in their territories;[11] and another provision requires a similar responsibility for magical games played in particular territories.[12] This law appears to have constitutional supremacy over national laws that are inconsistent with it, although it is unclear how this supremacy is enforced.

Accordingly, if a witch or wizard comes into conflict with a Muggle, the Muggle world must never know the conflict occurred. Commonly this requires a memory charm to be used on the Muggle, but other techniques are used. So far as we are shown, even murders of Muggles by wizards are rarely reported or investigated: Dumbledore, referring to suspicious recent events in book IV, remarks on a generally unacknowledged disappearance: "one which the Ministry, I regret to say, does not consider of any importance, for it concerns a Muggle."[13] We are told that some "extreme" members of wizard society believe Muggles should be legally classed as nonsentient creatures,[14] but Dumbledore's comment about the Ministry of Magic's inaction implies that to regard Muggle issues as irrelevant, and Muggles as not worthy of attention, is not an extreme position but a norm that is officially sanctioned.

Although this issue is initially introduced as a moral one, its legal consequences are subsequently explored. In *Chamber of Secrets*, Hermione is the victim of abuse when Draco Malfoy calls her "Mudblood"—a derogatory term for a wizard or witch from a purely Muggle background. Ron roundly condemns this attitude—"It's mad. Most wizards these days are half-blood anyway. If we hadn't married Muggles we'd have died out"[15]—although his choice of words is telling, implying as it does that he believes originally wizards *were*, in some sense, a different species. Harry's position is more complex: the Muggles with whom he lives are unpleasant to the point of being abusive and have made no attempt to foster his talents. Nonetheless, he can clearly distinguish between dislike of unpleasant individuals and prejudice against the group of which they form part, and he decisively rejects the latter.

The isolation of the wizard community enforced by the 1692 statute seems to have created potentially dangerous naïveté about Muggles, with even "good" characters regarding them in a patronizing and paternalistic light. This is reflected by the way wizard law impacts upon Muggles. Ron's father, Arthur Weasley, is an entirely sympathetic wizard who has failed to achieve promotion at the Ministry of Magic because his fondness for Muggles means his superiors believe he lacks "proper wizarding pride."[16] He has promoted (and probably drafted) a "Muggle Protection Act." And while we learn little about this law except that other wizards, including Lucius Malfoy, are hostile to it,[17] it is possible to draw some tentative conclusions about its contents.

First, Arthur Weasley's enthusiasm for the Muggle world is only equaled by his extraordinary level of ignorance about it. It is therefore almost a given that no Muggle was consulted in the act's drafting. It cannot allow Muggles equal rights of access to wizard law, because that would contravene the 1692 statute. Furthermore, there is a reference in *Chamber of Secrets* that suggests that it in fact reinforces the obligation on wizards to keep themselves secret. "Protection" without knowledge of the law under which one is being protected, or of the system by which that law is enforced, puts one in the same position as an animal, who can benefit from the statutes preventing cruelty to animals, but cannot complain on its own behalf to the authorities nor have direct input into what behavior should be judged "cruel."

Further, in his work at the Misuse of Muggle Artefacts Office, Arthur Weasley relies heavily on use of memory charms on Muggles. They are neither asked for consent nor given any opportunity to refuse this brain modification. This he justifies as preventing traumatic recollections, although such charms can cause permanent memory damage. Furthermore, Rowling in *Chamber of Secrets* introduces the sinister possibility that memory charms can be used as a way of "rewriting" the facts when Gilderoy Lockhart reveals that his entire career has been based on appropriating other witches' and wizards' achievements and using memory charms to change their recollections. Lockhart acts as an unscrupulous private individual: Rowling subsequently shows that a tool such as a memory charm in the hands of the Ministry of Magic, who have institutionalized prejudice against Muggles and exercise arbitrary power with little judicial constraint, is damaging to wizards as well as to nonmagical humans.

In other examples, the Muggle witnesses to the Black/Pettigrew confrontation described in *Prisoner of Azkaban* subsequently have had their memories modified, so that Black would have had no possibility of calling them as witnesses, even if he had been allowed a trial. We also learn in the same book that Cornelius Fudge was one of the first ministry representatives on the scene, and we are already aware, especially from Hagrid's imprisonment in *Chamber of Secrets*, that Fudge's preference is for "tidy" conclusions rather than for correct ones. Dumbledore's earlier mentioned point about the lack of justice for Muggles, then, is that not treating Muggles as fully human is not only wrong, but is contrary to the wizard world's own self-interest, since it fosters a general disregard for human life.

Other Magical Beings

The wizard world is intensely hierarchical. Magical beings other than "pure" wizards are treated to greater or lesser degrees of discrimination, amounting to open persecution at times.[18] The first example we see is Professor Lupin, a popular and sympathetic teacher whom, we discover in *Prisoner of Azkaban*, is also a werewolf. Hermione works this out from clues deliberately dropped by Professor Snape, but keeps the secret even from her closest friends until circumstances convince her (wrongly) that he is in league with a murderer and presenting an actual danger to the three of them. Ron's immediate response is *"Get away from me, werewolf!"* followed by: "Dumbledore hired you when he knew you were a werewolf? ... Is he mad?"[19] By contrast, Harry, although in a very emotional state, is persuaded to listen to the story and shows hostility to Lupin only for what he believes he has done, rather than what he is. When the news of Lupin's lycanthropy spreads through the school, he is forced to resign and explains that he has been ostracized for his entire adult life, "unable to find paid work because of what I am."[20]

In *Goblet of Fire*, the theme of the wizards' discrimination against other magical beings is taken further: Ron and Harry overhear Hagrid confess to Madame Maxime that he is a half-giant (as he assumes, correctly, she is as well). Ron, quite clearly acting here as the expression of the general opinion in the wizard world, calls giants "vicious": "[I]t's in their natures ... they just like killing, everyone knows that."[21] When the revelation is made public, wizards who do not know Hagrid, and many who do, are overtly hostile. Hermione, however, reacts calmly in the face of what she identifies as social "hysteria": "[H]onestly, ... They can't *all* be horrible. ... " She compares the prejudice against giants to that against werewolves and asks, "It's just bigotry, isn't it?"

The sole counterexample to the prejudice against nonhumans is that Fleur Delacour seems proud of her grandmother's veela identity and suffers no apparent discrimination as a result. However, being attractive is part of the veelas' magic powers and may act as a protective mechanism.

Nonhumans suffer institutionalized legal disabilities. For example, during the house-elf Winky's examination when she is under suspicion of having conjured the Dark Mark, Amos Diggory draws attention to clause three of the Code of Wand Use: "No nonhuman creature is permitted to carry or use a wand."[22] From the way the ministry wizards describe matters, a wand is necessary to perform some sorts of magic. Limiting wand use limits the potential of other magical beings. However, house-elves clearly have powerful inherent magic of their own, which their masters need but also fear. The Code of Wand Use operates to curtail their powers so they cannot attempt to overthrow wizards, and reemphasizes the social distinction between human and nonhuman magical beings. This distinction is further highlighted by the convention that a house-elf, while in servitude, must not be given clothes.

The comfortable life-style of many wizards, including the staff and students at Hogwarts, depends on house-elves not looking for greater freedom. When Hermione realizes this, her response is to seek to increase their legal rights. Her short-term goals for the elves are "fair wages and working conditions," while among her long-term goals are changing the wand-use laws and getting an elf hired at the Department for the Regulation and Control of Magical Creatures, since they are "shockingly under-represented."[23] In each example we are given Hermione takes the lead in arguing for an equal consideration of people's actions rather than their natures, and the equal application of the law to those actions.

Peculiarities of Law Enforcement Resulting from Use of Magic

The assumed use of magic presents difficulties for law enforcement. The use of a Time Turner or Disapparation erodes the concept of an alibi. Identification proves unreliable where a witch or wizard may be an Animagus or ingest Polyjuice Potion, methods used by Peter Pettigrew and Barty Crouch Jr., respectively, to commit crimes. However, in theory, magic should also allow corresponding legal opportunities. Rita Skeeter uses her talents for investigative journalism but they are equally valuable for detection of crime. Mad-Eye Moody (or at least his alter ego) possesses numerous technical devices such as Sneakoscopes to detect dishonest activity in his vicinity. The *Prior Incantato* spell, which reveals the last spell cast by a wand, can be used to identify the murder weapon, even if it is dangerously misleading about the actual perpetrator. The Marauder's Map twice accurately identifies people who are within the Hogwarts grounds in disguise. Finally, *Goblet of Fire* introduces us to the Veritaserum Potion, which appears to be a reliable truth drug, the use of which is apparently controlled by strict ministry guidelines.

The opportunities highlighted above have been consistently missed by the witches and wizards of Rowling's series. In *Prisoner of Azkaban*, to take one example, Cornelius Fudge authorizes the dementors to perform their kiss on Sirius Black: an action that goes beyond capital punishment in that the victim is transformed into an empty shell whose soul is gone forever. No suggestion of testing his protestations of innocence under Veritaserum is entertained before this authorization is given.

DOES WIZARD LAW CARE ABOUT INTENTION?

The Muggle criminal law lays considerable stress on the distinction between *actus reus* and *mens rea*. *Actus reus* can be defined as the physical acts that may amount to a crime. *Mens rea* is the mental attitude of the perpetrator, which determines whether or not a crime has in fact been committed. For example, A stabs B fatally. The *mens rea* for murder is an intention to cause death or serious injury, or the voluntary commission of an act that is virtually certain to cause such a result while knowing that this is the likely consequence.[24] Without such an intention the act itself cannot add up to murder and may well not be a crime at all. For example, if A slips on a wet patch in the kitchen while carrying a kitchen knife from the sink to the drawer and B's consequent stabbing is a pure accident, there is no criminal issue.

It is less clear how far the *mens rea/actus reus* distinction applies in wizard law. As magic itself can work on the mind, will, and memory, it poses serious difficulties in assessing *mens rea*. One early indication of the Ministry of Magic's apparent disregard of the whole concept of intention appears in *Chamber of Secrets* when the house-elf Dobby first levitates and then drops a cream pudding in the kitchen of the Dursleys' house. Within minutes Harry receives a formal warning by owl from the Improper Use of Magic Office, which advises him that he is considered responsible for the use of a Hover Charm and that, as an underage wizard, a further offense will render him liable to expulsion from Hogwarts.

Before sending this letter, the ministry made no investigation as to whether Harry in fact committed the crime concerned (which he had been actively trying to prevent); it acts by unchallengeable administrative decree. Dobby was trying to frame Harry, and the ministry allows him to succeed with frightening ease. The incident also suggests that Harry and all other young witches and wizards may be under constant surveillance in case they carry out magic. This is a potentially worrying civil liberties issue and will be addressed in more detail in the human rights discussion below.

Although one of the most interesting aspects of *mens rea* occurs where house-elves are involved in criminal activities, wizards do not seem sensitive to the concept in this context. Elves possess an extremely limited degree of free will and are controlled by their ruling wizard family. If a house-elf commits a crime, therefore, the investigator should, as a matter of common sense, inquire if the elf is acting on its own account or under duress exerted by its ruling family.[25] In *Goblet of Fire*, however, Amos Diggory conducts a brief and hostile interrogation of the house-elf Winky on the night of the Dark Mark's appearance, in which his evident prejudice against nonwizard magical beings impedes his ability to obtain any useful information. Barty Crouch Sr., Winky's master, intervenes to prevent further interrogation; the other adult wizards present are ministry employees and forced to concur because of Crouch's seniority. This example not only shows that senior ministry employees can raise themselves above the law, but that Diggory's prejudice makes him less effective than he should be as an investigator. Indirectly this leads to his own son's death.

The wizard world is not without some concept of *mens rea*. The role played by the Imperius Curse in mitigating the guilt of apparent Voldemort supporters is mentioned on a number of occasions. However, wizard legal institutions appear so significantly lacking in procedural safeguards and the lawmaking power appears so haphazardly exercised that this concept is rarely applied.

INSTITUTIONAL CORRUPTION OF THE MINISTRY OF MAGIC

As indicated above, the absence of rule of law safeguards allows the ministry and its officials to act in a capricious and arbitrary way, and for unscrupulous individuals within the ministry to exploit matters for their own advantage. The incident of Buckbeak, the hippogriff in *Prisoner of Azkaban,* encapsulates all the concerns expressed to date about how life or death issues are approached by wizard authorities. Hippogriffs are legally "beasts": capable of understanding human speech although their comprehension is somewhat limited. Buckbeak injures Draco Malfoy, who has ignored his teacher's instruction never to insult a hippogriff. Malfoy persuades his influential father, Lucius, to complain formally to the ministry, and Buckbeak's representation on a capital charge is left to Hagrid, who is wholly untrained, and to the efforts of Harry, Ron, and Hermione.[26] Relevant precedents are disregarded by the Committee for the Disposal of Dangerous Creatures, which orders Buckbeak's execution. Although there is an appeal, those hearing it (including, contrary to natural justice, one of the committee who heard the original application) arrive with the executioner Macnair and with their minds clearly made up.[27] Finally, the innocent Buckbeak has to be *il*legally rescued by Harry and Hermione, at Dumbledore's instigation.

A symptom of the level of corruption in the ministry is that even "good" ministry employees have to use doubtful means to achieve just results. In book IV, junior ministry employees Arthur Weasley and Amos Diggory find themselves forced into an illicit conspiracy to prevent Mad-Eye Moody from suffering serious consequences for attracting Muggle attention by his response to a threat.[28] Moody has genuinely been attacked, his past career as an Auror making him an obvious target. However, as both Diggory and Weasley assume correctly, the ministry's Improper Use of Magic officers will neither investigate Moody's complaint nor take any mitigating circumstances into account.

The corruption of ministry officials is perhaps most evident in that both Hagrid and Sirius Black are imprisoned in Azkaban without trial at the instigation of senior ministry representatives. In both cases, the absence of a trial is primarily for cosmetic reasons. In Hagrid's case, it is apparent that the minister of magic is neither convinced of his guilt nor especially interested in finding the actual culprit behind the attacks.[29] Furthermore, any charge carrying a possibility of a custodial sentence in Azkaban is effectively a capital charge since conditions in Azkaban induce clinical depression in prisoners, and most go mad, many starving themselves to death. Thus, even though Hagrid's incarceration is expressed to be a temporary precaution, there is a high likelihood of his suffering permanent damage or death before his release. As will be discussed at more length below, the conditions in Azkaban, and the imprisonment of these two characters without trial, clearly would contravene each of Articles 2–6 of the European Convention on Human Rights, if they occurred under the Muggle system.

Contrary to Dicey's first principle, therefore, in the wizard world people *can* lawfully be made to suffer otherwise than for a distinct breach of law established in the ordinary legal manner before the ordinary courts. The wizard world lacks effective checks and balances on the administrative powers of the ministry.

WOULD A FORMALIZED RULE OF LAW CONCEPT MAKE ANY DIFFERENCE?

It would be absurd to suggest that a stated adherence to the rule of law automatically makes one legal system superior to another if in practice in the first system the liberties of the subject are routinely suspended, or if the method of enforcing them is too cumbersome, expensive, or corrupt to achieve its objective. Twentieth-century English law has seen its fair share of counterexamples to Dicey's optimistic (and typically chauvinistic) assertions.

Most relevant are the Defence of the Realm Acts, applicable during and for some time after World War I, and the equivalent World War II legislation[30] requiring persons to place "themselves, their services and their property" at the disposal of the Crown and allowing suspected persons to be interned without trial. More recently, the Prevention of Terrorism (Temporary Provisions) Act 1989 allowed for persons suspected of terrorist offenses to be held for an initial forty-eight hours without charge (capable of extension to five days on the authority of the Secretary of State), and Section 75 of the Terrorism Act 2000, which applies to Northern Ireland, allows for the trial of "scheduled offences" on indictment without a jury (formalizing the existing "Diplock courts").

It might, therefore, be argued that the period of the first Voldemort ascendancy[31] should properly be compared to the equivalent Muggle conditions. Even so, wizard law appears at a disadvantage. Voldemort almost certainly kills his father and grandparents during World War II,[32] possibly as early as 1944 when the previously referenced emergency powers were in force. The emergency conditions that necessitated these acts do not prevent the Muggle authorities in Rowling's novel from carrying out a careful investigation. When the cause of death cannot be established, Frank Bryce, the chief suspect, is released, retaining not only his freedom but his job. Human nature being the same in both wizard and Muggle society, he is convicted at the bar of public opinion and exists under suspicion for the next fifty years, but at least retains his liberty. One only has to compare his situation with the wizard world treatment of Hagrid or of Sirius Black to show that in the nonmagical human world, at least, the rule of law makes a difference.

Another relevant difference between the magical versus nonmagical worlds is the European Convention on Human Rights. The United Kingdom signed the convention on 4 November 1950 and was the first country to ratify it on 8 March 1951. However, until the Human Rights Act 1998, the convention did not form part of U.K. domestic law, meaning that English courts remained bound to enforce domestic legislation even if it conflicted with the convention.[33] In the 1990 Spycatcher case,[34] Lord Justice Balcombe stated it was valid to invoke the convention in domestic law: (1) to resolve an ambiguity in English primary or subordinate legislation; (2) to consider principles upon which the court should act in exercising a discretion; (3) when the common law (including doctrines of equity) is uncertain; or, (4) to consider the conformity of U.K. law with the convention.

Prior to the direct effect of the European Convention on Human Rights in English law, enforcement was only performed by the European Court of Human Rights. Currently, the Council of Ministers is charged with ensuring states' compliance with the decisions of the European Court of Human Rights. The court's judgment is limited to recording that a violation of the convention has occurred, giving reasons for its findings, and awarding compensation and costs where appropriate. A signatory state to the convention is required to report at least twice a year on the steps it is taking to abide by court decisions. Even before it became directly effective in English law, therefore, the existence of the convention offered powerful moral authority in restraining administrative action and cases were regularly brought before the European Court of Human Rights. A finding against the government produced considerable embarrassment and not infrequently forced a change in the offending legislation.

The examples of Ministry of Magic procedure cited above all contravene the Convention on Human Rights in the most blatant manner. The existence and administration of Azkaban can be found wanting under Article 2, Right to Life,[35] and Article 3, Prohibition of Torture.[36] Hermione would find support for her house-elves campaign in Article 4: "No-one shall be held in slavery or servitude." On the topic of criminal investigations and prosecutions, no wizard trial or imprisonment we have so far seen, with the possible exception of that of Ludo Bagman, complies with subclause 4 of Article 5, Right to Liberty and Security: "Everyone who is deprived of his liberty by arrest or detention shall be entitled to take proceedings by which the lawfulness of his detention shall be decided speedily by a court and his release ordered if the detention is not lawful," or Article 6, Right to a Fair Trial: "In the determination of his civil rights obligations or of any criminal charge against him, everyone is entitled to a fair and public hearing within a reasonable time by an independent and impartial tribunal established by law." No matter how imperfect the Muggle system may be, the convention, which derives directly from rule of law thinking, provides a standard against which Muggle law and procedure may be compared and a just procedure assessed. It is now directly applicable in U.K. law. The wizard world offers no equivalent.

CONCLUSION

The mood at the end of *Goblet of Fire* is somber. Voldemort has committed murder but will escape justice. Characteristically preferring administrative action to open trial, the minister of magic has allowed Barty Crouch Jr. to be "kissed" by a dementor, removing any possibility of his giving testimony against Voldemort and Pettigrew; Fudge is also seeking to conceal all evidence that murder has occurred. Harry is regarded as unsound—and his testimony disregarded—because of his friendship for Lupin, a werewolf, and Hagrid, a half-giant. Further, Fudge has re-emphasized the ministry's self-serving corruption, defending Macnair from Harry's claims that he is a Voldemort supporter, apparently on the sole grounds that the executioner works for the ministry. He refuses any suggestion of approaching the giants in an alliance against Voldemort because of his fear of the reaction from the xenophobic wizard community and his own obsession with "purity of blood."

The rule of law in the wizard world, therefore, remains in abeyance. The struggle that is developing is not only that of Good against Evil, but of Structure against Chaos. One can only hope that Harry, Ron, and Hermione will continue to carry the torch successfully for what Lon Fuller referred to as "the internal morality of law," sometimes called "the procedural theory of natural law."[37] As Fuller pointed out, these "natural laws" resemble "the natural laws of carpentry, or at least those laws respected by a carpenter who wants the house he builds to remain standing and serve the purpose of those who live in it.... "[38] Therefore, even if Voldemort is defeated, the wizard world will need a great deal of rebuilding, and only those who have a feel for structure will be able to build something that will last longer than the world we see crumbling before us as the series progresses.

NOTES

In writing this chapter, I gratefully acknowledge the assistance of Dylan Roberts, who helped with the research, Diana Rossell, who sorted out the spelling and format, and Heidi Tandy and Russell Baldwin, who read it in draft and made valuable suggestions. The opinions expressed here are my sole responsibility.

1. J. K. Rowling, *Harry Potter and the Philosopher's Stone* (London: Bloomsbury, 1997) [published in the United States as *Harry Potter and the Sorcerer's Stone* (New

York: Scholastic Press, 1997)]; J. K. Rowling, *Harry Potter and the Chamber of Secrets* (London: Bloomsbury, 1998); J. K. Rowling, *Harry Potter and the Prisoner of Azkaban* (London: Bloomsbury, 1999); J. K. Rowling, *Harry Potter and the Goblet of Fire* (London: Bloomsbury, 2000).

In addition to the four novels, I cite from the two shorter works by Rowling writing under pseudonyms: Kennilworthy Whisp, *Quidditch through the Ages* (London: Bloomsbury/Whizz Hard, 2001), and Newt Scamander, *Fantastic Beasts and Where to Find Them* (London: Bloomsbury/Obscurus, 2001).

2. The convention will be adopted for the purposes of this essay of referring to nonmagical humans as Muggles.

3. A. V. Dicey, *Introduction to the Study of Constitutional Law,* 10th ed. (Basingstoke: Palgrave, 1985), 187–95: "[N]o man is punishable or can be lawfully made to suffer in body or goods except for a distinct breach of law established in the ordinary legal manner before the ordinary courts of the land. In this sense the rule of law is contrasted with every system of government based on the exercise by persons in authority of wide, arbitrary, or discretionary powers of constraint. . . . [N]o man is above the law, . . . every man, whatever be his rank or condition, is subject to the ordinary law of the realm and amenable to the jurisdiction of the ordinary tribunals. . . [T]he general principles of the constitution (as for example the right to personal liberty, or the right of public meeting) are with us the result of judicial decisions determining the rights of private persons in particular cases brought before the courts."

4. Rowling, *Philosopher's Stone,* 207.

5. The period referred to in this chapter as the first Voldemort ascendancy lasts for a period of approximately eleven years. It ends with the murder of Harry's parents and the abortive attack on Harry himself, when Harry is about fifteen months old. The dating and length of the first Voldemort ascendancy are derived from the comment of Dumbledore in respect to the wizard celebrations occurring on the day of Voldemort's fall—that the wizard community has had little to celebrate for eleven years (*Philosopher's Stone,* 13)—and from Hagrid's reference to Voldemort as having risen to power about twenty years before, a comment made on Harry's eleventh birthday (ibid., 49). The start of the second Voldemort ascendancy occurs in *Goblet of Fire* on 24 June 1995 (the reasoning for dating *Goblet of Fire* in 1994–1995 is given more fully below).

6. Ursula K. Le Guin, *The Farthest Shore* (London: Puffin, 1973), 212.

7. Scamander, *Fantastic Beasts,* Introduction, footnote 9.

8. The use of these curses gives the bearer complete control of another's will and actions, the ability to torture, and the power to levy death.

9. Rowling, *Philosopher's Stone,* 21.

10. Rowling, *Chamber of Secrets,* 21.

11. Scamander, *Fantastic Beasts,* xvi.

12. Whisp, *Quidditch,* 16.

13. Rowling, *Goblet of Fire,* 522.

14. "We are all familiar with the extremists who campaign for the classification of Muggles as 'beasts.'" Scamander, *Fantastic Beasts,* xiii.

15. Rowling, *Chamber of Secrets,* 89.

16. Rowling, *Goblet of Fire*, 617.

17. See Rowling, *Chamber of Secrets*, 247.

18. In *Fantastic Beasts*, Scamander explains the division of the magical world into beings, beasts, and spirits (x–xiii). A being is "any creature that has sufficient intelligence to understand the laws of the magical community and to bear part of the responsibility in shaping those laws." Beasts are living creatures that do not fit this definition. Spirits are dead beings. There are exceptions to the neat division, with creatures of high intelligence but irreversibly brutal natures falling into the beast category, and centaurs and merpeople opting into beastdom apparently as a protest about the way the wizards run things.

19. Rowling, *Prisoner of Azkaban*, 253.

20. Ibid., 261.

21. Rowling, *Goblet of Fire*, 374.

22. Ibid., 119.

23. Ibid., 198.

24. *R. v. Nedrick* (1986) 8 Cr. App. R. (S.) 179. 1 WLR 1025: necessary intention for murder is to cause death or serious bodily harm. Where the simple direction to the jury is insufficient, the jury should be directed that they are not entitled to infer the necessary intention unless they feel sure that death or really serious bodily harm was a virtual certainty (barring some unforeseen intervention) and that the defendant appreciated that such was the case. Approved by the House of Lords in *R. v. Woollin* (1999) 1 Cr. App. R. 8. 3 WLR 382.

25. In the previously mentioned case, Dobby is acting on his own account, but within limitations imposed by his servitude. Certainly the Malfoys would not object if his actions lead to Harry's being expelled from Hogwarts.

26. This is not to underestimate the efforts the children put in: Hermione in particular researches the case in a remarkably thorough and professional way with a very adult grasp of what makes a relevant and applicable precedent. Perhaps she has a barrister aunt to go with those dentist parents?

27. Rowling, *Prisoner of Azkaban*, 235. Macnair is revealed as a closet Voldemort supporter in *Goblet of Fire*.

28. Rowling, *Goblet of Fire*, 141–44.

29. As he fidgets with his hat, Fudge states: "Look at it from my point of view.... I'm under a lot of pressure. Got to be seen to be doing something.... " Rowling, *Chamber of Secrets*, 193.

30. Defence (General) Regulations 1939; Emergency Powers (Defence) Act 1940 and associated secondary legislation.

31. Of the examples given above, Sirius Black's original imprisonment and those of the individuals whose trials appear in the Pensieve, including the younger Barty Crouch, occur during or immediately after the close of the first Voldemort ascendancy.

32. Rowling, *Goblet of Fire*, 7–8. The date of the murders is described as "fifty years before" the events described in the remainder of the book. The main action of *Goblet of Fire* probably commences in August 1994. There is no particular reason the Quidditch World Cup should take place in the same month and year as the soccer World Cup, but

there are very significant (and probably deliberate) parallels between the soccer World Cup of 1994 and the Quidditch World Cup. First, and most unusually, each of England, Wales, and Scotland failed to make it to the finals in 1994 (cf. *Goblet of Fire*, 59), whereas both Ireland and Bulgaria, the Quidditch finalists, did appear in the soccer tournament with Hristo Stoitchkov of Bulgaria the joint highest goal scorer (Bulgaria was knocked out in the semi-finals) and wild public enthusiasm and support within Ireland for the unprecedented success of Charlton's team. More evidence as to the date appears in *Chamber of Secrets*, in which the 500th anniversary of Nearly Headless Nick's death on 31 October 1492 is celebrated. *Chamber of Secrets* is definitely two years before *Goblet of Fire*.

33. In construing any ambiguous provision, however, the courts would presume that Parliament intended to legislate in conformity with the European Convention on Human Rights. *R. v. Secretary of State for the Home Department, Ex Parte Brind* (1991) 1 A.C. 696.

34. *Attorney General v. Guardian Newspapers (No. 2)* (1990) 1 A.C. 109.

35. "No-one shall be deprived of his life intentionally save in the execution of a sentence of a court following his conviction of a crime for which this penalty is provided by law."

36. "No-one shall be subjected to torture or to inhuman or degrading treatment or punishment."

37. Lon Fuller, *The Morality of Law* (New Haven, CT: Yale University Press, 1969), 39.

38. Ibid., 96.

12

The Fallen Empire: Exploring Ethnic Otherness in the World of Harry Potter

Giselle Liza Anatol

[J]ust as Britain tried to impose Western cultural ideals and behaviors in Africa, India, the Caribbean, and elsewhere, British adults try to impose adult cultural ideals of thought and behavior upon children. Just as colonial subjects were voiceless—their lives are described for us by Westerners, not by themselves—children are also voiceless, depending upon adults to describe their lives for them. I do not see this as any sort of evil conspiracy by adults, but as a natural response to civilize and assimilate the "other" of childhood into the "subject" of adulthood.

—M. Daphne Kutzer[1]

Much of what children find intriguing is what lies beyond their borders—not only those metaphorical boundaries of license and socially sanctioned behavior, but also the geopolitical borders of the nation in which they reside. Overseas—including, in the case of nineteenth-century U. S. history, the space beyond the oceans of prairie claimed during the imperialist enterprise of Manifest Destiny—was a vast unknown, holding adventure and riches not available in the "civilized" homeland.

The wizarding world in J. K. Rowling's Harry Potter series has the potential to function as this overseas territory. Harry discovers that heart-racing escapades and treasures such as a substantial inheritance, Invisibility Cloak, and Marauder's Map await him. After a journey out of London on the Hogwarts Express, he and the other students end up in a place where the rules of the non-magical world, especially those of their everyday domestic lives under the roofs of their parents and guardians, no longer apply. In addition, away from the "civilized" space of contemporary England where social mores construct all magical folk as Other and inherently evil, Harry finds belonging and safety in a colony where *everyone* has wizarding powers. Rowling employs a discourse of difference—one that appears to embrace the landscape of the foreign and the situation of the outsider, heightening the books' appeal to children who remain outside of positions of power and agency in society.

Reading the Harry Potter novels for the first time, however, I was perturbed by the way that the postgraduate careers of Bill and Charlie Weasley after they leave Hogwarts seem to echo the British imperial enterprise. On several occasions, readers hear that Charlie works in Romania studying dragons, and Bill is employed by the Egyptian branch of Gringotts Wizarding Bank. The latter's official job title is Charm Breaker; he attempts to circumvent the spells that ancient Egyptian wizards put on tombs in order to discourage raiders. Responding to his mother's concern about his nonconventional appearance (i.e., long ponytail and earring), he states that no one at work cares how he dresses as long as he brings abundant treasure "home."[2] In other words, Bill does not hold a tedious paperwork position in banking or relocate to a foreign territory for the supposed education and benefit of the local people. Rather, he participates in excavations and thrilling adventures that deplete an area of historical and cultural treasures for British wizard-world profit. In the exotic yet primitive locales of eastern Europe and northern Africa, the Weasley brothers are engaged in ventures that bring apparently superior European knowledge and experience to the "frontier"—developing areas of the world—and, more importantly, that bring its rewards back "home" to the heart of the empire.

Analogously, Sirius Black, Harry's unofficial guardian, on the run from the law in book IV for a murder he did not commit, sends correspondence to his godson by large, vividly colored tropical birds instead of by the conventional owl. The feathered messengers are "flashy" and cause Harry to think of palm fronds, sparkling sand, and places where he hopes Sirius is enjoying himself, places that evoke images of a Caribbean paradise. Later, arguing for the length of time it would take Harry's owl to bring a letter from Sirius, Hermione suggests that he could be in Africa.[3] Both locations suggest the far reaches of the historical British Empire. For the escaped convict, trying to lose himself in these places cannot be a matter of appearances; as a white British man, Sirius will not readily blend into a predominantly black resident population. However, in the contemporary popular view of deserted Caribbean beaches, awaiting re-"discovery" by harried tourists seeking surf and sun, or of the overgrown African jungle, Sirius will have no trouble disappearing without magic.

Magical Britain, and Hogwarts in particular, thus become the magical metropole, despite their initial resemblance to a foreign landscape of Otherness. Everywhere else subsequently falls into the category of "periphery." I am reminded of a 1986 lecture given at York University in Toronto, in which Barbadian writer George Lamming described his audience, consisting primarily of Caribbean immigrants, as an external frontier of the archipelago. In doing so, the author inverted the conventional framework in which Europeans considered colonial possessions to be "outposts on the periphery of their world—the white, rich, politically and technologically powerful metropolis of Europe and

North America."[4] Unlike Lamming, Rowling seems to project a more traditional, nostalgic view of imperial Center and less-civilized Periphery in her Harry Potter series. Glancing over Elizabeth Schafer's sourcebook, I note that the critic describes Hogwarts as located in the "protective isolation of Britain," which "insulated Britain from the rest of tumultuous Europe and provided incubation for developing a culture rich in lore and steeped in tradition."[5] This romanticized interpretation fails to acknowledge Britain's often brutal history and confirms my worst suspicions about how the Potter books might be read. Schafer's idealistic view neglects the fact that on its way to becoming recognized as one of the most culturally advanced countries in the world, England was constantly involved in activities of colonial domination and exploitation.

What I aim to do in this chapter is examine the Harry Potter novels from a postcolonial perspective. This framework does not mean to suggest, as the term *postcolonial* might indicate, that colonialism is dead and gone: theories can be used to interrogate the ways that the old colonial system has found its way back into society as neocolonialism, a revived push by dominant forces to maintain or reinvigorate their positions of social and cultural privilege. Postcolonial readings attempt to "rethink, recuperate, and reconstruct racial, ethnic, and cultural others that have been repressed, misrepresented, omitted, stereotyped, and violated by the imperial West with all its institutions and strategies for dominating the non-Western."[6] Attributing this damage to the entire "imperial West" is a claim too broad to allow us to unravel the complexities of our current historical situation, or for us to adequately take into account Rowling's definitively nondominant subject position as a woman and former welfare recipient. However, I hope that by engaging with children's literature in the spirit of Xie's definition, I can challenge traditional and Eurocentric ways of seeing that are both represented within the narratives and with which many of us have been trained to interpret texts.

I begin with the question of whether Rowling simply continues in the tradition of what Martin Green in *Dreams of Adventure, Deeds of Empire* identifies as "the energizing myth" of imperialism. Popular children's literature published during the height of Britain's imperialist era "were, collectively, the story England told itself as it went to sleep at night; and ... they charged England's will with energy to go out into the world and explore, conquer, and rule."[7] I argue that although the Potter series attempts to embrace ideas of global equality and multiculturalism, the stories actually reveal how difficult it is for contemporary British subjects such as Rowling to extricate themselves from the ideological legacies of their ancestors.

Through children's literature, many European nations of the eighteenth, nineteenth, and twentieth centuries instilled the imperialist and colonizing values of the adult population. As Patrick Brantlinger notes: "Much imperialist discourse was ... directed at a specifically adolescent audience, the future rulers of the world."[8] However, the ideology of imperialism, colonialism, and xenophobia is often encoded so deeply—both in the text itself and in our own perception of the world—that it becomes almost invisible. Rowling's novels seem particularly influenced by the British adventure story tradition, which promoted "civilized" values—resourcefulness, wits, ingenuity, and hierarchy headed by a *legitimate* democratic authority—and demonstrated their desirability in the wild territories beyond England's borders. Because imperialists often condemned the indigenous peoples of Africa, India, and the Americas as wasteful of the incredible natural resources that lay around them, in imperialist literature, the empire and its agents are typically depicted as best for everyone concerned. In other words, when all behave according to the plan, the colonials gain the majority of capital but can be reassured that the indigenous peoples have had "their standard of living raised somewhat, and their moral natures raised quite a lot."[9]

The adventure story genre had its origins in Daniel Defoe's *Robinson Crusoe* (1719), frequently adapted for eighteenth-century children. In the spirit of this obviously imperialist text, with its European protagonist who civilizes both landscape and the Amerindian Friday, Johann David Wyss's *Swiss Family Robinson* (originally published in Germany in 1812 but gaining a great deal of notoriety when translated into English) also featured nature tamed and controlled by humans.[10] Victorian-era literature includes G. A. Henty's propaganda novels, featuring heroic young English boys: healthy, ultra-masculine, honest, and chivalrous. The values of imperialism were further supported by public school stories: tales of institutions where boys first learned what it took to be successful members of the colonial class and future leaders of the empire.

World War I marked the official start of the end of the British Empire, and children's literature often provided the escape for a society whose borders appeared to be closing in. A. A. Milne's *Winne-the-Pooh* (1926), published in the time between the wars, focuses on retreat from the harrowing experiences of the adult world, into the safety and purported innocence of childhood and childhood imagination, symbolized by the animals' adventures in the Hundred Acre Wood.[11] In the post–World War II period, a surge of fantasy novels for children seemed to reflect the perspective of British citizens taking measure of the empire's dwindling remains. Hunt and Sands note an increased number of British "animal fantasies," such as Margery Sharp's *The Rescuers* (1959), which patriotically emphasize the importance of remaining at "home" and staying true to one's English-ness. The prominence of assimilationist themes appears to correspond with the increased flow of colonized subjects into Britain, searching for economic and educational opportunities: "When the story centers on an outsider coming to England, that character's only hope for acceptance is to forget his or her past life and take on purely English ways."[12] Assimilationist narratives include H. A. Rey's *Curious George* (1941)—the monkey is taken out of the African jungle and only too happy to be brought to "civilization" and put into captivity in a zoo at the end of the book—and Michael Bond's *A Bear Called Paddington* (1958), in which the bear from "Darkest Peru" (though the phrase also invokes Africa, the so-called Dark Continent) eventually sacrifices his native language and name in favor of the name of the London train station where he is found and the British family that adopts him.[13]

In the last quarter of the twentieth century, children's books emphasizing a powerful Britain, such as Susan Cooper's 1970s series, *The Dark Is Rising*, can also be linked to the nation's waning international influence. Without explicit reference to empire, Cooper's narratives reveal a desire to return to past splendor and magnificence in order to defeat a Dark Lord. As Welsh and English characters work together toward victory, nostalgia for the faded glory of the empire replaces pride in contemporary imperial holdings. Hunt and Sands state of these moves toward introspection: "As Britain in reality grows less and less important in the world, British ... fantasy delights in isolationism, tradition, and monoculturalism."[14]

And so how do the Harry Potter novels fit into this tradition? Harry's option of staying at home with the Dursleys is obviously a dire one. As I mentioned previously, it is easy to interpret Harry's journey into the wizarding world as one into a thrilling and promising foreign space, separate from the metropole of Muggle England. Hogwarts and the surrounding magical community are a territory where the natives might be technologically primitive, but they are morally enlightened, friendly, respected and respectful, and powerful in many ways. As Kutzer notes of many fantasy works, authors expend a great deal of energy providing the specifics of local flora, fauna, native customs, and behavior. "There is a kind of ethnographic gloss to these books that suggests to the reader that foreign lands are not made-up fantasy lands, but real places that can provide real adventures, if only one can get to them."[15] Accordingly, Harry spends a great deal of time in the wizarding world learning about new plants and creatures, such as mandrakes, hippogriffs, and unicorns, and unfamiliar practices and customs—from the Sorting Hat procedure to how to send mail by Owl Post, travel by Floo powder, and de-gnome a garden.

Beneath this aspect of foreignness, however, lies the fact that the excursions to Hogwarts are not *away* from the homeland and *to* a symbolic colonial outpost, but rather journeys back to Harry's true homespace. In the wizarding world he finds acceptance among people of his own magical kind. As he reaches his dormitory room on the first night back at school for his third year, he feels as if he is "home at last."[16] Thus, on one hand Rowling depicts Hogwarts and its environs as a space of difference, inhabited by the Other, and quite separate from the "real" and flawed British sphere; on the other hand, however, this sphere also serves as an accurate reflection of British reality. Because the wizarding world overlaps and intersects with the Muggle world, Harry is allowed to remain in the very heart of Britain as he supposedly travels to a foreign space, discovers himself, and is initiated into adulthood. British cultural centrism and isolationism are effectively maintained.

Rudyard Kipling's fiction provides an interesting point of comparison with Rowling's series. Both writers seem trapped as they attempt to negotiate the space between longings for empire and a recognition of its potential for destruction. The novel *Kim* (1901), for example, celebrates life in India, and the diversity of people, wildlife, and landscapes of the region, but it simultaneously praises the young protagonist's induction into the British secret service—a collaboration that helps the British to rule India. Rowling appears to experience the same wavering desires between nostalgia for and opposition to neocolonial attitudes. When the Muggle groundskeeper at the Quidditch World Cup campsite suspiciously asks Mr. Weasley if he is "foreign" and remarks that the grounds have been overrun,[17] he gives voice to a conservative anti-immigrant sentiment that Rowling overtly writes against. The divergent attitudes of Ron and Hagrid and Harry and Hermione emphasize this point. Hagrid claims that the less one has do with foreigners, the happier one will be—"Yeh can' trust any of 'em"[18]—and Ron refuses to try the unfamiliar bouillabaisse at the Tournament welcome dinner. In contrast, Harry responds to Hagrid that Viktor Krum is "all right!," and Hermione not only enjoys the French dish but develops a romantic relationship with Krum as well. Together, Harry and Hermione suggest that although the wizarding world can be more insular than the Muggle world in some ways, as the "next generation" of wizards and witches, they will encourage more tolerance and an international outlook.

This tolerance, however, seems linked to the rather banal versions of "multiculturalism" that plague certain late twentieth-/early twenty-first-century communities: visions of "open-mindedness" to the Other function primarily on the level of the enjoyment and consumption of particular goods these foreigners have to offer, such as foods, film, music, and clothing. In spite of the progress that Rowling's narrative ostensibly offers, it can be observed that the underlying discourse of her work supports many of the very ideas she tries to counter. Thus, although she inverts traditional binaries and blurs the lines between domestic and foreign, civilized and savage, because the magical world is located within Britain's borders, the true center of intellectual, spiritual, and cultural enlightenment is not shifted out of the British realm.

Kipling's *The Jungle Books* (1894–1895) provide ground for further comparison between the two authors' sentimentality for certain aspects of imperialist ideology.[19] Many of the stories in Kipling's collection center on themes of invasion. In "Rikki-tikki-tavi," for example, the cobras despise the British colonial family that has moved into the bungalow because the humans threaten the snakes' dominion and the certainty that the snakes' offspring will grow up healthy, strong, and in control. The reptilian antagonists plot for the time when "the garden will be our own again."[20] Representative of India's brown-skinned indigenous peoples, the black snakes are cast as evil, vicious, and dangerous, needing to be exterminated so that the white British colonizers can live peacefully in the land they have appropriated. For the imperialist plan to be successful, however, the white invaders require the native assistance embodied in the mongoose, Rikki-tikki-tavi. The mongoose hero calls the family "his," and this loyalty essentially subverts "the *natural* animosity" between the species, situating the mongoose clearly and *willingly* on the side of the Europeans/humans.[21] By the end of the tale, the borders of the colonized garden are secure: Rikki-tikki-tavi "kept that garden as a mongoose should keep it ... till never a cobra dared show its head inside the walls."[22]

Rather than perpetuating traditional Christian concepts of serpents as evil, Rowling at first appears to contest Eurocentric norms. Hogwarts students initially shun Harry for being a Parselmouth.[23] In *Harry Potter and the Goblet of Fire*, newspaper reporter Rita Skeeter's twisted article about the "disturbed" Harry Potter quotes a member of the Dark Force Defense League, who intimates that others should be "highly suspicious" of anyone who can talk to snakes—creatures embodying the worst forces of Dark Magic and possessing a historical association with "evildoers."[24] Minister of Magic Cornelius Fudge later reiterates the sentiment when he calls Harry's trustworthiness into question specifically because the young wizard can converse with serpents.[25] Rowling suggests here the irony of their bigotry. In the same way that witches are ostracized in the Muggle world for having the rare gift of being able to perform magic, members of wizarding society censure Harry for his linguistic gift. Rowling's critique is clear in that Fudge is both prejudiced and a political coward, and Skeeter is detestably unethical. Harry, able to speak Parseltongue, has a link to the natural world, and, despite a demonstration of the ingenuity and resourcefulness highly regarded in early imperialist adventure stories, he chooses to employ this connection to commune with nature rather than to control and exploit it.

At the same time, however, Rowling relies on the discourse of imperialism in her use of snakes in the narrative. The word "Parseltongue" closely resembles the word "Parsee," the name of a religious community in India concentrated in Bombay. For British readers, references to Parsees might unconsciously evoke images of fakirs and other mystics who perform feats of magic or endurance, such as charming snakes from baskets and walking on coals. As Kutzer notes, the political and cultural lives of India, the "jewel in the crown" of the British Empire, and England have been inextricably entwined since the end of the nineteenth century: "Indian words had become English words: jodhpurs, verandahs, pukka, and so forth."[26] I would therefore assert that Rowling depends upon the reader's assumption of the exotic qualities of India—romantic associations with palm readers, snake charmers, and the like—to connect snakes to fear, particularly fear of the foreign. Just as the cobra antagonists in Kipling's "Rikki-tikki-tavi" are "highly emblematic of India itself. ... Visual shorthand for 'the Orient,'"[27] snakes in the Potter books symbolize inherent femaleness, seductiveness, duplicity, sensual excess, skulking silence, and, above all, danger.[28] Victims of the basilisk in *Harry Potter and the Chamber of Secrets* can be killed by the serpent's stare;[29] in *Goblet of Fire*, Voldemort must milk the female snake Nagini to build up his strength and malevolent powers. Voldemort himself possesses a flat, snakelike face, replete with red gleaming eyes before his transformation,[30] and afterwards, a ghostly white visage with a nose as "flat as a snake's" with slits for nostrils.[31] Furthermore, Voldemort is strengthened by a ceremony that casts him as an anti-Christ—he is the "son" renewed, the "master" revived,[32] and the foe "resurrected"[33]; the end of the chapter ominously states that "*Lord* Voldemort had *risen again*"[34]—effectively reinforcing traditional connections between snakes and Satan.

The anxiety over foreign invasion, far from being dispelled by a narrative that embraces difference, predominates in the Potter books. Danger typically comes from outside national borders. In *Harry Potter and the Sorcerer's Stone*, the three-headed dog, Fluffy, comes from a Greek;[35] in *Chamber of Secrets*, Aragog the giant spider informs Harry and Ron that he, too, arrived from a distant territory.[36] Hagrid found Aragog a mate and their family has grown exponentially in the Forbidden Forest, waiting for the human flesh on which they prey. The fear of immigrant entry, reproduction, and take-over seems evident in this subplot. Wizards and witches constantly worry about the threat of Muggles discovering and invading the magical realm; the antagonism against Muggle-borns stems, in part, from a distrust of their motives after years of persecution at the hands of the nonmagical. Looking for a location for the International Quidditch World Cup, the Ministry of Magic seeks arenas Muggles cannot penetrate and works for months setting up "anti-Muggle precautions" and repelling charms to ward off potential invaders.[37] Voldemort threatens to assail people's minds, hearts, and souls in an attempt to reestablish himself and come to power once again. The turbaned Professor Quirrell, who has been travelling in Albania, proves to be the weak link to national security in book I; easily manipulated by Voldemort, he brings the Dark Lord back to Britain and allows him to penetrate the halls of learning and protection.[38] Similarly, in book IV, Bertha Jorkins holidays in Albania, which leads to her capture, torture for ministry knowledge, and murder, further intimating the perils of travelling abroad.

The motif of invasion and militarized borders grows most prominent in *Harry Potter and the Prisoner of Azkaban*. Hogwarts is cast as a vast empire; it takes students ten minutes to walk to the top of the North Tower from the dining hall. Professor Trelawney remarks that she does not often descend from the tower into "the hustle and bustle" of the main buildings,[39] suggesting a territory of diversity, with both rural and urban spaces. The students learn that powerful enchantments and spells prevent people from entering the castle by stealth or magically apparating, and the groundskeeper Filch knows all of the secret passages to keep guarded. The Marauder's Map shows Harry the secret passages that lead to the village of Hogsmeade, including some of which Filch is unaware; however, these ways *out* also mean that there are ways back *in*, holding an important statement about the repercussions of the imperial enterprise: if explorers and adventurers leave the security of England and establish routes to the far reaches of the empire, these routes are left open for those members of foreign societies to negotiate their way back into England.

Headmaster Albus Dumbledore reluctantly agrees to have dementors[40] stationed around the entrances to the Hogwarts grounds to protect the school from invasion by wizard Sirius Black, at this point a feared escaped convict. The anxiety of infiltration by those who are supposed to be protecting the frontier, however, also runs high: Dumbledore proclaims that no dementor will cross over into the castle while he is the headmaster.[41] Once-strong borders are soon revealed to be quite penetrable, however. When over one hundred dementors enter the Quidditch stadium during a match, Professor Lupin claims that the "restless" spirit of these guards had been swelling for some time.[42] The phrase "the natives are restless" comes to mind, and the dementor attack on Harry after he learns the truth about his parents' murder confirms the dread of the foreign as a force that can suck the soul out of the citizens of the empire. Similarly, after Black's second break-in into the castle, an ominous-looking set of security trolls is hired to guard the entrance to Gryffindor Tower. They patrol the hallways in "a menacing group," grunting instead of speaking in an identifiable (civilized?) language and comparing the size of their clubs.[43] One cannot fail to recall the troll that found its way into Hogwarts in book I of the series and threatened the lives of the students and faculty.

In this way, rather than functioning as symbolic of the colonial territory, the school of magic comes to symbolize the imperial center that unenlightened foreigners threaten to infiltrate, leading to the obliteration of its people. Is it significant that Voldemort and his forces, like Kipling's black snakes, are portrayed in terms of darkness, and to be "dark" is to be evil? Perhaps not. However, the ancient castle clearly stands as a beacon of safety for the side of good, and represents the longevity and stability of Britain's history and civilization.

Hogsmeade, identified as "the only entirely non-Muggle settlement in Britain,"[44] prides itself on the racial purity symbolized by the homogenous magical identity of its residents. The village inn is renowned as the headquarters for the 1612 Goblin Rebellion, reminding visitors of the goblins' uneasy place in magical British history. Goblins of the present day have "dark, slanting eyes"[45] and are described as quite clever, resonating with images of Asian peoples in popular discourse. Extremely self-assured, they are potentially dangerous but fair and trustworthy; they run Gringotts Bank and are polite to customers. Their refusal to assimilate completely (and "properly"?) after the rebellions is suggested by the presence of a Goblin Liaison Office at the Ministry of Magic, and the comment that their English isn't very good. Similarly, the merpeople exist within Hogwarts's boundaries, in the larger magical world that is contained within British borders, but they lead distinct lives, rarely interacting with magical humans. Apparently more primitive than wizards and witches, their rock paintings resemble prehistoric cave drawings, they carry spears, live in crude stone structures, and have no magical abilities.

Harry first encounters the merpeople during the Triwizard Tournament of book IV. This event, which serves as the framework for *Goblet of Fire*, is described as a seven-hundred-year-old tradition, established as a friendly competition between the three largest schools of magic. Its purpose is to lay the foundation of relationships between young wizards and witches of various nationalities. While the message of international camaraderie and cooperation is a positive one and emphasized throughout the story, it is quite noticeable that none of the schools represented comes from outside of the Eurasian continent. We know, for example, that there are schools in the Americas—Bill had a pen-pal at a magic school in Brazil and Harry sees witches from The Salem Witches' Institute at the World Cup.[46] In spite of this, Africa, south and southeast Asia, Australia, North and South America are not merely Other at the tournament—they are invisible. The Others in *Goblet of Fire* are foreign, but still European: students of Beauxbatons and Durmstrang. Rowling's novels do little to alter the Western notion that "outlying regions of the world have no life, history, or culture to speak of, no independence or integrity worth representing without the West."[47]

Madame Maxime, Beauxbatons's headmistress, attires herself in black satin, dresses her hair in a simple yet elegant knot, and wears sparkling opals on her neck and fingers. Her students speak French, dress in expensive silks, and have well-cultivated tastes in cuisine and the arts. The Durmstrang students, on the opposite end of the spectrum, wear cloaks made of a shaggy, matted fur, suggesting an emphasis on function over fashion and a more primitive nature. Impressed by the starry black ceiling of the Great Hall and the golden plates and goblets on which they are served, they seem awed by the refined culture of Hogwarts, situated as more civilized than their own. Nonetheless, they remain silent and stoic, exhibiting tremendous endurance for both their cruelly demanding headmaster and coach—intimating the notoriously exacting trainers of world-renown athletes from Eastern bloc nations—and the harsh winter climate, suggesting their East German-Slavic-Russian connections.

In using these characterizations to emphasize the differences among the rivals, Rowling succeeds in perpetuating certain national and ethnic stereotypes against the British wizards' competitors. While they are cultured and fashionable, the Beauxbaton students are also haughty and snobbish. Fleur Delacoeur laughs derisively at Dumbledore's wish for a comfortable extended visit; she claims Hogwarts delicacies are "too heavy," the furnishings gauche, and musical accompaniments plodding. And although readers eventually come to trust Viktor Krum, he and the rest of the Durmstrang team appear vaguely sinister for most of the novel. Durmstrang pupils learn the Dark Arts as a part of their formal education, and the school does not admit Muggle-borns. Headmaster Karkaroff, a former Voldemort supporter, constantly threatens to withdraw his students from the tournament and accuses Hogwarts and the British ministry of political treachery and corruption in order to manipulate his own champion's success.[48]

Hogwarts's position on the ethical high ground, with its students and teachers of superior character, shines through further when Dumbledore invites all of the foreign pupils back to Hogwarts at any time they wish to visit. He urges bonds of friendship and trust in order to successfully defeat Voldemort: cultural and linguistic differences are "nothing at all if our aims are identical and our hearts are open."[49] The British school promotes international goodwill, the inspiration for the battle against evil, and stands as the emblem of enlightened thought.

The obvious question: what would the result of this policy of open borders be? Amongst conventional children's adventure stories, non-European cultures are established as the inferior Other, and non-white, non-European characters who are central to the plots are either well-assimilated into the mainstream or comic in their attempts to blend in. The position of the students of color in their Hogwarts surroundings is therefore telling as to Rowling's conception of multiculturalism. While most discussions of race and racism in the novels operate on a symbolic level, analyzing Rowling's representation of metaphorical Others in the human wizarding world, including Muggle-borns, giants, trolls, and house-elves, I would like to explore the depiction of literal Otherness in the predominantly white, British environs of Hogwarts.[50]

Cho Chang, the Patil twins, Dean Thomas, Lee Jordan, and Angelina Johnson reveal that a diversity of races and ethnicities are represented at Harry Potter's school. Cho Chang's name suggests that she is Chinese; Parvati and Padma Patil's names similarly point to South Asian identity. During the first-year sorting, Dean is described as "a Black boy even taller than Ron,"[51] and, while not a definitive racial marker, Lee Jordan's dreadlocks hint at possible African-Jamaican ancestry. In *Goblet of Fire*, Rowling describes Angelina as the "tall black girl" who plays one of the Chasers on Gryffindor's Quidditch team.[52]

Noticeably, however, the inclusion of people of color does not mean the inclusion of any representation of ethnic difference and cultural practices. Parvati's and Cho's ethnicities are evident in their names, but *only* in their names. And while all of the students mentioned might be visually apparent to the characters within the fictional storyline, their visual difference for the reader quickly disappears and their racial identities fade into the background. In a world where white people are the dominant social group, whiteness becomes the "default" for unmentioned race; it is interpreted as the norm and assumed when unstated. Rowling thus finds herself in an ideological bind—while she perhaps attempts to display a "colorblind" society where everyone is distinguished solely by magical ability, she makes it supremely easy for the reader to forget (or ignore) the multiethnic surroundings that she initially seeks to establish.

When Fred and George spot Lee Jordan in Diagon Alley in book II, for instance, his race goes unmentioned; he is simply "their friend," and, throughout the series, their partner in mischief and the spirited commentator of the Hogwarts Quidditch matches. Likewise, no physical description accompanies the introduction or numerous subsequent mentions of Dean Thomas in book II or in book III, where he is identified only as one of Harry's "fellow Gryffindors," "good with a quill," and the only one bold enough to hope for a vampire as the next Defense Against the Dark Arts teacher.[53] It is somewhat of a surprise to learn in book IV, after three novels and over thirteen hundred pages of text, that Angelina is of African descent. This lack of specificity is quite remarkable when compared to the repetition of the most striking physical features of most of the white characters, whether they are central to the plots of each novel or simply familiar faces among the student body. Neville Longbottom is consistently described as round-faced in each book of the series; Seamus Finnigan's sandy-colored hair is often highlighted; Professor Snape's hooked nose, long, greasy black hair, and crooked yellow teeth come up time and time again. Mad-Eye Moody's introduction includes wonderfully sharp details about his scarred face, nose with a missing chunk of flesh, grizzled mane of grey hair, and the beady dark eye paired with the rolling magical blue one. On Ron's first appearance in the series, his bodily characteristics are carefully enumerated: "He was tall, thin, and gangling, with freckles, big hands and feet, and a long nose." The same is true of Hermione: she has "lots of bushy brown hair, and rather large front teeth."[54] The Weasleys' "flaming" red hair and freckles continue to be a site of grounding for the reader, and much is made of the size of Hermione's teeth and the wooliness of her hair throughout the series, as well as her tanned skin after a summer vacation in France. And, perhaps most obviously, references to Harry Potter's frail build, green eyes, unruly black hair, and the lightning-bolt scar all work to heighten the reader's identification with the protagonist, and simultaneously reveal how being physically unusual can be admirable.[55]

Rowling makes a strong move towards encouraging multiculturalism, especially with her messages condemning the bigotry of both normative Muggles like the Dursleys, pure-blood witches and wizards who scorn "Mudbloods," and all magical folk who assume the natural inferiority of house-elves and fear and persecute giants and werewolves.[56] On a more literal level, Hogwarts enrolls several students of color, who are mentioned numerous times throughout the books, and many of the couples at the Yule Ball during Harry's fourth year at Hogwarts are interracial—Cedric and Cho, Fred and Angelina, Ron and Padma, and Harry and Parvati.[57] All suggest the integration of people of various races at the school and the hope for tolerance among people of the larger magical community. At the same time, however, Rowling undermines this reading; to date, the novels portray not integration and acceptance, but the complete assimilation of Dean, Lee, Angelina, Parvati, Padma, and Cho into the all-white landscape of Hogwarts students and teachers.[58] In stressing a liberal humanist message of "we are all the same beneath the surface" and asserting that race and ethnicity *should* not be important in judging another person, Rowling's text conveys the message that race and ethnicity *are* not important for those who experience life from this position—hardly true of late twentieth/early twenty-first century Britain, Canada, the United States, or much of the rest of the world.

One possibility for why racial identity *cannot* be mentioned in Rowling's texts is that the works wobble between seeking a way out of the imperialist agenda and experiencing a certain nostalgia for the safety and security attributed to the empire. In order to perpetuate the notion that her characters of color are "true Brits" and belong to the national landscape, they must symbolically disappear from this landscape—visually, if not physically. My concern lies in how this translates for young readers: just beneath the surface, the novels propose that in order to be accepted, popular, and successful, one's differences must be ignored. And, although the *existence* of differences may be a reality, *acknowledging* these differences is taboo. As postcolonial critic Shaobo Xie proclaims, "commonality must not be exaggerated as a license for eliminating cultural or social specificity. ... [T]he imperialism of the [S]ame has reigned for over two thousand years; it provides the dominant discourse or social group with power to dominate and control difference."[59]

The literature of most anglophone, or English-speaking, countries has been strongly influenced by the British Empire. As Jean Webb notes, during their formative years, the colonies (including America) were economically unable to produce their own children's books. These materials were imported from the industrial powerhouse of England, "and therefore the ideological forces derived from imperialist England were also carried along."[60] In our current era of so-called globalization, it is interesting to note that while approximately 70 percent of children's books in France have been translated into French from other languages—predominantly English—less than 1 percent of books published in English are translations. British (and U.S.) texts still dominate the market throughout the English-speaking Caribbean and Africa as well. All of these figures have tremendous implications for the cultural, political, and social ideas that get spread throughout the world. Because literature can so readily be wielded as a weapon of assimilation, we must understand the imperialist ideology encoded within—especially when it is ensconced in the discourse of postcolonial resistance, proposing to support the position of the minority—and contest it within our daily lives.

NOTES

1. M. Daphne Kutzer, *Empire's Children: Empire and Imperialism in Classic British Children's Books* (New York: Garland, 2000), xvi.

2. J. K. Rowling, *Harry Potter and the Goblet of Fire* (New York: Scholastic Press, 2000), 62.

3. Ibid., 150.

4. Frank Birbalsingh, Introduction, *Frontiers of Caribbean Literature in English*, Frank Birbalsingh, ed. (New York: St. Martin's Press, 1996), ix–xxiii, ix.

5. Elizabeth D. Schafer, *Beacham's Sourcebooks for Teaching Young Adult Fiction: Exploring Harry Potter* (Osprey: FL: Beacham Publishing Corp., 2000), 117.

6. Shaobo Xie, "Rethinking the Identity of Cultural Otherness: The Discourse of Difference as an Unfinished Project," in *Voices of the Other: Children's Literature and the Postcolonial Context*, Roderick McGillis, ed. (New York: Garland, 2000), 1–16, 1.

7. Quoted in M. Daphne Kutzer, *Empire's Children*, 66.

8. Patrick Brantlinger, "Victorians and Africans: The Genealogy of the Myth of the Dark Continent," *Critical Inquiry* 12, no. 1 (Autumn 1985): 166–203, 200.

9. Kutzer, *Empire's Children*, 56.

10. The same is true of R. M. Ballantyne's *The Coral Island* (1858). As Kutzer lays forth, the novel also clearly instructs readers in what traits are to be esteemed in the

colonizer: Avatea, the Samoan woman whom the cannibals plan to sacrifice, provides the young British hero Jack with the chance to prove his chivalry and manhood without the risk of marriage, domesticity, or, as Kutzer fails to mention, miscegenation.

11. At the same time, as Kutzer maintains, the narrative contains a submerged concern over trouble cropping up throughout the empire. Labor rebellions and demands for political independence and social equality are domesticated in *Pooh*: tigers, kangaroos, and elephants—symbolic of colonial territories and dominions—are all stuffed animals for children.

12. Peter Hunt and Karen Sands, "The View from the Center: British Empire and Post-Empire Children's Literature," in *Voices of the Other: Children's Literature and the Postcolonial Context*, Roderick McGillis, ed. (New York: Garland, 2000): 39–54, 47.

13. Jean de Brunhoff's *The Story of Babar, the Little Elephant* (1931) also fits the trend: at its conclusion, Babar is made king of his herd because he has been to the city, wears fancy clothes, and drives an impressive car. The adoption of European culture and ostensibly "civilized" ways seems to serve as evidence of his superiority and right to rule.

14. Hunt and Sands, "The View," 48.

15. Kutzer, *Empire's Children*, 2.

16. J. K. Rowling, *Harry Potter and the Prisoner of Azkaban* (New York: Scholastic Press, 1999), 95.

17. Rowling, *Goblet of Fire*, 77.

18. Ibid., 563.

19. Rudyard Kipling, *The Jungle Books*, 1894–1895 (New York: Signet, 1961).

20. Ibid., 102. Interestingly enough, Kipling's snakes are called Nag and Nagina; Voldemort's snake in book IV is called Nagini.

21. Kutzer, *Empire's Children*, 26, emphasis added. Similarly, in the Mowgli stories, Mowgli serves as an intruder in the jungle, but one welcomed by the "good" natives/animals. Mowgli's Mother Wolf confesses to him: "child of man, I loved thee more than ever I loved my cubs." Kipling, *Jungle Books*, 29.

22. Kipling, *Jungle Books*, 109.

23. One able to speak with snakes.

24. Rowling, *Goblet of Fire*, 612.

25. Ibid., 706.

26. Kutzer, *Empire's Children*, 68.

27. Ibid., 26.

28. See Edward W. Said's *Orientalism* (New York: Vintage Books, 1979).

29. J. K. Rowling, *Harry Potter and the Chamber of Secrets* (New York: Scholastic Press, 1999).

30. Rowling, *Goblet of Fire*, 640.

31. Ibid., 643.

32. Ibid., 641.

33. Ibid., 642.

34. Ibid., 643, emphasis added.

35. J. K. Rowling, *Harry Potter and the Sorcerer's Stone* (New York: Scholastic Inc., 1999).

36. Rowling, *Chamber of Secrets*, 277.

37. Rowling, *Goblet of Fire*, 69.

38. Quirrell's turban connects a specific cultural item of clothing with the dangers of concealment, further suggesting xenophobia and a deceptive nature in Arabic people.

39. Rowling, *Prisoner of Azkaban*, 103.

40. Guards from Azkaban Prison who absorb all positive feelings and memories from their human captives.

41. Rowling, *Prisoner of Azkaban*, 166.

42. Ibid., 187.

43. Ibid., 270.

44. Ibid., 76.

45. Rowling, *Goblet of Fire*, 446.

46. One might also assume the same of the other continents, although this is more of a long shot, since they are represented in sports at the World Cup but not explicitly in an academic context: Bartemius Crouch speaks of organizing portkey magical transports over five continents, Harry sees three African wizards in the campground, and the Ugandan team beats Wales in one of the matches. Notably, Britain has not hosted the Quidditch World Cup in thirty years, suggesting the decline of the nation's preeminence in the international world. During the finals, England falls to Transylvania in a shockingly bad performance, Wales loses to Uganda, and Scotland is soundly defeated by Luxembourg. We see here the symbolic end to the British dynasty, and a dynamic described by C. L. R James in his influential *Beyond a Boundary* (1963), which analyzes the role of cricket in the former colonies.

47. Edward W. Said, *Culture and Imperialism* (New York: Vintage Books, 1994), xix.

48. See Rowling, *Goblet of Fire*, 561–62.

49. Ibid., 723.

50. Schafer's discussion of race, for example, focuses almost exclusively on the question of Mudbloods and Muggles in the narratives: she identifies racism as central to the plot of book II, but speaks of it only in terms of castes and pedigrees.

51. Rowling, *Sorcerer's Stone*, 122.

52. Rowling, *Goblet of Fire*, 261.

53. Rowling, *Prisoner of Azkaban*, 55, 151, and 429, respectively. In the last case, perhaps this hope arises because he understands the position of being the Other?

54. Rowling, *Sorcerer's Stone*, 93 and 105.

55. Certain physical traits work to bias the reader towards particular characters, and later reveal the danger of falling for beauty that is only skin deep. However, it seems that the lesson does not extend to the characters whose appearance violates accepted gender roles. Most notably, although Madame Maxime is incredibly large, she is still established as perfectly feminine: she wears elegant satin dresses, elaborate jewelry, dances gracefully, and styles her hair tastefully. In contrast, Rita Skeeter's curls stand rigid on her head and appear quite odd on her "heavy-jawed face." Although she has long fingernails, they resemble daggers; her fingers are thick and her large hands are "mannish" with an astonishingly powerful (i.e., manly) grip. Rowling, *Goblet of Fire*, 307 and 303, respectively. The journalist's masculinity ties in disturbingly with her antagonistic and untrustworthy nature.

56. In *Prisoner of Azkaban*, Professor Lupin serves as a racialized Other; he has been "passing" for human at Hogwarts in order to achieve acceptance in the same way that people of African descent have long passed for white in European-dominated societies. Late in the text, Ron avoids Lupin's touch, gasping, *"Get away from me, werewolf!"* Rowling, *Prisoner of Azkaban*, 345. He uses "werewolf" much like a racial slur, exhibiting the socially indoctrinated fear of difference. During the course of writing this essay, I came to think of Lupin's identity less in terms of its racial significance and more in terms of the discourse of disease, and AIDS in particular. He was bitten as a child, when there was no cure; he recalls hiding his diagnosis upon entering school because other parents would not want their children "exposed" to him. Rowling, *Prisoner of Azkaban*, 353. Lupin's primary concern when he forgets to take his potion after capturing Pettigrew is to escape into the Forbidden Forest and then resign because he can't risk infecting others. The language is that of immunity, contagion, the threat of infection, and social ignorance about disease transmission.

57. Dean calls the twins "the best-looking girls" in their school class, but he has asked neither one to the dance. Rowling, *Goblet of Fire*, 411. Is anything to be made of the fact that all the female students in the list of interracial couples are of color, while all the male students mentioned are white? Might this apparent pattern be tied to the old necessity of preserving the purity of white womanhood? Hunt argues that Burnett's *The Secret Garden* (1911), Kenneth Grahame's *The Wind in the Willows* (1908), and Rider Haggard's *King Solomon's Mines* (1885) "chart aspects of the decline of empire (corruption, instability, and resistance) without necessarily damaging the central ideas of white male supremacy." Peter Hunt, *Children's Literature* (Malden, MA: Blackwell Publishers Ltd., 2001), 260. Perhaps the same is true of *Goblet of Fire*; the boys are cast as varying models of desirability.

58. Rowling's depiction of certain creatures further subverts her more overt antiracist message. The mandrakes in book II are raised for wizard use—to be cut up and stewed for the revival of the petrified victims of the basilisk. Although these anthropomorphic plants wail like babies and mature to party like teenagers, their harvest and essential death for wizard consumption is portrayed as for the good of Hogwarts's empire. In a similar vein, the small, leathery gnomes, with their large, knobby, bald heads "exactly like a potato"—though not explicitly brown—are characterized by Ron as "not too bright." As he hurls one twenty feet out of his family's garden, it lands with a thud, and he claims: "It doesn't *hurt* them. ... " Rowling, *Chamber of Secrets*, 37. How does Ron *know* that the creatures experience no pain? I am reminded of the rhetoric supporting the extensions of the empire: "Whatever the actual reasons behind imperial conquests— be they mercenary, missionary, or military—there is a need to justify, if not idealize, one's often brutal actions in the pursuit of empire. One way of justifying one's actions is to demonize the native population." Kutzer, *Empire's Children*, 4–5. Rowling softens her portrayal of the antagonism between garden gnomes and wizards in *Goblet of Fire*, where a gnome, running from Hermione's cat, giggles maniacally as it escapes.

59. Xie, "Rethinking the Identity," 9.

60. Jean Webb, "Text, Culture, and Postcolonial Children's Literature: A Comparative Perspective," in *Voices of the Other: Children's Literature and the Postcolonial Context*, Roderick McGillis, ed. (New York: Garland, 2000), 71–88, 71.

13

Class and Socioeconomic Identity in Harry Potter's England

Julia Park

In J. K. Rowling's phenomenally successful children's series about young wizard Harry Potter, readers are ostensibly treated to a world divided in two, between wizards and Muggles, the nonmagical humans. In the wizard world, we hear whether one is a pureblooded wizard or a "Mudblood"—a derogatory name for wizards of Muggle parentage—but we do not hear direct discussions of social class. Or do we? What does the story of an orphaned wizard-in-training reveal about England and British class structure? And, more specifically, what does Rowling reveal about her own experience of English society? The author's perspective is inescapably written into the stories; when Rowling writes about Harry Potter, we learn as much about Joanne Kathleen Rowling as we do about Harry.

Rowling, whose rags-to-riches story improves with each media retelling, is a scion of the British middle class. Much like Charles Dickens, she reveals her attitudes toward social rank through character and scene. For example, her view of the upper classes can be determined by examining her portraits of Lucius and Draco Malfoy and the private "public" school world. Similarly, one can conjecture her feelings towards the working classes by looking at her caricatures of Hagrid, the house-elves, and various other bit players. Rowling illustrates the perfect model for the middle class via Harry Potter himself. I will argue that only the middle class—Rowling's class—seems to escape general criticism, with one notable exception: Potter's Muggle relations, the cartoonish Dursleys.

For Rowling, the middle class is a comfort zone, a place where she feels most familiar. In her own life, as has been documented in numerous sources, she accepted public assistance; however, as befits a member of the bourgeoisie, she has also expressed feeling shame about receiving this financial support. As is the case with most members of society, Rowling holds some seemingly indelible prejudices and biases towards those with money and the status that comes with it, and those without. As literary critic Pam Morris suggests, the middle class believes that "wealth [is] a reliable signifier of virtue, while poverty [is] the outward sign of moral lack." This "social myth" functions by allowing members of the middle class to construct their "own class identity through difference, and for justifying the condition and status of the working class as the result of their own irresponsible degradation."[1] In the Potter books, however, a distinct difference also seems to be drawn between those who inherited wealth and those who "earned" it—a throwback to the Industrial Age and the rise of the modern middle class.[2]

In this chapter I will show how Rowling's staunchly middle-class worldview colors every aspect of the four novels published to date. And in spite of the inevitable comparison, Rowling is no Dickens; despite halfhearted attempts at social commentary, she is still bound by her English middle-class upbringing. Her experience of British class structure and society is reflected in the wizard world she has created, and what a rigid, structured world it truly is. She thus reveals her own prejudices with her portraits of the magical and nonmagical worlds.

Rowling is a great borrower of themes and motifs, which critics have acknowledged in many articles about her work. One of the instantly recognizable features of the Harry Potter books is their resemblance to familiar fairy tales.[3] "The plots of the first four novels thus far resemble the structure of a conventional fairy tale: a modest little protagonist, typically male, ... does not at first realize how talented he is and departs from his home on a mission."[4] A strict social class characterizes fairy tales of the European sort: the poor girl in rags marries the prince, and voilà, they discover that she was a nobleman's daughter after all. What seems like a rags-to-riches story often merely confirms the status quo, and generally, there is not much movement down the social ladder; despite having fallen into poverty or other dire circumstances, a noble still has his or her blue blood. Thus Cinderella, though forced to sleep in the fireplace, is always still a nobleman's daughter, as is Snow White, who temporarily becomes a domestic for the dwarves, and both marry according to this birth status.

This paradigm holds true in Rowling's tales. We find that although Harry Potter is a mistreated orphan who sleeps under the stairs, he is the only son of two socially beloved, powerful, wizard parents. At the age of eleven, Harry experiences his coming of age—his invitation to Hogwarts School of Witchcraft and Wizardry, knowledge of his parentage, a cache of gold held in trust for him, and his destiny as one of the strongest wizards ever born. Thus Harry claims his birthright and social class in the wizard world, following the pattern of all fairy tales: he will become a great wizard in his own time, he is no longer poor, and he will, most likely, eventually get the girl (though will it be Cho Chang, Ginny Weasley, or Hermione? We await the final three novels for that answer).

Interestingly, however, despite this newly acquired money and status, Harry is never catapulted into the highest echelons of society. Most obviously, he rejects Draco Malfoy's offers of allegiance on board the Hogwarts Express in book I and chooses to remain by the side of Ron, who, although he possesses a long-standing family name and pure-blood pedigree, occupies lower rungs of the class hierarchy than both Draco and Harry because of his family's poverty. Furthermore, Rowling's hero is only too happy to distribute his wealth rather than hoard it. In *Harry Potter and the Sorcerer's Stone*, Harry describes going without money for his entire life until the visit to Gringotts; once his pockets are full of wizarding money, however, he proceeds to buy a pile of treats for Ron and himself on the train to Hogwarts.[5] In book IV, he generously gives his Triwizard Tournament winnings to Fred and George, Ron's twin brothers, again demonstrating a preference for socioeconomic equity and minimizing the distance between himself and the Weasley family. It is never made clear how the Potters ended up with so much gold to bequeath to Harry in the first place: Lily Potter is from a middle-class family, as her sister Petunia Dursley makes very apparent, and James Potter is from a wizard family of unstated financial status. In comparison with the Malfoys, however, though he has a good bit of gold, Harry clearly belongs to a different class—both by choice, upbringing, and the scale of his possessions.

More intriguing than Harry's character arc is Rowling's own personal mythology, whether created by the public relations department of her publisher or too many journalists scrambling for a scoop. One biographer gushes:

Often the story behind the author is as interesting, if not more so, than what is written. In the case of J. K. Rowling, the story has a little bit of everything. There is happiness and love. There is also some sadness. The story of J. K. Rowling is also one of bravery, determination, and triumph over seemingly overwhelming odds. And finally there is the happy ending. The life of J. K. Rowling sounds very much like the stories she writes and is, in a way, a fairy tale come true.[6]

Another journalist interviewed Rowling and came away with this observation:

Perhaps the most amazing aspect of this story is the woman behind it all. Seven years ago Joanne Kathleen Rowling was an unemployed single mother who spent her afternoons staying warm in Edinburgh coffee shops, writing while her baby slept. Today, with three of the world's all-time best-selling books to her credit, the 34-year-old author is 25th on the *Forbes'* list of the world's 100 most powerful celebrities.[7]

Critic Jack Zipes pinpointed the situation precisely when he wrote about the appeal of the now legendary story of J. K. Rowling, Single Mother on Welfare: "This myth is the old rags-to-riches story and in our day and age has been spread through the mass media. It is the fairy tale about the diligent, hardworking girl who is recognized as a princess and lives happily ever after."[8] The various interpretations of the facts exemplify how a person's history can become mythologized to serve a particular purpose—whether this be skillful marketing, inspiration of the masses, or calming the anxieties of a public decrying the inequalities of their social systems.

In point of fact, Rowling is the daughter of a factory manager and a lab technician—both solidly middle-class jobs. She went to Wyedean Comprehensive, where she received high marks and was named head girl in her final year.[9] She then attended Exeter University, and during that time spent a year in Paris studying French. After university, Rowling spent two years researching human rights violations for Amnesty International and worked for the Manchester Chamber of Commerce, among other administrative jobs. She took a job teaching English in Portugal, where she met and married her husband. (The marriage was short-lived but produced a daughter.) Rowling moved to Scotland to be near to her sister, and, by her own admission and that of her biographer, she went on public assistance for a year as she finished the manuscript for *Harry Potter and the Philosopher's Stone*, published as *Harry Potter and the Sorcerer's Stone* in the United States.[10]

Rowling's own life choices disprove the fairy-tale allusion. Her biographer writes that when moving to Scotland, "Joanne knew she would have no trouble finding another teaching job. But to do that would mean there would be no time left for writing." In other words, her "descent" into indigence was willful and clearly temporary. When Prime Minister John Major called welfare mothers "freeloaders," Rowling felt particularly offended. "Yes, she was a single mother with a child. But she was also a college graduate with no shortage of skills."[11] After earning a grant from the Scottish Arts Council, Rowling taught French at the Leth Academy in Edinburgh, and later at the Moray House Training College. Thus, by the time she received a publishing contract from Bloomsbury and the first Harry Potter title hit the stands, she had long been gainfully employed. When the royalty checks began to arrive, she no longer needed to work as a teacher and the rest is fairy-tale golden: Rowling possesses wealth, fame, and general acclaim, as well as the luxury of finishing the Potter series without financial struggle and the limits that a full-time job would put on her time.

The often-drawn comparisons between Rowling's life and a fairy tale existence are therefore moot. Except for the one year she chose to take off from work, the successful children's book writer never endured any long-term and/or dire poverty. Her year in Paris and her jobs with Amnesty International, the Chamber of Commerce, and teaching English abroad, though not necessarily luxury jobs, still kept her squarely in the middle-class world she had always known. Rowling, rather than suffering economic hardships, seemed instead to suffer from those middle-class afflictions: ennui, low self-esteem, and parents who did not understand her career desires. As a teenager, she stated outright that she wanted to be a writer. According to an article in *School Library Journal*, Rowling notes, "My parents were the kind of parents who would have thought, 'Ah, yes, that's very nice, dear. But where is the pension plan?'"[12]

If moral support was thin on the ground, Rowling's imagination was clearly fertile enough, and she has used her experience of middle-class suburbia and her daily childhood exposure to the rigid class system of British schools to build a world for Harry—a world that clearly exhibits the same sort of social order.

As an English schoolgirl, Rowling undoubtedly would have been exposed to Charles Dickens. Indeed, I would argue that Dickens is the author whom Rowling most resembles: like her literary forefather, Rowling writes in fairy-tale mode; as well, she writes from her personal worldview. As critic Michael Kotzin asserts, much of Dickens's fiction can be interpreted through his personal experiences. "His insistent, recurring portrayal of the deserted child, for example, doubtless owed much to his own childhood 'desertion,' which came when his father went to prison for debt."[13] Many of Dickens's characters were "innocent children deprived of care by cruel or unproviding parents or stepparents and threatened by villains"[14]—a description that fits Harry Potter exactly.

Like Dickens, Rowling often names her characters onomatopoeically, also utilizing foreign associations and phonetics when naming her creations. "Naming her characters was one of the most enjoyable parts about writing Harry. [She was] long a collector of unusual names and clever when it came to creating her own."[15] Where Dickens offers Chuzzlewit, Choakumchilde, and Scrooge, among other memorable names, Rowling gives us Snape, Malfoy, Filch, Quirrell, and Lupin. Names function as character tags, suggesting something of the characters' personality and demeanor. Snape snipes at his students, Malfoy is of bad faith, Filch is a sneaky fellow, and Quirrell is the quivering, frightened teacher who succumbs to Voldemort's powers.[16] Lupin is, appropriately, a werewolf.

In terms of social and economic issues, Dickens felt the need to try to expose some of the more egregious social ills of his time, including child labor and the use of the workhouse to punish debtors and other social misfits. Rowling is not quite so efficacious. As Zipes says,

In the last novel [*Harry Potter and the Goblet of Fire*[17]], Rowling seemed to be touching on some serious problems such as violence ... and union organizing. However, she never explores these topics in depth. For example, Hermione's support of the house-elves is generally mocked by the boys, and Rowling also depicts the elves (common laborers) resisting Hermione's attempts to organize them because they enjoy their work and slavery. Is Rowling trying to show us that workers have such a low political consciousness that they will not listen to an enlightened leader like Hermione?[18]

By contrast, Dickens was tortured by the social conditions of the poor and wrote frequently about the seamier side of London. "As social critic, artist and tormented man, Dickens was never far from the fairy tale. ... Part of the horror was of man's making—the result of social conditions which, it seemed, could be corrected, and Dickens called upon the medium of the fairy tale in an attempt to bring about change."[19] Rowling has yet to reach that kind of depth;[20] she too often reverts to stereotypes rather than original creations, and these stereotypes most vividly reveal her middle-class prejudices.

Rowling accurately portrays the world of the British boarding school in her depictions of Hogwarts School of Witchcraft and Wizardry. All of the pupils are called by their surnames except by bosom friends; much like children all over the world, they either covet or scoff at the position of prefect or head boy or girl. The students' (and indeed, the entire wizard world's) devotion to the game of Quidditch equates to the British love for soccer and cricket, and students display their patriotism by supporting national Quidditch teams and attending the World Cup. They also show loyalty and support for their individual houses by spirited competition, whether on the field or in the classroom. Social Darwinism prevails, and indeed, teachers encourage such behavior; Professor McGonagall acts as keen for her house to win the annual house cup as her students.[21] Rowling's use of Latin or pseudo-Latin for the magical spells learned at Hogwarts—incantations like *"Expeliaramus"* or *"Priori Incantatem,"* for example—also alludes to another aspect of British education: a Victorian awe for science and love of classifying. Knowing Latin names became associated with intellectualism and the schooling of the elite class.[22]

In the traditional social order of the magical school, comparable to that of British private schools for the privileged, what matters is how ancient one's family is, how much wizard gold they possess, and of course, where they stood in the Dark Times when Voldemort rose to power. Those of mixed blood or little money receive sneers from the wealthier, and those whose families held power with Voldemort grudgingly await their return to favor.

Draco Malfoy and his father represent the stereotypical upper classes of British society. As Rowling describes them, they have pale skin and fair hair—an Aryan-like appearance that perhaps alludes to whiteness being equated with virtue.[23] Overtly, however, the Malfoys associate their wealth and pure-blood heritage with virtue. Their attitude of entitlement enables them to sneer and bully their way through life. When Draco gets caught in mischief with Harry and receives detention, for example, he complains that the punishment is "servant stuff," inappropriate for students to do.[24] Draco would far prefer the intellectual though tedious exercise of writing a hundred sentences than to be out chasing unicorns in the Forbidden Forest; Dickens scholar Pam Morris identifies this outlook as a fear of "the perceived degradation of manual labor."[25] Likewise, to exemplify the upper class's need for "conspicuous consumption and display," Malfoy regularly mocks the Weasleys for their lack of money. He shows off his new broomstick—the fastest, most expensive model available, the Firebolt—and his father soon purchases enough Firebolts to outfit the entire Slytherin Quidditch team. As Morris writes, "[T]he spectacle of wealthy style … is intended to intimidate those it separates off as 'common.'"[26]

When Dickens writes of the upper classes, he frequently shows a yearning on the part of the nobility to incarcerate the poor, criminalizing poverty and the "crime" of want. Rowling's characters exhibit this same desire when Draco Malfoy attempts to use his influence to get Hagrid fired and sent to Azkaban, the wizard prison.[27] And Malfoy is at least temporarily successful at that. Rowling does not necessarily believe in her upper class characters' inherent goodness or evil, but I would argue that a common urge exists among all people to envy and resent those farther up the social ladder. It would be difficult to believe that Rowling had completely escaped being influenced by these ideas.[28]

Hagrid, the Hogwarts gamekeeper, is one of many representatives of the lower classes in the Potter series. He reflects this position in his speech, complete with fractured grammar, muttered expletives, and a deafeningly loud voice, emblematic of a lack of education, not only in the formal rules of language arts but also in the social graces. His manners are uncouth, to say the least; he wipes his mouth on the backs of his hands, belches and honks loudly into huge handkerchiefs. Hagrid lacks restraint, partaking in frequent drunken binges—he always seems to have a huge tankard of ale at hand—and displaying an inability to contain his temper or to resist temptations such as the dragon's egg or Fluffy, the three-headed dog. His intense fondness for all types of animals provides a reason for the upper classes to sneer at him continually, but especially in the trial and execution of Buckbeak in book III. Hagrid often gambles down at the pub and was expelled from school as a youth. And, despite their affection for the gamekeeper, Hermione, Ron, and Harry cannot stomach his rustic cooking. When he offers them stoat sandwiches, they refuse; they also quail at the proffered beef casserole in which huge talons lurk. These details distance Hagrid's food from the delicacies prepared in the school kitchens and symbolically mark Hagrid as distinctly lower class.

Rowling's house-elves function in ways that resemble Hagrid's place in the texts—primarily in their farcical roles. Besides Hagrid and the elves, the only characters who weep openly are female: Hermione, Ron's sister, Ginny, and Mrs. Weasley. The lower classes, as characterized by the gamekeeper and Dobby and the other elves, exist symbolically outside the social system represented by Hogwarts and are therefore not subject to a need for a stoicism that could be connected to upper-crust frigidity. While Hagrid and Dobby regularly cry without regard for the jeers of the upper classes, as represented by the students, faculty, or the elves' masters, their outbursts are typically portrayed as a cause for the reader's amusement. Correspondingly, members of the upper classes rarely display any emotions other than anger or smugness.

Rowling's physical description of the house-elves—creatures with large ears like bats', bulbous green eyes, and each resembling a "very ugly doll"[29]— proves eerily similar to descriptions of the creatures from the 1984 U.S. movie *Gremlins*. According to social critic Ed Guerrero, this film furnishes society with allegorical ways to work out dynamics of power and domination. He notes that the "good" Gremlin is "passive, diminutive and aims to entertain and please the family," a description that suits the house-elves' obsequy perfectly.[30] House-elves bow and scrape and flagellate themselves for even thinking badly of their owners. Rowling means to draw a parallel to slavery, but, once again, because she frequently uses the elves for comic effect, she spoils her effort at social commentary. There is nothing funny about slavery, and the author's depiction of an enslaved class as something to entertain her readers is reprehensible. Her demeaning use of these characters, written in a way that suggests their plight as humorous in and of itself, betrays her middle-class patronizing attitude toward all types of laborers, and specifically unpaid/underpaid workers. As Guerrero would say, "[M]onsters in the horror, sci-fi, and fantasy genres [represent] the incessant return of those repressed fears and problems that society cannot articulate or cope with openly."[31]

As we turn to the middle class, we must examine the figure of Ron Weasley, faithful friend to Harry Potter. Overall, Ron and the Weasley family are positive characters; however, Rowling depicts them in a subtly mocking, stereotypical view of the Irish. Ron, the youngest son from a large family of wizards, has red hair and freckles. He is also dirt-poor, stuck with hand-me-downs and too many siblings, and the butt of the wealthy Draco Malfoy's taunts. Mrs. Weasley—her Christian name is Molly, a proper Irish name, if you please—has so many children that she cannot remember that Ron hates corned beef (that traditional Irish meat) on his sandwiches. Mrs. Weasley takes Harry under her wing and sends him a hand-knit emerald green sweater for his first Christmas at Hogwarts; when the Weasleys travel by Floo powder in *Harry Potter and the Chamber of Secrets,* it turns the fire an emerald green as well, and when they attend the Quidditch World Cup in book IV, they are, without question, rooting for Ireland to win. Rowling names the Weasleys' home *The Burrow,* suggesting rabbits and how they breed; she also describes the structure as looking like a large stone pigpen, animalizing the family in yet another unflattering way.[32] And although most other Rowling characters possess Dickensian names, mostly comic-descriptive, the Weasleys' name sounds like a slur; its associations are hardly charming. Is there anything redeeming about being a weasel or weasel-like? Thus, the Weasleys are shabby-genteel. They belong to the middle class, but with the taint of too little money and too many children.

"[E]vil is elusive in the Harry Potter novels, and yet it lurks around every corner and on almost every page. Even in Muggleland, or suburban England, evil exists in the shape of the Dursley family."[33] The Dursleys, Harry's non-magical relations, present an excruciating parody of the middle class. Aunt Petunia, a horse-faced woman, spends her free time spying on the neighbors, partially in a bizarre attempt to "keep up with the Joneses," while Uncle Vernon, an overlarge, self-important man, runs a company that makes drills. Their greatest pride is that they are perfectly normal, as Rowling writes.[34] Petunia and Vernon live in a "perfect" house at Privet Drive, where they dote upon their son, Dudley, who grows fatter and crueler to Harry every year. His very size emphasizes the family's obsession with excess and luxury as they constantly strive to prove their financial and social standing.

In stark contrast to the hoard of food given to Dudley, the Dursleys punish Harry with short food rations, or no food at all. Food critic Bee Wilson comments on Rowling's ability to link food to characters:

Aunt Petunia is mean and pretentious when it comes to food. She is mean with Harry, providing two slices of bread and a lump of cheese for his birthday supper; but she is pretentious with posh guests, for whom she fashions "a huge mound of whipped cream and sugared violets." By contrast, the down-to-earth Mrs. Weasley cooks vast, comforting breakfasts—eight or nine sausages and three fried eggs a head—and sends Harry homemade cakes.[35]

In a stab at a particular set of middle-class values, Rowling reveals that the Dursleys want for nothing and yet they stingily dole out the things that Harry, their own flesh and blood, needs. The Weasleys, on the other hand, who have so little to share, give what they have without reservation.

The Dursleys—"materialist philistines," according to Zipes—also lack any type of creativity. "Their home is more like a prison than anything else, or to be more precise, it is the domain of banal reality. *The Dursleys and their kind are devoid of imagination.*"[36] This is one of the greatest evils that dwells in Muggle suburbia—perhaps a subconscious jab at her parents and an upbringing that focused on money and pensions instead of the fulfillment of desires. Significantly, Harry recognizes that the most important aspect for an undisturbed life with the Dursleys is not to ask questions,[37] leaving the contentment that comes from passive acceptance of one's situation unperturbed.

Linked to that banal, drab existence is the egregious sin of middle-class conformity. Rowling tries to make a point of Harry's difference, the main reason he cannot seem to fit in at his local grammar school or among his Muggle relatives. Even among the wizards, he always stands out because of the scar on his forehead, the magical mark that sets him apart and represents his connection to Lord Voldemort. However, as Zipes points out,

[I]s Harry really different? He is white, Anglo-Saxon, bright, athletic and honest. The only mark of difference he bears is a slight ... scar. Otherwise he is the classic Boy Scout. He does not curse, he speaks standard English grammatically, as do all his friends; he is respectful to his elders; and he has perfect manners. He would definitely help a grandmother cross the street, perhaps even fly her across on his broomstick.[38]

So much for Harry's "difference": he is the perfect child of the middle class.

Many critics, librarians, reviewers, and parents have noted that at some point Harry Potter stopped being a fictional character and became a phenomenon. In Zipes's view, that isn't necessarily a good thing:

In American and British culture, the quality of what rises to the top is always appropriated, and if the phenomenon does somehow contain some qualities that are truly different, they are bound to be corroded and degraded, turning the phenomenon against itself and into a homogenized commodity that will reap huge profits until the next phenomenon appears on the horizon. Difference and otherness are obliterated in the process.[39]

What a general dispersal of the Harry Potter books does among the readers, both child and adult, is further disseminate the same old stereotypes of dark villains, the profligate poor, the cruel rich, the brave middle-class boy-hero who saves the day.

Marketing statistics show that most of the Harry Potter series buyers and readers are affluent white children and their parents; one might argue, therefore, that when Rowling's books repeat the same Eurocentric, hetero/patriarchal, class biases of conventional classical fairy tales, no "harm" is done. In effect, the author is, as the saying goes, preaching to the converted.[40] Furthermore, to give Rowling her due, she does follow the old saw about "writing what you know." Though she does not live in a wizard world among broomsticks and incantations, she has re-created an environment that she knows intimately well—the rigid socioeconomic structure of English society. With the astounding, world-wide success of the novels, the author may be accused of working a little magic herself. No amount of magic, however, can spirit Rowling out of her middle-class worldview; this view, therefore, is inevitably projected onto the fictional realm of Harry Potter's England.

NOTES

1. Pam Morris, *Dickens' Class Consciousness* (New York: St. Martin's Press, 1991), 64.

2. During that era, working in trade lost some of its taint and the nouveau riche of the merchant classes became part of the new landed gentry.

3. See Elaine Ostry's chapter for an extensive discussion of this topic.

4. Jack Zipes, *Sticks and Stones: The Troublesome Success of Children's Literature from Slovenly Peter to Harry Potter* (New York: Routledge, 2001), 177.

5. J. K. Rowling, *Harry Potter and the Sorcerer's Stone* (New York: Scholastic Inc., 1997), 100–102.

6. Marc Shapiro, *J. K. Rowling: The Wizard behind Harry Potter* (New York: St. Martin's Griffin, 2000), xiv.

7. Malcolm Jones, "The Return of Harry Potter! Exclusive: J. K. Rowling Talks about Her Success, Her Daughter, Her Readers, the Upcoming Film and, of Course, Harry Potter, Teen Wizard." *Newsweek* (10 July 2000): 56–60, 56.

8. Zipes, *Sticks and Stones*, 173.

9. Wyedean is a secondary school in Sedbury, Chepstow, in Gloucestershire near where Rowling lived as a child. It is a comprehensive school, coeducational, and "takes all pupils, usually regardless of their ability, aptitude, or whether they have been selected for a place at a selective school," according to BBC British education statistics. By these figures, Wyedean appears to have been an average school for those of average ability; Rowling would have been surrounded by pupils from the middle classes, if not also some lower class students. See "BBC News/Education/School League Tables," *Education: School League Tables: Wyedean School (GM)*, http://news.bbc.co.uk/hi/english/static/education/school_tables_1998/england/9165415.html (accessed 12 August 2001).

10. J. K. Rowling, *Harry Potter and the Sorcerer's Stone* (New York: Scholastic Inc., 1997).

11. Shapiro, *J. K. Rowling*, 62–65.

12. Ibid., 24.

13. Michael C. Kotzin, *Dickens and the Fairy Tale* (Bowling Green, OH: Bowling Green University Popular Press, 1972), 71.

14. Ibid., 50.

15. Shapiro, *J. K. Rowling*, 56.

16. Voldemort is another word-association name: *death rat*, or *flight of death*, among other interpretations. See Zipes, *Sticks and Stones*, 181.

17. J. K. Rowling, *Harry Potter and the Goblet of Fire* (New York: Scholastic Press, 2000).

18. Zipes, *Sticks and Stones*, 183.

19. Kotzin, *Dickens*, 44.

20. Just because Rowling writes for children does not mean the characters cannot be fully rounded, as E. M. Forster would have them. As it happens, one of the common complaints of critics about the Potter series has been a certain shallowness. Book critic Anthony Holden, for example, condemned the books and their author "for not being multicultural enough, feminist enough, politically engaged enough, socially aware enough, the whole caboodle, finishing with the final flourish that people will think Britain is terribly old-fashioned if they read these books." Sophie Masson, "So What's All This about Harry Potter?" *Quadrant* (December 2000): 68–70, 68.

21. Rowling, *Sorcerer's Stone*, 152.

22. NB: The use of Latin associated with witchcraft and spells also has to do with a traditional British anti-Catholicism. The term "hocus-pocus" comes from the Latin words for "This is my Body, which was given up for you," the sacred words of the institution said by Catholic priests during the blessing of the Eucharist. After Henry VIII, this sort of anti-Catholicism became commonplace, and Rowling would have undoubtedly been exposed to her share of this bias in her public school. See further discussion of Ron Weasley and Irish stereotyping and, by extension, anti-Catholicism in this chapter.

23. For an expanded discussion of this point, see Ed Guerrero, "Slaves, Monsters, and Others," in *Rereading America: Cultural Contexts for Critical Thinking and Writing*, 3rd ed., Gary Colombo, Robert Cullen, and Bonnie Lisle, eds. (Boston: Bedford Books of St. Martin's Press, 1995), 407.

24. Rowling, *Sorcerer's Stone*, 250.

25. Morris, *Dickens' Class*, 73.

26. Ibid., 144.

27. J. K. Rowling, *Harry Potter and the Prisoner of Azkaban* (New York: Scholastic Press, 1999).

28. Morris, *Dickens' Class*, 116.

29. J. K. Rowling, *Harry Potter and the Chamber of Secrets* (New York: Scholastic Inc., 1999), 12.

30. Guerrero, "Slaves, Monsters and Others," 405.

31. Ibid., 403.

32. Rowling, *Chamber of Secrets*, 32.

33. Zipes, *Sticks and Stones*, 181.

34. Rowling, *Sorcerer's Stone*, 1.

35. Bee Wilson, "Pottering in the Kitchen," *New Statesman* (21 August 2000): 36–37, 36.

36. Zipes, *Sticks and Stones*, 176, emphasis added.

37. Rowling, *Sorcerer's Stone*, 20.

38. Zipes, *Sticks and Stones*, 179.

39. Ibid., 175.

40. Ibid., 186.

14

Cinderfella:
J. K. Rowling's Wily Web of Gender

Ximena Gallardo-C. and C. Jason Smith

J. K. Rowling's imaginary world abounds in glittering mystery, nail-biting suspense, and colorful images peppered by cute neologisms such as "Muggles," "Quidditch," and "Parseltongue." At the same time, the series is hardly groundbreaking: its basic premise comes right out of "Cinderella," key scenes allude to an array of children's literature from C. S. Lewis to Enid Blyton, and its clever language echoes Roald Dahl's. Most importantly, the Harry Potter books resonate with gender stereotypes of the worst sort; as Christine Schoefer argues in her review of the first three books in the series, "From the beginning ..., it is boys and men, wizards and sorcerers, who catch our attention by dominating the scenes and determining the action. ... Girls, when they are not downright silly or unlikable, are helpers, enablers and instruments."[1] Any thinking parent, argues Schoefer, cannot and should not "ignore the sexism" of the series.

Schoefer has a point, but by offering a proactive feminist interpretation of Rowling's fiction, we argue that there are alternative, radical readings of the series for both children and adults. While the novels do not actively critique gender stereotyping, the narrative does challenge standard constructions of gender and gender roles in several ways. First, cyclical moves from passive subject at home (Cinderella as servant) to active subject at Hogwarts (Cinderella at the ball) drive the series and inevitably lead to the hero's "blooming." This tie to a traditionally "girl tale" feminizes Harry in ways that allow female readers to identify strongly with a male protagonist. Second, feminine symbols (e.g., caves) accompany the usual phallic representations (e.g., swords) in the series, and Harry's symbolic actions evidence a preference for the feminine. Third, the series' growing obsession with understanding "otherness" (represented by witches, giants, Muggles, house-elves, and so on) opens the narrative to gender critique, albeit in displaced form. Fourth and finally, though the Harry Potter series does not support radical feminism, it is radical as children's literature and therefore has ample material to support feminist readings.

GIRLS JUST AREN'T ANY FUN

Simply stated, the world of the Harry Potter books, even the magical part of that world, does not offer particularly progressive gender roles: while men and boys tend to get into trouble and share knowing winks, women mostly putter around the kitchen and scold boys for stepping out of line. Still, the majority of conflicts do not arise—as adults might read—between male and female, the mundane and the magical, or even good and evil; instead, they arise from tensions between children and adults, as suits a story intended for children. Thus, a look at gender in Harry Potter's world must take into account the way children read fiction and the world. Most psychologists, for instance, agree that children develop primary gender identification very early (usually by age three) and that their perception of the gendered world predictably tends towards the stereotypical as they are operating on a more essential level than adults.[2] While authors can (and do) construct stories for children that normalize alternative gender roles and sexual orientations, they typically resort to displacement and metaphor to make these ideas more palatable to children. Stories for children and adolescents that most effectively address issues of gender do so not by creating adult-inspired utopias or dystopias, but by mirroring the child's real world experiences in a slightly altered form. For example, Maurice Sendak's *Where the Wild Things Are, In the Night Kitchen,* and *Outside over There* each explore issues of gender identification and embodiment—often read as stages of the Oedipal drama—by displacing these issues into fantasy worlds.[3] In the most widely read of this trilogy, *Where the Wild Things Are,* Max—and by proxy the child reader—faces his fear of the punishing mother by adventuring to a faraway island where he learns to control his anxiety and thereby to better understand his own aggressive, "animal" nature.

Readers of all ages and genders can identify with the Harry Potter stories, not *in spite of* the gender inequality but *because* they see in the stories a reflection of their own experiences of gender disparity. (Adult readers, of course, are more conscious of this identification.) We will argue that the Potter series contains ample material to justify a reading against the apparently misogynist portrayal of gender, but first we must explore its gender trouble.

Rowling's narrative reinforces traditional categories of labor, as it presents women primarily as wives and mothers. Petunia Dursley, true to the wicked old stepmother stereotype, dotes on her selfish, spoiled, malicious son, Dudley, and mistreats her orphaned nephew Harry. On the other hand, there are the good mothers, such as the hardworking Molly Weasley, who keeps house for five children (out of seven) and a forgetful if easygoing husband, who makes at least as much trouble as the teenage boys. A formidable woman feared by all the males in her family, she strives to keep them on the good path, reinforcing the image of women as the civilizers of men. The most important mother—though absent—is Lily Potter, who sacrificed herself to save her son, Harry, from Lord Voldemort and whose love envelopes Harry in an ever-present protection from evil. The maternal ideal extends to other female characters as well. Winky, the female house-elf, nurtures the evil Barty Crouch Jr. back to life in *Harry Potter and the Goblet of Fire*. Even Harry's friend Hermione, like Professor Minerva McGonagall, eventually becomes a mother figure for Ron and Harry. Clearly, the text implies that the primary role of women in society is the care, socialization, and education of men *at any cost*.

For the most part, the working women in the series teach at Hogwarts School of Witchcraft and Wizardry. Although this handful of witches specializes in nonstereotypical magical arts that range from the "complex and dangerous" Transfiguration to the apparently inexact Divination, Rowling's choice of teaching as the main form of public labor for women certainly is conventional. In comparison, men work outside the house, filling most of the highly ranked jobs in the Ministry of Magic. They also have the glamorous, exciting, and classified jobs: Charlie Weasley studies dragons in Romania, and his brother Bill goes on secret missions for Gringotts, the central bank of the magical world.

The series also stereotypes females as emotional or sensitive to the point of irrationality. As Schoefer notes, "again and again, we see girls so caught up in their emotions that they lose sight of the bigger picture. We watch them 'shriek,' 'scream,' 'gasp' and 'giggle' in situations where the boys retain their composure."[4] Even Professor McGonagall, the authoritarian deputy headmistress of Hogwarts and Head of Gryffindor House, constantly struggles to refrain from emotional outbursts. Schoefer observes, for example, that at the end of *Harry Potter and the Chamber of Secrets*,[5] when Harry returns from defeating the basilisk, Professor McGonagall "clutches her chest, gasps and speaks weakly while the all-knowing Dumbledore beams."[6] Likewise, in *Goblet of Fire*, McGonagall loses control and falls into a furious, though ineffective, rage when Cornelius Fudge, the Minister of Magic, brings a dementor into Hogwarts; alarmed, Harry notices that her face turns red with "angry blotches" and she balls her hands into fists.[7] Even more telling is the cause of her anger: the immorality of Barty Crouch's death at the hands of the soul-sucking dementors. Dumbledore, in comparison, concerns himself with the long-term effects: Crouch, even if guilty, would have been useful in the battle against Voldemort.

Professor Sibyll Trelawney, Hogwarts's Divination teacher, exemplifies another side of the "sensitive" female stereotype. As a bumbling psychic considered ridiculous and irrational by almost everyone except a few girls, Professor Trelawney does get to reflect "the big picture" (the imminent rise of Lord Voldemort), but only under a trance so that she is never aware of what she has revealed to Harry. Such "real" predictions rarely come from her and, as the "mildly impressed" and half-joking Dumbledore explains in *Harry Potter and the Prisoner of Azkaban*, now that her real predictions total two, perhaps he should give her a raise in salary.[8] Trelawney may have power, but in contrast to the headmaster, her power becomes useless as the true predictions go unheard in the mass of humbug she usually produces.

Other female stereotypes in the series include the chatterbox (in *Harry Potter and the Sorcerer's Stone,*[9] Hermione irritates the boys with her constant talk and, most importantly, her extensive bookish knowledge); the groupie (in *Chamber of Secrets,* both Hermione and Mrs. Weasley fall head over heels for the vain and fraudulent Gilderoy Lockhart, while Ginny Weasley has a wild crush on Harry); and the nosy gossip (Petunia Dursley spends her spare time spying on her neighbors, and *Daily Prophet* reporter Rita Skeeter writes sensational, untrue stories for her paper, causing unnecessary trouble in *Goblet of Fire*). Woman as sex object is represented by the hyper-female veela, irresistible *femme fatales,* and the trophy wife comes in the form of Draco Malfoy's mother, Narcissa, whose name suggests that she is vain and self-absorbed.

In contrast to the women, the men in the series seem more fun, mostly because they are curious, if not downright adventurous. Mr. Weasley displays a childlike fascination for Muggle technology that repeatedly lands him in trouble with Mrs. Weasley and the Ministry of Magic. The creative and boisterous Weasley twins, George and Fred, devise "Weasley's Wizard Wheezes," a set of wonderful magic toys with a tendency to smoke, explode, and balloon tongues to massive size. Even the sensible Dumbledore exercises wonder as well as wisdom. Most interestingly, in the numerous adventures and trials of the series, Harry, Ron, James Potter, and Sirius Black exemplify the motto of Gryffindor House: "brave and daring," whereas the female Gryffindors (Hermione, Professor McGonagall, and Mrs. Weasley) profess responsible rule-enforcement. This last division illustrates the general message of the series—"Men are interesting, women are good"—and would explain why no female characters actively work for Lord Voldemort ... yet.

CINDERFELLA

In his review of *Sorcerer's Stone,* Michael Dirda elaborates on the familiar nature of the Harry Potter story: "We have all been here before—in Roald Dahl, Ursula Le Guin, 'Star Wars,' Dune. But in the right hands we're always happy to make the trip again."[10] In truth, most aspects of Harry's childhood, such as the identifying mark, the evil stepparents and the competition with favored stepsiblings, the virtual enslavement and emotional abuse, the recognition from without and magical assistance, all point to a long tradition of myths and fairy tales. Of these, Potter critics most often cite the King Arthur myths.[11] And though it may seem natural to compare Harry's story to the other "lost boy tale" of King Arthur, Rowling's protagonist really has little more than superficial similarity to the Arthurian legends. Rather, if we look closely at Harry's background and experiences we may locate a more revealing model for the series. Harry Potter—the hidden and abused child, hunted by evil and often afraid of failure, never fully escapes the loathsome conditions of his upbringing, reminding us not so much of King Arthur but of Cinderella, caught in a perpetual loop of slavery and liberty, abuse and triumph, inadequacy and power.

Of the nearly 700 extant versions of the Cinderella story,[12] we have chosen the Grimm Brothers' "Aschenputtel" as our primary reference because its thematic content remains uncensored; the elements we discuss, however, can be found in virtually all renditions of the narrative. Like the Harry Potter story, "Aschenputtel" is a dark little tale of parental abuse. The wicked stepmother and stepsisters subject Aschenputtel to numerous indignities including forcing her to pick peas from the ash bin and making her sleep on a filthy hearth. When her ineffectual father leaves for the fair, he asks each daughter what she would like. The vain and beautiful stepdaughters ask for jewels and finery, but Aschenputtel requests "The first twig, father, that strikes against your hat on the way home; that is what I should like you to bring me."[13] He returns with her humble gift, a branch from a hazel tree, and she promptly plants it on her mother's grave. The branch grows rapidly into a tree that grants her wishes. Attired in clothing provided by the tree, Aschenputtel repeatedly attends the royal ball, where she dances with the prince, who predictably falls in love with her. When the prince visits the family estate with her lost shoe, at their mother's bidding, one stepsister cuts off her big toe to fit the slipper, while the other cuts off her heel. Unfortunately for them, seeping blood gives each away. As punishment, the magic tree sends forth birds to pluck out the stepsisters' eyes after the prince recognizes Aschenputtel.

Connections between "Aschenputtel" and the Harry Potter story abound: for instance, both Aschenputtel's and Harry's mothers are dead, and yet their love, represented as "magic," continues to protect and guide the children. Both characters have an identifying physical characteristic associated with the power of the mother: Harry's scar is analogous to Ashenputttel's foot not only as a method of identification, but also in the association of the tiny glass slipper to the mother's magic that provided it. A bird in Aschenputtel's tree warns of deceit just as Harry's scar warns of the proximity of Voldemort. Further, "Aschenputtel" is one of few fairy tales that features a protagonist who actually casts spells herself. Though she is not called a witch in the story, the implication is clear, and thus later sanitized versions have displaced her spell-casting with that of a fairy godmother or the help of friendly, intelligent animals.

Most importantly, Harry's story, like Aschenputtel's, operates in a cyclical pattern: from the drudgery and abuse at home, Harry progresses to the glamour of the magical world where one and all recognize him as a miracle, and then back to home again. Cyclical "boy tales" do exist ("Jack and the Beanstalk," for example), but this type of spatially recursive narrative centered in the home appears most often in tales about women. Though Arthur finds fame only to become embroiled in a domestic drama, no one would suggest that he return home for the summer to virtual slavery with nasty Muggle relatives. Thus

Harry reminds us more of a woman warrior like Spenser's Britomart, who sallies forth to fight evil but sooner or later must return the armor to the closet.

This rooting of Harry Potter in a cyclical, domestic "girl tale" rather than a linear "boy tale" has several interesting effects. Appearing within a traditionally feminine narrative structure, Harry, in essence, is a boy caught in a girl's story. As these stories normally involve feminine themes—abandonment, rape, loss of the protecting mother or father, menses, and pregnancy, to name a few—and feminine, often magical, power, Harry's inclusion within this tale-type not only modifies the themes to include a boy, but also tells us something about Harry himself and the world in which he lives. Harry may be sexed male, but he is passing through a world where many females have walked before him and triumphed.

SEXED SYMBOLS, GENDERED CHOICES

An intricate contextual framework of sexed objects, sexed spaces, and gendered actions further destabilizes sex and gender in the Harry Potter novels. In order to differentiate between the passive reception of symbolic meaning and active interaction in the sex-gender system, we use the term "sex" to refer to both the physical and symbolic characteristics of objects (a phallic sword or vaginal cave, for instance) and "gender" to indicate the more fluid interaction between subjects and society. At its most general, the sex-gender web of the series reveals a gender-transgressive narrative: Rowling takes a boy, places him into a Cinderella story set in the mundane, logical, masculine world, and then, toting a magic wand and wearing dresslike robes, sends him off to a witch and wizarding school where his greatest joy will be riding a flying broom! Interestingly, while the broom is the wizarding equivalent of a sports car, it is still, as Xavière Gauthier states in her essay on feminism and witchcraft, "A slight modification of the housewife's tool."[14] Therefore, even if Harry's *use* of the broom to play a dangerous sport recodes the broom as active/masculine, this appropriation still operates in connection with the transgressive magic world of (female) witches. Whatever Harry's (fictional) sex, his association with the magical world makes him a feminized "other."

Rowling's first book implicates Harry in a search for the Philosopher's Stone,[15] the *lapis* or *philosophorum* that symbolizes wealth and eternal life and joins the masculine principles of the sun and purification with the feminine principles of the moon and reproduction.[16] Harry's first quest, then, prefigures his growth arc towards a well-rounded, thinking individual with a flexible understanding of gender that transcends biological sex: the Philosopher's Stone embodies masculine and feminine principles in a duality that is one, "the crowned hermaphrodite" (*aenigma regis*).[17]

This initial symbolic connection with ambivalent gender sets the stage for Harry's exploration of the feminine. The young wizard's pewter cauldron, long robes and pointed hat, his pet owl, and even the Potions and Herbology classes all serve as reminders of the "soft," nontechnological nature of Harry's experiences and operate in metaphorical association with the world of women and women's work. The cauldron, black robes, and pointed hats are classical and often parodied representations of the powerful female witch. The feminine symbolism continues with Harry's familiar, Hedwig, who is not only female but also a white owl in the classical tradition of Bubo, the owl of the warrior goddess Athena—also worshipped as the goddess of wisdom—who served as the protector of the ancient Greek heroes Heracles, Perseus, and Odysseus. Even the majority of the courses Harry takes are associated with woman's work: Herbology brings to mind the "kitchen garden" of traditional homemakers, and Potions—the "misuse" of the same herbs to brew magical concoctions—has long been associated with witchcraft in contrast to the traditionally "masculine" art of alchemy, which is not as yet a class at Hogwarts. To further the point, the male Potions master, the malevolent Professor Snape, clearly hates teaching the class even though he excels at it. He covets the more dangerous—and therefore "manly"—Defense Against the Dark Arts position.

The most important symbol in the series, Harry's lightning-shaped scar, serves as his magical third eye. The scar functions not only as an outward symbol of the protagonist's supposed power against evil, but also operates as a reminder, like the mark of Cain, of the very evil it protects against. The symbolism runs even deeper when considering the Hindu god Shiva—the destroyer of all material forms—whose vertical third eye, centered in his forehead, "blazes with the fire of ten million suns, and can consume any creature with flame."[18] Shiva's power, sometimes indicated by the thunderbolt, bears a striking resemblance to Harry's destructive effect on Voldemort.[19]

As Lee Siegal notes, "Harry's scar is not only evidence of a deep emotional injury but, more consequentially, it is also the sign by which everyone in the wizard world recognizes him as the famous Harry Potter, the boy who defeated the villain Voldemort."[20] Indeed, for Harry, "the body is its scars," as feminist theorist Elaine Scarry suggests.[21] Harry's visible, outward sign of difference operates both as an indicator of the phallic, aggressive power of Voldemort and the passive protection of his mother. Further, the scar as a sign of a previously opened "feminine" body, a wound or gash healed, indicates the vulnerability of the supposedly solid, masculine body. Because the text posits the nature of Harry's defining mark as both masculine and feminine, weapon and wound, phallus and vagina, the closed and open body, we sense no transgression when we see a young girl at a book signing wearing a lighting bolt tattoo on her forehead—a transgression we might sense if she were carrying a sword.

Harry also inhabits "feminine" spaces. He starts buried in a cupboard under the stairs and then moves to the "other" world of magic, where he will reside at Gryffindor Tower in Hogwarts castle. Though phallic in appearance, the tower is identified with the feminine because of its defensive, protecting role. Unlike the sword, the tower does not penetrate but rather defends against penetration.

For this reason, the tower is a common symbol of virginity and the Virgin Mary; alchemists thus often built their athanors (alchemical furnaces) in tower shape.[22] The feminine nature of the symbol is reinforced by the fact that Professor Minerva McGonagall leads Gryffindor House, and that the Fat Lady guards the "round opening" to the Gryffindor dormitories.

Interestingly, Gryffindor's rival, Slytherin House, is most often associated with Hogwarts' dungeons. This apparent contrast between the visible and virginal power of the tower and the hidden dark femininity of the dungeon or cave actually completes the traditional feminine dyad of virgin and crone (Hufflepuff and Ravenclaw are rarely part of the equation). Thus, Hogwarts castle itself constitutes a feminine space, full of secret passages and secret chambers, all of which Harry must explore; indeed his father would be disappointed, Professor Lupin tells us, if he *didn't*.

In brief, from the series of rooms housing the Philosopher's Stone through the Chamber of Secrets and hidden tunnels leading to the Shrieking Shack, dragon's nest, lake, and maze of *Goblet of Fire*, Harry must discover and explore feminine spaces. As Clarissa Pinkola Estés writes:

The cellar, dungeon, and cave symbols are all related to one another. They are ancient initiatory environs; places to or through which a woman descends to the murdered one(s), breaks taboos to find the truth, and through wit and/or travail triumphs by banishing, transforming, or exterminating the assassin of the psyche.[23]

In these places Harry does indeed find truth—not only about the camouflaged enemies within Hogwarts's midst, such as Scabbers/Peter Pettigrew, Professors Quirrell, Moody (Barty Crouch in disguise), and, to some extent, Lockhart, but also about his friendships and his own true identity. He is initiated into his role as a worthy opponent of Lord Voldemort and the future savior of the wizarding world. In these feminine spaces, Harry plays a restorative role and corrects the damage done by those (males) before him.

As a whole, the network of sexed symbols and spaces provides a framework for Harry's tests and decisions. In *Sorcerer's Stone*, for example, we learn early that the wand that "chooses" Harry is the "brother" wand to Voldemort's, connecting Harry with the Dark Lord and preparing him for the first of many important choices: whether to go to Slytherin House or Gryffindor House. In this case, we learn that the decision is up to the magical Sorting Hat, which understands each candidate's "true essence" and sends her to the house where she will fit best. "Difficult. Very difficult," says the hat, as it not only identifies Harry's courage and magical talent, but also his desire to prove himself and his potential for greatness. "*Not Slytherin, not Slytherin*," thinks Harry, and the Sorting Hat places him in Gryffindor.[24] The young wizard's wand may have chosen him, but Harry rejects the ambition of Slytherin for the friendship and bravery exemplified by the Gryffindor lion. Thus, Harry not only distances himself from the nasty Draco Malfoy and the evil Voldemort but also from the phallic power and ambition that they represent.

Harry is "rewarded" for his choice with two loyal friends, Ron and Hermione (the masculine principle and the feminine principle, respectively). Of these two, however, the boys-will-be-boys Ron almost always points Harry in the wrong direction while Hermione typically suggests the action leading to Harry's personal growth and success. In *Sorcerer's Stone*, for example, when Harry ignores Hermione and chooses, as Ron wants, to meet Draco Malfoy for an all-male showdown in the Hogwarts trophy room, he is nearly caught breaking curfew (a serious offense at Hogwarts) and then nearly killed by Fluffy, the vicious three-headed dog that guards the forbidden corridor leading to the Philosopher's Stone.

The residential houses at Hogwarts play another important role in displacing the usual gender-specific groups that children devise; no one at Hogwarts says "No Girls Allowed," except perhaps the Slytherins, who do not have girls on their Quidditch team—and they certainly are not role models. The series acknowledges gender difference (real boys and girls often play differently) but does not advocate gender cleavage (same-sex groups). The Sorting Hat, for example, makes its judgments based on inner characteristics—talent, personality, and disposition—and not on biological sex.

In *Chamber of Secrets*, the Sorting Hat appears again, this time as the delivery device for the sword of Godric Gryffindor, which Harry *chooses* to pull from it. Harry's use of the sword and hat (or crown)—traditional symbols of masculine and feminine power as well as creation when conjoined—again proves his mastery in negotiating gender roles. Though Harry does not at first know "what to do with" the hat, he does draw what "he needs" from it—namely the phallic power of the sword—and he slays the Slytherin basilisk sent to kill him by Voldemort.

In fact, most of Harry's major choices in the first four books belie a preference for the feminine. In *Prisoner of Azkaban*, Harry must decide between revenge and mercy. Haunted by his mother's dying screams, the angry Harry confronts the two men implicated in his parents' murder at the Shrieking Shack. He cannot, however, bring himself to kill Sirius Black even though he believes Black betrayed his parents, and he is rewarded with the truth that Black is not only innocent, but his godfather as well. This act of clemency foreshadows his later sparing of the two-timing Peter Pettigrew, the real servant of Voldemort. If Harry had opted for the masculine act of revenge, he would never have established a relationship with his godfather or learned what really happened to his parents. Even worse, he would be acting in the same vein as Voldemort.

Focusing on competition in the form of the Triwizard Tournament, *Goblet of Fire* betrays an obsession with tests and the consequences of right and wrong actions. Again, Harry responds to such a masculine enterprise by acting fairly, working within his limitations, accepting help, and sharing the triumph at the end of the maze. In the end, though, Harry's choice to share the victory with Cedric Diggory—only to be magically transported into the hands of Voldemort and almost certain death—warns that winning and the ambition it represents are not necessarily good or healthy.

Most importantly, the narrative of the Triwizard Tournament contrasts with the subplot of courtship and attraction surrounding the Yule Ball. While Harry's age makes his participation in the tournament unauthorized and transgressive, he and others of his Hogwarts class are required to participate in the ball. A formal introduction into heterosexuality, the ball illustrates the necessity of dating rituals to gender construction—both of which cause sheer panic. The ball also highlights the subjectivity of gender performance: all the boys wear long flowing "dress robes," and yet Ron frets over the lace trim on his hand-me-down costume. Similarly, Harry and his friends understand that failing to "win" a date and attend the dance will make them "losers." Predictably, the Yule Ball proves an unsettling affair as both Hagrid and Ron try foolishly to impress the "wrong" girls and Harry himself battles Ginny Weasley's crush on him and his own crush on Cho Chang. Hermione, on the other hand, successfully negotiates her transformation from an insecure, overachieving bookworm into a "real girl": as she enters the Great Hall, she looks so elegant in her blue robes, with sleek, shiny hair and magically improved teeth, that Harry does not recognize her at first. The contrast between all of these narratives serves as a warning against the dangers of premature experiences. For while social pressure forces the unprepared Harry into the dangers of the adult world and the awkwardness of the dating world as well, the Yule Ball allows Hermione to choose an authorized entrance into gender and sexuality. Interestingly, we see that Harry's failure to date Cho Chang becomes mirrored and amplified in the disastrous capture of the Triwizard Cup: the "winner" of the date with Cho, Cedric Diggory, loses his life at Voldemort's hands.

In all cases, Rowling's world conjoins realities: there is no technology without magic, no good without evil, no pleasure without pain and suffering, and no triumph without failure. At every turn the text reminds us of the gendered duality of Harry's existence, and the hero is consistently associated with the feminine side of this dyad. From the beginning of the series, for instance, we have a somewhat generic division between the "hard," technological, masculine world of the Muggles—symbolized in Dudley's TV, VCR, and computer and Uncle Vernon's drill factory—and the "soft," magical, feminine "other" world of the witches and wizards. Later, the reader becomes aware of a second generic division in the magical world: that of the "good" magic people associated with Hogwarts and the "evil" magic people allied with Lord Voldemort. Tellingly, the Hogwarts opponents of the aggressive and power-hungry Voldemort resist his ability to penetrate, wound, and kill by exhibiting kindness, selflessness, a desire for intimacy with others, and responsibility. Thus, whereas the series apparently favors characters of the *male sex*, this preference continually conflicts with a context of symbols and actions that are *gendered feminine*. Female readers can identify with Harry in spite of his fictional sex because they have a similar experience of the world: the world is masculine, aggressive, oppressive, and only collectively can the wolf be kept from the door. In the end, all of Harry's choices throughout the texts tend towards feminine values, and he is often punished or put into peril for making masculine decisions. Male honor of the traditional sort supported by Ron Weasley just doesn't work for Harry. Rather, the protagonist succeeds by recognizing the less obvious "other choice." Somewhere in that "other" land, between the advice of his best friends Ron and Hermione, between the masculine and the feminine, Harry stands as a true symbol of the possibility of the Philosopher's Stone.

EXPLORING THE OTHER

Every trip to platform nine and three-quarters reminds us that the magical world of Harry Potter exists *somewhere in-between.* To get to the Hogwarts Express, a person must walk through the barriers dividing platforms nine and ten at King's Cross station in the real London. The liminal magical world, then, exists parallel to the Muggle world and inside of it, so that like most fantasy and science fiction it both mirrors reality and offers alternatives to it by displacing controversial issues onto other Others.

Kylene Beers, creator of an online discussion guide, identifies the separation of Self and Other in the series as a division in terms of race and class: "A caste system is well established: wizards and witches are better than Muggles and Mudbloods; giants are outcasts; and house-elves are considered as sub-human."[25] Hermione, not Harry, becomes the outspoken champion of the marginal in this caste system, partly because she herself is marginal, as pointed out in *Chamber of Secrets* when Draco Malfoy dubs her a "Mudblood" (born of nonmagical parents). As the "other" hero, however, she resists clear-cut definitions of who can or cannot be a wizard or witch, since she is the most accomplished student in Hogwarts. Her "Mudblood" state never shows but in Malfoy's name-calling.

Throughout the series, Hermione befriends the underdogs at all costs. From the beginning she helps the clumsy Neville Longbottom, a borderline "Squib," or wizard who lacks natural magical abilities. In *Prisoner of Azkaban,* she covers up Professor Lupin's werewolf identity because she knows he will be ejected from Hogwarts if discovered; she also helps the half-giant Hagrid to defend one of his pet hippogriffs in front of the Committee for the Disposal of Dangerous Creatures; and finally, along with Harry, she saves both the hippogriff and Sirius Black from being executed. Hermione's boldest initiative is to start an organization to help the enslaved house-elves in *Goblet of Fire.* Hermione as newly discovered unionist brings forward issues of slavery and oppression that had been passed over in the previous books. While the acronym for her Society for the Promotion of Elfish Welfare (S.P.E.W.) sounds like an in-joke, her actions to help the house-elves parallel those of the wise Dumbledore, who has started paying Dobby the house-elf to work in the Hogwarts kitchen, and make Harry wonder if the elves *like* to be enslaved, as Ron argues. Hermione appropriately recognizes the injustice of the house-elves' servitude because as a "Mudblood" and political minority, *but also as a woman*, she can see discrimination where others see tradition. The house-elves are the "women" of Hogwarts, regardless of their sex.

By far the most transgressive acceptance of the female other is Rowling's *de facto* redemption of the slanderous term "witch."[26] Witchcraft is not the "dark art" in Rowling's magical world; rather, it exists as an art that can be used for good or evil and symbolically represents our inner power: the "magic and wonder" within all of us. In the spirit of tolerance, the series neither advocates nor denies any god or religion, thus thankfully liberating the term "witch" from its paranoid and misogynistic overtones, which have resulted in the ostracism and deaths of millions of men and women around the world. As in the *Oz* books, witches and wizards can be either good or evil, but Rowling's witches and wizards are not Baum's bubbleheads or humbugs. Instead, they represent the possibility of real power. Separated from all direct associations with Satanism, and even poking fun at those who would make the connection, witchcraft in the Harry Potter series becomes a technique rather than an evil.

The secularization and normalization of witchcraft ties Rowling's narrative closely to the feminist project of interrogating and reclaiming women's spaces, as expressed by the title of the French feminist journal *Sorcières* (*Witches*) edited by Xavière Gauthier. In the introduction to the first issue, Gauthier explains the connection: "If the figure of the witch appears wicked, it is because she poses a real danger to phallocratic society. We do constitute a danger for this society which is built on the exclusion—worse, on the repression—of female strength."[27]

CONCLUSION: IS *HARRY POTTER* RADICAL?

In his book *Should We Burn Babar?*, Herbert Kohl devises requisites for a radical children's literature. His framework addresses feminist concerns for critiquing traditional, patriarchal culture. A radical children's literature should (1) not focus on the individual hero, but depict a community or "natural social group larger than the family" as a central element; (2) organize conflicts around a group larger than the nuclear family: a "community, class, ethnic group, nation, or even the world"; (3) focus on collective rather than individual action; (4) portray a three-dimensional antagonist or enemy who is not inherently evil, nor evil in all situations; (5) highlight comradeship, friendship, and different types of love; and (6) not force a happy ending or resolution to the problem. As Kohl summarizes, "Radical tales should nurture the social imagination and at the same time not be dogmatic or preachy. They have to be personal, intimate, and funny as well as honest about pain and defeat."[28] Tales such as these are radical, not simply because they address issues of racism, sexism, or poverty, but because their narratives give children ways of seeing that differ from the great majority of didactic texts they encounter in school, at home, and especially on television.

Although Rowling draws long and deep from a fairy-tale and fantasy tradition steeped in misogyny and gender stereotyping, she is seldom at its mercy. The great majority of fantasy narratives recycle stereotypical gender roles; Rowling's Potter series, however, engages in self-reflective critique on many levels and therefore belongs to a "new" type of children's literature that interrogates and deconstructs traditional expectations of gender roles. While the Harry Potter books may not be as ironic and revisionist of fairy-tale narratives as Dreamworks's animated fantasy film *Shrek* (2001), Harry's story does operate on many subtle levels to the same effect. Based on the original "girl tales," starring a cross-dressing orphan, set in a coeducational school, and highlighting defensive rather than offensive action, the series speaks to modern families who, while still craving familiarity, are aware that the same old stories will no longer do. Because nothing in Rowling's series is quite as familiar as it first seems, readers of all ages can actively rethink the old tales in new nonmisogynistic ways that liberate the text and reader from conventional, phallogocentric narratives.

Readers see that Harry is never the self-centered, independent hero, but instead relies on his inclusion in a larger group: his friends, Gryffindor House, Hogwarts, and the entire non-Muggle world. Further, the series valorizes collective action, as the conflicts *always* require action by cohesive communities (children, adults, good wizards, bad wizards, Muggles, and house-elves). Though the magical world, like the Muggle world, suffers from gender stereotyping and sexism, it is a world in the process of change: Hogwarts is not only coeducational, but mixed-sex groups have the advantage over same-sex groups in classes, sports, and friendships. This tendency to question the status quo extends throughout the series and invites readers to cultivate a more critical approach to societal norms. Finally, rather than the linear, closed "happy-ending," the series to date highlights openness and continuing growth. All of these elements in sum work to interrogate simplistic dichotomous propositions such as masculine and feminine, good and evil, friend and enemy, self and other. On these grounds, then, the Harry Potter series is radical. Based in the "opposing social forces involved in social struggle" which Kohl advocates,[29] Rowling has created the context for an active discussion of social issues including, as we have shown, sex and gender.

NOTES

1. Christine Schoefer, "Harry Potter's Girl Trouble," 13 January 2000, http://www.salon.com, 1 (accessed 25 January 2000).

2. See, for example, E. E. Maccoby and C. N. Jacklin, *The Psychology of Sex Differences* (Stanford, CA: Stanford University Press, 1974).

3. Maurice Sendak, *Where the Wild Things Are* (New York: HarperCollins, 1963); *In the Night Kitchen* (New York: Harper and Row, 1970); *Outside over There* (New York: Harper and Row, 1981).

4. Schoefer, "Girl Trouble," 5.

5. J. K. Rowling, *Harry Potter and the Chamber of Secrets* (New York: Scholastic Press, 1999).

6. Schoefer, "Girl Trouble," 5.

7. J. K. Rowling, *Harry Potter and the Goblet of Fire* (New York: Scholastic Press, 2000), 702.

8. J. K. Rowling, *Harry Potter and the Prisoner of Azkaban* (New York: Scholastic Press, 1999), 426.

9. J. K. Rowling, *Harry Potter and the Sorcerer's Stone* (New York: Scholastic Press, 1997).

10. Michael Dirda, "The Orphan and the Ogres," *Washington Post,* 3 January 1999, xii.

11. For an extended comparison, see "Potter as Legend" in Elizabeth D. Schafer's *Exploring Harry Potter* (Osprey, FL: Beacham Publishing Corp., 2000), 148–49.

12. Jim Trelease, *The Read-Aloud Handbook* (New York: Penguin Books, 1995), 77.

13. The Brothers Grimm, "Aschenputtel," in *Household Stories* (1886), Lucy Crane, trans. (Dover: New York, 1963), 119.

14. Xavière Gauthier, "Why Witches," Erica M. Eisinger, trans., in *New French Feminisms,* Elaine Marks and Isabelle de Courtivron, eds. (New York: Schocken Books, 1981), 199.

15. The original English title, *Harry Potter and the Philosopher's Stone,* was changed to *Harry Potter and the Sorcerer's Stone* for publication in the United States. The title substitution was perhaps motivated by fears that the American audience would either not understand the alchemical reference or react in a puritanical way, associating alchemy with witchcraft. The substitution in the title has the additional effect of occluding the hermaphroditic symbolism of the philosopher's stone as "sorcerer's stone" does not have a clear (cultural, mythological, or psychological) referent.

16. See, for example, J. E. Cirlot, *A Dictionary of Symbols,* 2d ed., Jack Sage, trans. (New York: Philosophical Library, 1971), 119, 145–46.

17. Carl Gustav Jung, *Psychology and Alchemy,* 2d ed., R. F. C. Hull, trans. (Princeton, NJ: Princeton University Press, 1993), 112. See also Jung's *Mysterium Coniunctionis,* R. F .C. Hull, trans. (Princeton, NJ: Princeton University Press, 1989) and *Alchemical Studies,* R. F. C. Hull, trans. (Princeton, NJ: Princeton University Press, 1983).

18. Neil Philip, *Myths and Legends* (New York: DK Publishing, 1999), 112–13. See also Carl Gustav Jung, *Symbols of Transformation,* 2d ed., R. F. C. Hull, trans. (Princeton, NJ: Princeton University Press, 1990), 209, pl. XXIII; and J. E. Cirlot, *Dictionary of Symbols,* 342.

19. Furthermore, Shiva is often depicted in hermaphroditic form, physically combined in one body with his wife Parvati. See Jung, *Symbols of Transformation,* 209, pl. XXIII.

20. Lee Siegal, "Harry Potter and the Spirit of the Age: Fear of Not Flying," *Contemporary Literary Criticism,* vol. 137, C. Riley, ed. (Detroit: Gale Research Co., 2000), 322, and *New Republic,* 22 November 1999, 40.

21. Elaine Scarry, *The Body in Pain* (New York: Oxford University Press, 1985), 31.

22. Cirlot, *Dictionary of Symbols*, 345.

23. Clarissa Pinkola Estés, *Women Who Run with the Wolves: Myths and Stories of the Wild Woman Archetype* (New York: Ballentine Books, 1992), 59.

24. Rowling, *Sorcerer's Stone*, 121.

25. Kylene Beers, "Harry Potter: Discussion Guide for Books I–IV," 4 May 2001, http://www.scholastic.com/harrypotter/books/guides/index.htm (accessed 26 March 2001). For a brief explanation of the origins of the class system for witches and wizards with a connection to the Harry Potter series, see Schafer, *Exploring Harry Potter*, 57. For a more extensive discussion of the racial allegories at work in Rowling's fiction, see the chapters by Elaine Ostry and Brycchan Carey in this collection.

26. For a summary of witchcraft and the Harry Potter series, see Schafer, *Exploring Harry Potter*, 191–209.

27. Gauthier, "Why Witches," 203.

28. Herbert Kohl, *Should We Burn Babar? Essays on Children's Literature and the Power of Stories* (New York: The New Press, 1995), 66–68.

29. Kohl, *Burn Babar*, 67.

Selected Bibliography

Acocella, Joan. "Under the Spell." *The New Yorker,* 31 July 2000: 74–78.

Armitstead, Claire. "Wizard but with a Touch of Brown." *Guardian Unlimited* Archive. 8 July 1999 http://books.guardian.co.uk/Print/0,3858,3881430,00.html, (accessed 19 February 2003).

Beam, Lindy. "What Shall We Do With Harry?" Plugged In: Focus on the Family, July 2000, http://www.family.org/pplace/pi/genl/A0008833.html (accessed 5 May 2001).

Bettelheim, Bruno. *The Uses of Enchantment: The Meaning and Importance of Fairy Tales.* New York: Vintage, 1976.

Blais, Jacqueline. "A Magical Breakfast of Potter Champions." *USA Today,* 9 October 2000: 8D.

Booth, Jenny. "Friendly Witches Earn School Ban for Potter." *Scotsman,* 29 March 2000.

Center for Studies on New Religions (CESNUR) website. "Harry Potter—Culture and Religion." http://www.cesnur.org/2001/potter/index.htm (accessed 21 May 2001).

Colbert, David. *The Magical Worlds of Harry Potter: A Treasury of Myths, Legends and Fascinating Facts.* Toronto: McArthur and Company, 2001.

Floyd, Jacquielynn. "Most Folks Are Just Wild About Harry." *The Dallas Morning News,* 4 December 1999: A37.

Fraser, James H. *Society and Children's Literature.* Boston: David R. Godine Publishers, 1978.

Freud, Sigmund. *New Introductory Lectures on Psychoanalysis.* New York: W.W. Norton, 1933.

Gauthier, Xavière. "Why Witches," Erica M. Eisinger, trans. In *New French Feminisms,* Elaine Marks and Isabelle de Courtivron, eds. New York: Schocken Books, 1981.

Green, Martin B. *Dreams of Adventure, Deeds of Empire.* New York: Basic Books, 1979.

Guerrero, Ed. "Slaves, Monsters, and Others." In *Rereading America: Cultural Contexts for Critical Thinking and Writing,* 3d ed., Gary Colombo, Robert Cullen, and Bonnie Lisle, eds. Boston: Bedford Books of St. Martin's Press, 1995, 400–410.

Harrington, Roberta. "Fundamentalists in a Frenzy over Power of the Occult," *Sunday Herald/Scottish Media Newspapers Ltd.,* 17 October 1999, 10.

Hunt, Peter. *Children's Literature.* Malden, MA: Blackwell Publishers Ltd., 2001.

———, ed. *Literature for Children: Contemporary Criticism.* New York: Routledge, 1992.

Jacobs, Alan. "Harry Potter's Magic." *First Things: A Monthly Journal of Religion and Public Life* (January 2000): 35–38.

Jones, Malcolm. "The Return of Harry Potter! Exclusive: J. K. Rowling Talks about Her Success, Her Daughter, Her Readers, the Upcoming Film and, of Course, Harry Potter, Teen Wizard." *Newsweek* (10 July 2000): 57–60.

Jung, Carl Gustav. *Alchemical Studies*, R. F. C. Hull, trans. Princeton, NJ: Princeton University Press, 1983.

———. *The Archetypes and the Collective Unconscious*, 2d ed., R. C. F. Hull, trans. Princeton, NJ: Princeton University Press, 1968.

———. *Psychology and Alchemy*, 2d ed., R. F. C. Hull, trans. Princeton, NJ: Princeton University Press, 1993.

———. *Symbols of Transformation*, 2d ed., R. F. C. Hull, trans. Princeton, NJ: Princeton University Press, 1990.

Kirkpatrick, Robert J. *The Encyclopedia of Boys' School Stories*. Aldershot, UK: Ashgate Press, 2000.

Kutzer, M. Daphne. *Empire's Children: Empire and Imperialism in Classic British Children's Books*. New York: Garland Publishing, 2000.

MacCann, Donnarae. *White Supremacy in Children's Literature: Characterizations of African Americans, 1830–1900*. New York: Routledge, 2001.

Masson, Sophie. "So What's All This about Harry Potter?" *Quadrant* (December 2000): 68–70.

McGillis, Roderick, ed. *Voices of the Other: Children's Literature and the Postcolonial Context*. New York: Garland, 2000.

Moore, Sharon A. *We Love Harry Potter*. New York: St. Martin's Griffin, 1999.

Murray, John Andrew. "Harry Dilemma," Teachers in Focus: A Web Site of Focus on the Family, 2000, http://www.family.org/cforum/teachersmag/features/a0009439.html (accessed 20 May 2001).

Natov, Roni. "Harry Potter and the Extraordinariness of the Ordinary." *The Lion and the Unicorn* 25, no.2 (2001): 310–27.

Nikolajeva, Maria. *From Mythic to Linear: Time in Children's Literature*. London: The Children's Literature Association and The Scarecrow Press, 2000.

Noel-Smith, Kelly. "Harry Potter's Oedipal Issues." *Psychoanalytic Studies* 3, no.2 (2001): 199–207.

O'Brien, Michael. "Harry Potter and the Paganization of Children's Culture." *Catholic World Report* (April 2001): 52–61.

Parsons, R. "Cathedral Shouldn't Welcome Harry Potter." *Western Daily Press/Bristol United Press*, 26 February 2001: 9.

Patterson, Troy. "J. K. Rowling: Every Muggle in America Has Read Her Books—And That May be Harry Potter's Ultimate Magic Trick: Kids Are Reading Again." *Entertainment Weekly*, 24 December 1999: 32+.

Philip, Neil. *Myths and Legends*. New York: DK Publishing, 1999.

Reis, Elizabeth, ed. *Spellbound: Women and Witchcraft in America*. Wilmington, DE: Scholarly Resources, Inc., 1998.

Rowling, J. K., as Newt Scamander. *Fantastic Beasts and Where to Find Them*. London: Bloomsbury/Obscurus, 2001.

———. *Harry Potter and the Chamber of Secrets*. London: Bloomsbury, 1998. New York: Scholastic Press, 1999.

———. *Harry Potter and the Goblet of Fire*. London: Bloomsbury, 2000. New York: Scholastic Press, 2000.

———. *Harry Potter and the Philosopher's Stone*. London: Bloomsbury, 1997.

———. *Harry Potter and the Prisoner of Azkaban*. London: Bloomsbury, 1999. New York: Scholastic Press, 1999.

———. *Harry Potter and the Sorcerer's Stone*. New York: Scholastic Press, 1997.

———, as Kennilworthy Whisp. *Quidditch through the Ages*. London: Bloomsbury/Whizz Hard, 2001.

Sadler, Glenn Edward, ed. *Teaching Children's Literature: Issues, Pedagogy, Resources*. New York: The Modern Language Association of America, 1992.

Schafer, Elizabeth D. *Beacham's Sourcebooks for Teaching Young Adult Fiction: Exploring Harry Potter*. Osprey: FL: Beacham Publishing Corp., 2000.

Schoefer, Christine. "Harry Potter's Girl Trouble." 13 January 2000, http://www.salon.com (accessed 25 January 2000).

Shannon, Sarah. "Harry Potter Fails to Cast a Spell on U.S. Christians," *Evening Standard* (London). 1 October 1999: 18.

Shapiro, Marc. *J. K. Rowling: The Wizard behind Harry Potter*. New York: St. Martin's Griffin, 2000.

Sims, Sue, and Hilary Claire. *The Encyclopedia of Girls' School Stories*. Aldershot, UK: Ashgate Press, 2000.

Thacker, Deborah. "Disdain or Ignorance? Literary Theory and the Absence of Children's Literature." *The Lion and the Unicorn*, 24, no.1 (2000): 1–17.

Thomson, J. *Understanding Teenagers Reading: Reading Processes and the Teaching of Literature*. Sydney: Methuen, 1986.

Tomlinson, Carl M., and Carol Lynch-Brown. *Essentials of Children's Literature*, 4th ed. Boston: Allyn and Bacon, 2002.

Tucker, Nicholas. "The Rise and Rise of Harry Potter," *Children's Literature in Education* 30, no.4 (1999): 221–34.

Vallely, Paul. "Faith and Reason: Harry Potter and a Lesson for Adults." *Independent*. 1 April 2000: 7.

Warner, Marina. *From the Beast to the Blonde: On Fairy Tales and Their Tellers*. London: Chatto and Windus, 1994.

Weir, Margaret. "Of Magic and Single Motherhood," Salon Mothers Who Think, *Salon*, 31 March 1999, www.salon.com/mwt/feature/1999/03/cov_31featureb.html (accessed 28 August 2001).

Wilson, Bee. "Pottering in the Kitchen." *New Statesman* (21 August 2000), 36–37.

Zipes, Jack. *Breaking the Magic Spell: Radical Theories of Folk and Fairy Tales*. London: Heinemann Educational Books, 1979.

———. *Spells of Enchantment: The Wondrous Fairy Tales of Western Culture*. Toronto: Penguin, 1991.

———. *Sticks and Stones: The Troublesome Success of Children's Literature from Slovenly Peter to Harry Potter*. New York: Routledge, 2001.

Index

About the Contributors

GISELLE LIZA ANATOL is an assistant professor of English at the University of Kansas. She specializes in Caribbean, African-American, and children's literatures and has published on the works of Paule Marshall, Audre Lorde, and Jamaica Kincaid. In addition to *Reading Harry Potter,* she is currently working on a manuscript exploring representations of motherhood in Caribbean women's writing.

BRYCCHAN CAREY holds the position of lecturer at London University, where he also completed a Ph.D. dissertation entitled "The Rhetoric of Sensibility: Argument, Sentiment and Slavery in the Late Eighteenth Century." Forthcoming articles include writings on late-eighteenth-/early-nineteenth-century literature and slavery and on the work of Thomas Day, author of *Sandford and Merton,* arguably the first children's novel in English.

LISA DAMOUR is a clinical psychologist who treats children, adolescents, and adults in her private practice. She also teaches part-time in the Department of Psychology at John Carroll University (Cleveland, Ohio) and is a psychoanalytic trainee at the Cleveland Center for Research in Child Development. Dr. Damour is currently writing a textbook on abnormal psychology.

XIMENA GALLARDO-C. works as an assistant professor of comparative literature at Glenville State College (Glenville, West Virginia) and currently serves as cochair of the science fiction and fantasy area for the Southwest and Texas Popular Culture Association and American Culture Association. Research interests include postcolonialism and Shakespeare, drama as performance, and gender approaches to science fiction and fantasy. Dr. Gallardo-C. is currently working on a book that explores the construction of gender in the *Alien* film series.

SUSAN HALL graduated from St. Anne's College, Oxford, with a first class degree in law. Her University of Toronto master's thesis focused on the social and legal issues behind compulsory licensing of pharmaceuticals. She currently works as a partner in a Manchester (United Kingdom) law firm, specializing in copyright, designs, patents, and the law of information technology.

LISA HOPKINS is a senior lecturer in English in the School of Cultural Studies at Sheffield Hallam University (United Kingdom). She also serves as the editor of the peer-reviewed electronic journal *Early Modern Literary Studies*. Her publications include "John Ford's Political Theatre," "The Shakespearean Marriage: Merry Wives and Heavy Husbands," and "Christopher Marlowe: A Literary Life."

CHANTEL LAVOIE is a lecturer with the English Department at the University of Toronto. Her focus is eighteenth-century poetry and women writers, as well as history of the book and early literary anthologies. Other areas of interest include children's literature and Canadian literature.

ALICE MILLS serves as a senior lecturer in children's literature at Australia's University of Ballarat (Victoria). She has published in the fields of children's literature and fantasy, including a paper on *Pollyanna* in the 1999 volume of *Children's Literature*. She has edited a book of scholarly essays on the grotesque, and a second volume, on the unspeakable, is forthcoming. Dr. Mills is also a creative writer.

MARGARET J. OAKES is an associate professor of English at Furman University in Greenville, South Carolina. After a five-year stint as an attorney, Professor Oakes matriculated at Stanford University for the Ph.D. Her research interests are in British Renaissance literature and gender issues, British children's literature, and British detective fiction.

ELAINE OSTRY holds the position of assistant professor of English at SUNY–Plattsburgh, where she teaches children's literature, young adult literature and nineteenth-century literature. She is the coeditor of *Utopian and Dystopian Writing for Children and Young Adults* and the author of *Social Dreaming: Dickens and the Fairy Tale*, both forthcoming from Routledge Press.

JULIA PARK has been a professional journalist for eighteen years, and she is currently the editor of San Francisco's *Alameda Sun*. Her creative nonfiction, fiction, reviews, and poetry have been published in *The Sun, Americas Review, Green Fuse, Sacred River, Prophetic Voices, The San Francisco Chronicle*, and elsewhere in the United States, Britain, and Japan. Ms. Park is also a Jane Austen scholar and reporter for the national newsletter of the Jane Austen Society of North America.

VERONICA L. SCHANOES is a graduate student working toward her Ph.D. in English at the University of Pennsylvania. Her areas of interest include feminist theory, women's writing, and children's literature.

C. JASON SMITH is an assistant professor of Foundations English and director of the Writing Clinic at Glenville State College (Glenville, West Virginia) and currently serves as cochair of the science fiction and fantasy area for the Southwest and Texas Popular Culture Association and American Culture Association. Dr. Smith has taught, presented, and published on a wide variety of topics including Robert Penn Warren, gender theory, and children's literature.

KAREN MANNERS SMITH is an associate professor of history at Emporia State University (Emporia, Kansas). She received her B.A. in English and American literature from Brandeis University and her Ph.D. in American history from the University of Massachusetts. Manners Smith is the author of *New Paths to Power: American Women from 1890–1920* (Oxford University Press, 1994) and a number of articles on nineteenth-century women writers.

REBECCA STEPHENS works as an assistant professor of English at the University of Wisconsin–Stevens Point, where she teaches young adult literature, writing, and drama. Her research interests include nationalism, identity politics, and memory studies.

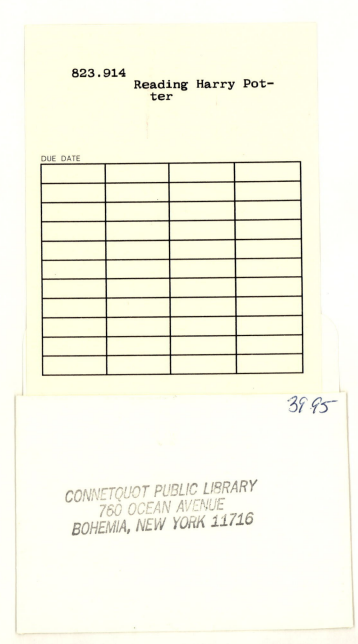